EDMONTON OILERS
H O C K E Y   C L U B

CELEBRATING 25 YEARS IN THE HEARTLAND OF HOCKEY

RAY TURCHANSKY
FOREWORD BY KEVIN LOWE

Published by:
Edmonton Journal Group Inc.
10006 – 101 Street
Edmonton, Alberta, Canada T5J 0S1

National Library of Canada Cataloguing in Publication

Turchansky, Ray, 1950-
Edmonton Oilers Hockey Club: Celebrating 25 Years in the Heartland of Hockey / writer, Ray
Turchansky; editor, Bob Boehm.

ISBN 0-9690184-4-4

1. Edmonton Oilers (Hockey team) I. Boehm, Bob, 1959- II. Title.

GV848.E35T87 2003   796.962'64'09712334   C2003-905945-6

Printed and bound in Canada at Friesens
First edition, first printing, 2003

EDMONTON OILERS
1979-2003

—— TABLE OF CONTENTS ——

OWNERS' MESSAGE

In March of 1998, a group of community and business leaders came together under the Edmonton Investors Group (EIG) banner and raised $70 million US to help preserve NHL hockey in Edmonton. Their bid to buy the Oilers defeated Houston-based investor Les Alexander's efforts to purchase the club. The EIG kept the Oilers in Canada—under Canadian ownership.

Thirty-eight individuals — "the team behind the team" — came together to save the city's NHL team, without any profit motive. The deal was done because it was good for Edmonton, for Alberta — and, in the wake of both Winnipeg and Quebec City losing their franchises, for Canada, as well.

After the sale, NHL Commissioner Gary Bettman praised the new ownership group: "The roots of NHL hockey are in Canada," he said. "The League is pleased to see this unique resolution to preserving Canada's heritage."

With the current economic state of the National Hockey League, the challenges for the EIG in their quest to preserve top-level professional hockey in Alberta's capital only grow in nature.

In 2001, the EIG responded to a $4-million cash call to meet the financial challenges of running a major-league hockey franchise, another sign of its commitment to the city.

During the recent off-season, NHL player salaries continued their upward trend and the EIG still has to deal with the weak state of the Canadian dollar when it comes to having to pay expenses in U.S. currency.

If the EIG's track record is any indication, Oilers fans should be confident that the group will meet the challenge head-on.

The Oilers' owners are committed to staying the financial course until the NHL and the NHLPA (the players' union) hammer out a new collective bargaining agreement prior to 2004.

True to their mandate of keeping the Edmonton Oilers Canadian, the owners continue to run their day-to-day Oilers business as cost-effectively as possible. This is unique in a league where the ownership of many of the other teams is primarily in the hands of people who often subsidize team operations from other sources. The Oilers, unlike other NHL teams, are not a simple cog in a corporate wheel. EIG shareholders don't even get to enjoy free tickets to Oilers games—in fact members of the group spend over $3 million a season in ticket purchases, suite rentals, advertising and sponsorship. As well, members of the ownership group have stepped up to help the Oilers in unique and creative ways; for example, the Oilers' highly acclaimed third jersey was designed by one of the owners.

With a vibrant season-ticket base, Edmonton's hockey fans have answered the challenge and are doing their part to keep NHL hockey here. The fans can rest assured that the EIG will not jeopardize the team by spending recklessly. Through prudent financial management, the EIG can pass its next significant test — keeping the Oilers a competitive NHL entity after the ink dries on the new collective bargaining agreement in 2004.

— Cal Nichols, Chairman, Edmonton Investors Group

PRESIDENT'S MESSAGE

We believe that it is very difficult to find another franchise in all of professional sport that can boast the kind of success over the last 25 years as the Edmonton Oilers.

Not only has the hockey club provided its home town with five championships and a myriad of mind-boggling scoring records, it has helped put Edmonton into the minds of people across the world. If you ask someone in Helsinki, Finland or Hoboken, New Jersey about Edmonton, they will likely mention the Oilers—the team has become the city's greeting card to the rest of the world.

What has made Oilers' hockey so successful? Great management, great coaches, great players and—our greatest asset of all—an outstanding fan base. Edmonton has proven itself as one of the premier NHL cities thanks to fans who sell out the arena on a February Wednesday when the mercury dips to –25 C or who show the rest of the league what it means to "Go Crazy" during the playoffs.

From our season-ticket customers and executive suite tenants to the fans who come from all across the prairies to catch a game, this organization cannot thank you enough for your support. I hope that our dyed-in-the-wool fans will enjoy this look back at our first 25 NHL years; after all, this book is for you.

As well, this book will commemorate our silver anniversary season, highlighted by the Nov. 22 Molson Canadian Heritage Classic, which will feature the first outdoor game in NHL history at Commonwealth Stadium, reminding us of an era when the Thistle Rink was the premier spot in Edmonton to see world-class teams like the Eskimos and Dominions take to the ice.

Edmonton is a city with a proud hockey tradition, from the Allan Cup champion Flyers of 1948 to the Olympic gold-medal winning Mercurys of 1952 to the Oil Kings that won Memorial Cups in 1963 and 1966. The Edmonton Oilers are proud to be part of this city's great hockey story.

— Patrick LaForge,
Edmonton Oilers President
and Chief Executive Officer

FOREWORD

As a player, I was proud to be part of one of the greatest hockey dynasties the game has ever seen. Today, I am just as proud to be the general manager of one of the most exciting franchises in the National Hockey League — the Edmonton Oilers.

Shortly after I first arrived in Edmonton in 1979, I learned what a great sports community this was. The city rallied around the newest members of the NHL, embracing us wholeheartedly, and the undying support of Edmonton's hockey fans helped push us to new heights.

In time, it became apparent that the talented group of players I laced up the skates with every day was special. We were a young group of kids, all with the same drive and determination to succeed, and together we grew into Stanley Cup champions.

And what a ride it was — making the playoffs and lining up against the Broad Street Bullies in our first year in the league; enduring power outages in the Boston Garden; watching Wayne's amazing feats on ice; and finally bringing the powerful dynasty of the New York Islanders to its knees to clinch our first Stanley Cup.

There were so many great moments, and so many incredible team efforts, that the phrase "Oilers hockey" soon became a well-worn catch-phrase throughout the league to describe the style of high-energy, fast-paced hockey that brought five Stanley Cups home to the City of Champions.

After 25 years in the league, the Edmonton Oilers are still recognized as one of the greatest sports teams in hockey history — a statement that was endorsed in February of 2003 by *ESPN Magazine*, when they ranked the Oilers 9th out of all 121 professional sports franchises in North America.

Throughout this 25th anniversary season, the Edmonton Oilers will take the time to salute the superstars and the role players, the skilled athletes and the great characters who helped make the past 25 years so memorable. As part of our anniversary celebrations, we offer this yearbook as a keepsake for our fans. We know that it will bring back many great memories, and hope that it captures the same Oilers legacy that inspires a saying we have in our dressing room: "Once an Oiler, Always an Oiler."

As the current general manager of the Edmonton Oilers, I will continue to build on that great Oilers tradition — to be an innovative team, playing a style of hockey the way this game should be played.

Here's to another great 25 years of Oilers Hockey.

— Kevin Lowe, Edmonton Oilers General Manager

ACKNOWLEDGMENTS

I was nicely coasting into early retirement at the *Edmonton Journal* when deputy editor Allan Mayer called me into his office.

The Edmonton Oilers had commissioned *The Journal* to write a book on the team's 25 years in the National Hockey League, and he wondered if I'd be interested in writing it.

The deadline? Yesterday.

I mentioned the offer at home, and my sons Zak and Jay got even more excited than the day Jay got hit in the cheek by a puck at an Oilers' open practice, when team management gave the boys a signed picture of Tommy Salo and a puck autographed by Mike Comrie.

I didn't know at the time that during the 1980s, *The Journal* had carried more than 1,700 stories with an Edmonton Oiler reference in each of the seasons the team won the Stanley Cup. The number dropped to a paltry 1,400 in years they didn't win the Cup. And during the strike season of 1994-95, with only 48 games and the team missing the playoffs, there were still more than 700 Oiler stories.

Sifting through them was a delightful exercise in reliving not only how the Oilers evolved, but also how Edmonton grew up, and how *The Journal* wrote and sometimes rewrote history. When I wanted to get Glen Sather's exact fire hydrant quote when he traded Blair MacDonald in 1981, I found four slightly different versions.

The original quote surfaced: "A fire hydrant could score 40 goals playing with Gretzky."

I have borrowed liberally from the writings of my original *Journal* colleague, Jim Matheson, who rightfully sits in the Hockey Hall of Fame. I have also used the words of many other *Journal* writers over the ages, notably Cam Cole, Terry Jones, Norm Cowley, Mark Spector, Robin Brownlee, Curtis Stock, Joanne Ireland, Dan Barnes and Paul Marck.

It was fitting that my writing should be edited by *Journal* copy editor Bob Boehm — a former Saskatchewan Junior Hockey League goalie editing the words of a former Alberta Junior Hockey League goalie. He made it a far better book.

And the excitement of graphic designer Joey Angeles, as he assembled old and new pictures for the layout, was infectious.

The photos were chosen out of thousands that came from the cameras of many *Journal* photographers and Oiler photographer Gerry Thomas. Those pictures were prepared for publication by Terry Elniski, Robert Flasha, Shaun Cooney and the rest of the *Journal* image supply department.

Making sure we were all still alive and working with some sense of deadline was Cindy Mah from the *Journal*'s marketing department.

For me the final signal to proceed came when Oilers president and chief executive officer Pat LaForge said he wanted a book that above all would be interesting, which meant a few warts would resurface. General manager Kevin Lowe was also keen to contribute to the project. Natalie Minckler, of the Oilers' corporate communications and marketing department, coordinator Darren Krill and vice-president Allan Watt, who was named after the Allan Cup his father Gordie won with the 1947-48 Edmonton Flyers, provided background information. Steve Knowles of the Oilers and Darlene Dean of Quality Color came up with the statistics.

I must thank my boys, Zak and Jay, for that initial encouragement, and my wife Lorraine, for putting up with a basement adorned with Edmonton sports memorabilia I've accumulated over 50 years. I told you it would come in handy one day.

And a final thanks goes to the late Bill Hunter, my former general manager with the Oil Kings junior team and my source for many hockey and curling stories. We all owe the Edmonton Oilers, the Skyreach Centre, and this book, to him.

— *Ray Turchansky*

INTRODUCTION

When it looked like the Edmonton Oilers were destined to leave for Houston or Hamilton back in the mid-1990s, I was torn by two thoughts.

One was that at least I had the wonderful fortune of being in the right place at the right time when the greatest player and perhaps the greatest team in NHL history were at their peak.

With magician Wayne Gretzky surrounded by a superb cast of assistants, the club had been the envy of sports fans around the globe. To have that assembled talent combined with a coaching staff that let it play at warp speed was the stuff of dreams for a spectator.

While the Oilers were winning five Stanley Cups, it was simply impossible to watch the action while sitting on your hands. If the Oilers were to leave Edmonton, at least one whole generation — myself included — had been treated to the very best. To expect more almost seemed selfish.

However, I had another thought.

Suddenly it seemed sad that a whole new generation — my sons included — might not have the chance to experience the joy of NHL action. Gone from school classrooms would be all those kids wearing Oiler jerseys. Heroes would evaporate. Dreams would be fewer.

But then the Edmonton Oilers Investors Group Partnership Limited came together and kept the team in Edmonton.

And it made a cognizant effort to reach back into the team's history. It admitted that the Oilers had been in the World Hockey Association, something the previous ownership had been reluctant to do.

Under the new management, Al Hamilton's No. 3, which had been retired after the 1979-80 season, was finally raised to the Skyreach Centre rafters in 2001.

And the Oilers publicly honoured Bill Hunter, the man who had founded the team, which in turn caused the building of the Coliseum (later renamed the Skyreach Centre), which attracted Wayne Gretzky to Edmonton, which attracted Edmonton to the NHL, which led to five Stanley Cups for the city.

So, thanks to the local ownership group, the Oilers have reached their silver anniversary in the NHL.

And there now exists a second generation of Oiler fans, ones who never saw Paul Coffey as an Oiler, ones who can't imagine a scoreboard without a Smooch Cam.

All of this means there are now two audiences for this book. For one it will rekindle memories of the way we were. For another it will serve as an education textbook.

And the year 2003 has offered more than the usual share of Oiler nostalgia. The club is celebrating its 25th anniversary in the NHL, goalie Grant Fuhr's number will be retired and fans will be treated to the outdoor Heritage Classic game.

But hanging over the season is the doomsday scenario that it could be the last hockey for a while, if a failure to come up with a new collective bargaining agreement wipes out the 2004-05 season.

So, what would Bill do?

Bill Hunter, the eternal optimist, would have believed that common sense will somehow prevail. Salaries will become manageable and small-market teams will survive.

And, in the spirit of Bill Hunter, I'll even go further and say that the calibre of play will improve. The dreaded neutral zone trap will fade.

I say that noting that in this book, Glen Sather said he came up with the idea of a firewagon brand of hockey for the Oilers after watching some peewees practise in Turku, Finland.

Well, right now in Edmonton, which still boasts the largest hockey tournament anywhere with Minor Hockey Week, a former Swede named Bjorn Kinding is spreading the word about a new way of coaching to people like myself.

He said that during the 1972 Canada-Soviet series, people charted where every Soviet player went on the ice. The assumption was they would move up and down lanes, in the Canadian tradition of Eddie Shore, who would tie a rope around a winger in practice to make sure he didn't get too far away from the boards.

Instead, it was discovered that Soviet players flowed everywhere and that if you superimposed charts of a player's movement over three periods, it would cover the entire ice surface.

As young players are nurtured to be creative and to react, all will be well with the game.

This book tells the story about one great era of Oilers hockey. Another isn't unthinkable. Enjoy.

— *Ray Turchansky*

1979-2003

WHAT THE OILERS MEAN TO EDMONTON

To fathom the importance of hockey and the Edmonton Oilers to central Alberta, one need only reflect on what life was like in 1964, or 14 BG (Before Gretzky).

Edmonton was an isolated pimple on the Prairies and the National Hockey League seemed like a million miles away.

Sure, the Detroit Red Wings had owned and operated the minor professional Edmonton Flyers in the old Western Hockey League and the junior Edmonton Oil Kings, so Edmontonians had a soft spot for the Wings. Many local players had graduated from the Oil Kings and Flyers and had moved on to star in Detroit — players like Norm Ullman, Eddie Joyal and Bruce MacGregor.

But the Red Wings folded the Flyers in 1963 and Edmonton went into a deep funk.

The city's psyche took another hit the same year when Edmonton's most famous professional athlete, quarterback Jackie Parker of the Edmonton Eskimos, was traded to Toronto. Parker put Edmonton on the sports map with three straight Grey Cups in the mid-1950s.

So central Albertans looking for a pro hockey fix in the mid- to late-1960s had to watch the Red Wings and other NHL teams on television or buy a ticket to the always sold-out Kinsmen Sportsmen's Dinner to meet superstars like Gordie Howe or Phil Esposito in the flesh.

Then in 1972, Wild Bill Hunter brought the rogue World Hockey Association to Edmonton. The WHA made a big splash by raiding the NHL for superstars like Bobby Hull and Howe, but it was still a second-rate league.

Gerry Cheevers, who once played goal for the Oil Kings against a touring Soviet team, explained the difference between playing for the Boston Bruins in the NHL and the Cleveland Crusaders in the WHA.

"In Boston, wearing No. 4 in front of me was Bobby Orr. In Cleveland, wearing No. 4 in front of me was Ralph Hopiavouri."

Hunter and the WHA Oilers concentrated on signing players with local ties — such as Ullman and MacGregor — but the team was never a huge draw. The only sellouts, except for the first few games after the Edmonton Coliseum opened in 1974, were when Howe and Hull and other WHA stars came to town to play the Oilers.

Everything changed in 1978.

Edmonton played host to the highly successful Commonwealth Games. The Eskimos won the first of five straight Grey Cups. And Peter Pocklington, owner of the WHA Oilers, acquired 17-year-old Wayne Gretzky from the WHA's Indianapolis Racers.

The Gretzky deal proved to be Edmonton's defining sports moment. It was no mere coincidence that the Oilers, who had struggled to make the playoffs every year, reached the Avco Cup final the season Gretzky arrived.

The next year, the NHL and WHA merged, and what seemed like an impossible dream in 1964 turned to reality — Edmonton had an NHL franchise.

Still there were doubters. During the merger talks in 1979, Eastern sportswriter Al Strachan wrote that allowing Edmonton into the NHL would debase the league. Chided then *Journal* publisher Pat O'Callaghan in a front page editorial: "Who would want to watch some 18-year-old kid called Gretzky performing miracles with a puck?"

Of course, Strachan couldn't have been more wrong. The Oilers would go on to win the Stanley Cup only five years later, and we could proudly puff out our chests and claim to be the City of Champions.

With Gretzky and friends hoisting the Cup over their heads on a regular basis, Edmontonians came to enjoy driving cars with bumper stickers that told Easterners to freeze in the dark. And even better, *Journal* writer Cam Cole was able to call Calgary "a city of large hats and small trophy cases."

Historically withdrawn Edmontonians were now shouting their joy on Jasper Avenue at 2 a.m. When boxing promoter Don King brought Mike Tyson to town and addressed the "Edmonites," instead of whimpering in protest, now we laughed. Self-confidence works wonders.

Despite the new feeling of self-worth, Edmonton was far from devoid of critics. In 1985, Montreal writer Mordecai Richler came to Edmonton to interview Gretzky, and then wrote: "There is hardly a tree to be seen downtown, nothing to delight the eye on Jasper Avenue. On 30-below-zero nights, grim religious zealots loom on street corners, speaking in tongues, and intrepid streetwalkers in mini-skirts rap on the windows of cars that have stopped for traffic. There isn't a first-class restaurant anywhere in town."

Harsh words indeed. But the article appeared in the *New York Times*. Hockey was putting Edmonton on the world map.

We lived our lives vicariously through the Oilers. When Gretzky was hobnobbing with John Candy, making public service announcements with Sally Struthers or being painted by LeRoy Neiman, we were along for the ride.

And forget Chuck and Di, we had our own Royal Wedding with Wayne and Janet.

The Oilers became our passkey to open doors all over the world.

When Gretzky retired in 1999, Edmonton Mayor Bill Smith said: "When I travel to Asia there are three things they remember. They know the Edmonton Oilers, Wayne Gretzky and West Edmonton Mall."

And there were the words of 67-year-old Rita Kelly, who braved the winter cold to attend the civic ceremony at City Hall honouring Gretzky: "The people who don't come to this are really missing one of the most important moments ever in this city."

What the Oilers mean to Edmonton was driven home in the mid-1990s, when there were threats of moving the franchise elsewhere.

The business community was understandably concerned about losing the team and ultimately pitched in to help keep the franchise in Edmonton. In economic terms, estimates suggest a professional sports franchise contributes about one per cent of a city's gross domestic product each year. That's small in terms of percentage, but huge in terms of actual dollars.

Yet the value of a franchise goes much beyond that.

A twentysomething clerk at a souvenir store in Disneyland, himself a netminder, empathized with the Edmonton tourist wearing a T-shirt depicting the evolution of the goalie mask.

"You can't have the NHL without Edmonton," protested the Anaheim lad.

"Edmonton is Gretzky. Hockey is Edmonton."

Funny. Around the year 14 BG, that's what Edmontonians used to think about Montreal and Toronto. And now, some youngster near Los Angeles was saying that about Edmonton.

It kind of made you feel good.

When Gretzky was hobnobbing with John Candy, making public service announcements with Sally Struthers or being painted by LeRoy Neiman, we were along for the ride.

CHAPTER 1

IN THE BEGINNING

*The World
Hockey Association*

1972-1979
THE WHA YEARS

For many fans, the Edmonton Oilers came alive when a long-haired, fresh-faced teenager named Wayne Gretzky jetted into town on a cold night in November of 1978, sold from one swashbuckling owner, Nelson Skalbania, to another, Edmonton's Peter Pocklington.

Without Gretzky, the Oilers had been one of the World Hockey Association's also-rans, missing the post-season twice and bowing out of the playoffs in the first round four times in six years.

Gretzky, still only 17, ignited the Oilers' offence with 46 goals and 110 points, catapulting Edmonton to the top of the WHA standings. The Oilers advanced to the league finals, finally falling to Bobby Hull and the defending champion Winnipeg Jets.

"It was the best money the franchise ever spent," *Edmonton Journal* hockey writer Jim Matheson wrote years later, of the deal to purchase Gretzky from Skalbania. "For the first time, people knew and even cared the team existed."

But by the start of the next season, the rogue WHA would be a distant memory, and Gretzky and the Oilers would become new members of the National Hockey League.

The WHA had been the brainchild of two California promoters, Dennis Murphy and Gary Davidson, best known for creating the American Basketball Association to compete with the National Basketball Association in 1967.

The two saw an opportunity to gain a foothold in the hockey world, too, and in 1971 incorporated the WHA to rival the NHL.

Shortly after, Edmonton's Bill Hunter entered the picture. Davidson and Murphy were scouting around for prospective WHA franchises, and Wild Bill, as he was known, was the owner of the highly successful junior Edmonton Oil Kings. Hunter agreed to usher in a new pro team in Edmonton and the Alberta Oilers were born.

"The first thing I realized was that these guys (Murphy and Davidson) knew absolutely nothing about the game of hockey," wrote Hunter, in his 2000 autobiography *Wild Bill*. "They were promoters, and they knew the timing was right. They knew they needed a hockey man. They had to get me on board and finally I agreed to join them."

Hunter became the general manager of the Edmonton-based team and helped orchestrate a special player lottery in February of 1972 for the league's first twelve teams, helping the WHA get off the ground later that year.

By the fall of 1972, Edmonton hockey fans had been without professional hockey for nine years. The Detroit Red Wings had folded their minor-pro team, the Edmonton Flyers, in 1963. So hockey-starved fans were at least moderately excited about the new team in town and the new league, which gained instant credibility when NHL superstar Bobby Hull signed on with the Winnipeg Jets for $1 million.

But while other WHA teams raided the NHL for such well-known stars as Bernie Parent, J.C. Tremblay, Gerry Cheevers, Derek Sanderson and the like, the Oilers settled for lesser-known players, many with a local connection, like former Oil

Opposite: Ray Kinasewich signs on as the Alberta Oilers' first-ever head coach, as general manager Bill Hunter looks on. Above: Hunter never strayed too far away from the bench, even taking over the coaching duties a couple of times when the team wasn't performing up to his expectations.

THE WHA YEARS

Kings defenceman Al Hamilton and Edmonton native Doug Barrie. The Oilers' biggest splash in that first year came when Toronto Maple Leafs centre Jim Harrison was lured away for the princely sum of $75,000. Ever the showman, Hunter announced the signing by setting up a photo opportunity with Harrison pushing a shopping cart full of dollar bills out of Wild Bill's Edmonton office, a picture of which ran in the *Edmonton Journal*. The Oilers also gave Harrison a new car and promised to transport his wife's horse from Eastern Canada to Edmonton.

The league's first-ever game, one of only six televised on CBC that season, saw the Alberta Oilers upend the Ottawa Nationals 7-4, with ex-Oil King Ron Anderson scoring the Oilers' and the league's first goal. The highlight of the first season came on Jan. 30, 1973, when Harrison set a major hockey league record with 10 points in one game — three goals and seven assists — against the New York Raiders, a mark later equalled by Darryl Sittler of the Toronto Maple Leafs in the NHL.

There were more lows than highs for the Oilers — renamed the Edmonton Oilers in 1973-74 — in the first few years. And the league had more than its share of growing pains as well. Teams folded, moved and were sold at an alarming rate, barely surviving on the strength of the stars it brazenly courted away from the NHL, the European players it brought over, the underage juniors it signed and the novelty of the Howe family — father Gordie and sons Mark and Marty playing together with the Houston Aeros.

Edmonton's franchise, owned by Hunter, Willard Estay, Dr. Charles Allard, Zane Feldman and Canadian Cablesystems, struggled financially, although an average of 4,900 fans braved the dank, dilapidated 5,200-seat Edmonton Gardens to watch

each game. After barely missing the playoffs in 1972-73, the team shot out of the gate in season two with an 11-1 record, prompting coach Brian Shaw to playfully boast, "We may never lose again."

Of course, that didn't happen, but the Oilers at least managed to qualify for the post-season, falling to the Minnesota Fighting Saints in the quarter-finals.

By the 1974-75 season, the team moved into the new 15,300-seat Edmonton Coliseum. A record-setting WHA regular season crowd of 15,326 showed up on Nov. 10, 1974, to christen the new building. That season, fans were treated to the resurrection of legendary Montreal Canadiens goaltender Jacques Plante, who, at the ripe old age of 45, signed on with the Oilers for two years at $150,000 a season. Plante turned back the clock, going 8-1 in one stretch with a 2.54 goals-against average. And although the Coliseum wasn't jammed for every game, an average of more than 10,000 fans came to watch Plante and Co., setting a league attendance record for the season of 418,150. Unfortunately, the team missed the playoffs for the second time in three tries.

By the 1975-76 season, Plante's contract had been terminated, replaced on the roster by another 40-year-old legend at the end of his career, centre Norm Ullman. It was a homecoming of sorts for Ullman, a native of Provost, Alta., who played with the Edmonton Oil Kings and the Edmonton Flyers before entering the NHL with Detroit in 1955.

Ullman lasted two years, with 87 points his first season, which included his 500th career goal on Dec. 11, 1975, against the Quebec Nordiques. "I wish it could have come in the National Hockey League," Ullman admitted, "but I guess it just

Opposite: Jim Harrison was the Oilers' high-profile signing in the team's first year, plucked from the Toronto Maple Leafs. Harrison set a pro hockey record with a 10-point night in 1973, a mark later equalled by Darryl Sittler in the NHL. Above: Norm Ullman joined the Oilers in the twilight of his career, and misses the net on this glorious chance against the Toronto Toros.

1972-1979

—— THE WHA YEARS ——

wasn't meant to be."

Changes came after the Oilers were knocked out in the first round of the 1975-76 playoffs to Winnipeg. A survey showed that 60 per cent of fans blamed GM Hunter for the team's ineptitude, and Wild Bill was stripped of his authority by Dr. Charles Allard, the Oilers' chairman of the board.

It was a bitter pill for super-salesman Hunter to swallow, after being largely responsible for bringing the team to town and getting the Coliseum built, but he resigned as GM. In a 73-paragraph speech, Hunter went out with a bang, blaming the "critics, rumour-mongers and sadists who have a field day expounding on their views" for his demise. Hunter stayed on as part-owner, but only until Allard sold half the team to Vancouver real estate tycoon Nelson Skalbania prior to the 1976-77 season.

Skalbania, who brought in Edmonton entrepreneurial golden boy Peter Pocklington as an equal partner, claimed the Oilers were in a mess.

"The team was terrible. Management had been dreadful. It just wasn't a businesslike operation. The contracts were crazy," said Skalbania. "There was one guy on the club with a contract that said if he went to another club we had to pay his wife $14,000 because she would have to change jobs."

Skalbania fared little better, however, although the team made a positive step by securing Glen Sather, another ex-Oil King, from the NHL's Minnesota North Stars as the Oilers' new captain. Sather became a playing coach when Bep Guidolin stepped aside as coach and GM in March of 1977.

"He said if I didn't take the job, I'd sit in the stands," said Sather.

Sather added some stability to the team, as player-coach in 1976-77 and behind the bench in 1977-78, although the Oilers saw early playoff exits both years.

Skalbania left before the 1977-78 campaign — at least in person — buying 51 per cent of the Indianapolis Racers for $1 while retaining his half-share in the Oilers. Eventually, he sold that share to Pocklington.

Then came November of 1978, when Skalbania made his most infamous of moves — unloading Gretzky, goaltender Eddie Mio and forward Peter Driscoll for $825,000 to Pocklington's Oilers. Pocklington spent several more thousand dollars to charter a Lear jet to bring the new Oilers to Edmonton. "In Nelson's eyes, he felt he was doing us a favour," said Gretzky. "He said Edmonton was the best city in North America."

The team in the best city in North America was in a league that had been teetering on the brink of financial ruin for most of its seven-year history, however.

Merger talks, which had been on-again and off-again for at least two years, led to a deal that would see the WHA fold and Edmonton, Winnipeg, New England and Quebec join the NHL in the fall of 1979.

And although Edmonton was the only one of the four never to have won a World Hockey Association championship, the Oilers would be the first of the WHA orphans to win a Stanley Cup.

Opposite: Legendary goaltender Jacques Plante donned the pads for the Oilers in 1974-75 at the ripe old age of 45. Above: Happy Birthday, 99! Whiz kid Wayne Gretzky, flanked by Oilers owner Peter Pocklington and 99's dad Walter, signs a 21-year personal services contract with Pocklington at a centre-ice ceremony at the Coliseum.

CHAPTER 2

A QUARTER CENTURY OF

Oilers Hockey

EDMONTON OILERS
LOWE KEVIN (QUEBEC)
EDMONTON
OILERS EDMONTON

EDMONTON OILERS
1979-1980
AN NHL TEAM IS BORN

For seven years, the National Hockey League and upstart World Hockey Association had battled each other until the financial competition for players emptied the pockets of both sides. Over two years, there were four different sets of talks held to bring the leagues together — a merger according to WHA spin doctors, an expansion according to the NHL.

Finally, in Chicago on March 30, 1979, the NHL board of governors voted 14-3 to accept four WHA teams into their fold — Edmonton Oilers, Winnipeg Jets, Quebec Nordiques and New England Whalers.

At long last, the NHL was coming to Edmonton. And the fans couldn't wait.

On the night of April 26, 1979, dozens of fans who had started gathering at noon that day spent the evening outside Northlands Coliseum, listening on radio to the Oilers playing a WHA game inside the building. At 9 the next morning, some 1,400 season tickets still available for the team's first NHL season would go on sale. As their numbers swelled, fans huddled in sleeping bags and sat on lawn chairs all night. By noon the next day, the 15,326-seat Coliseum had been sold out of season tickets for the Oilers' first NHL season, save the 700 being kept back for casual sales each game.

But entry into the NHL came not without a price. Oilers owner Peter Pocklington and the three other WHA teams would each pay a $6-million entry fee, plus an extra $1.6 million per team in indemnification fees to departing WHA teams Birmingham and Cincinnati. And even more of a killer, each surviving team would be able to protect only two skaters and two goalies. That's because the rights of unprotected players who had been NHL draftees or lured by the WHA reverted to their original NHL teams.

For Edmonton, one selection was a slam dunk. Seventeen-year-old Wayne Gretzky had come to the WHA Oilers in 1978 from the cash-strapped Indianapolis Racers. He led Edmonton with 46 goals and 110 points in the club's final WHA season. On Jan. 26, 1979, his 18th birthday, he had signed a 21-year personal services contract for $5 million with owner Pocklington.

The second skater never would play for the club in the NHL. The Oilers chose not to protect hard-hitting, all-star defenceman Dave Langevin, opting instead for 21-year-old Swedish right winger Bengt-Ake Gustafsson. But a month before the 1979-80 NHL season started, league president John Ziegler ruled that the Oilers did not have a valid contract with Gustafsson in place before the March expansion draft, and he was declared the property of the Washington Capitals.

It was the Aug. 9 entry draft that set in motion the wheels that would eventually provide Gretzky with a formidable supporting cast. Chief scout Barry Fraser chose Quebec Remparts captain Kevin Lowe in the first round, St. Albert product Mark Messier (an underage forward with the Cincinnati Stingers) in the second round and Olympic-bound Glenn Anderson of the University of Denver in the third. And a deal was also made to get back the rights to muscleman Dave Semenko.

When Messier held out for a contract before attending training camp, coach Glen Sather said: "The kid can be a helluva pro one day. He's big and strong and he might just be the tough centre I'm looking for. But he only scored one goal last season. He's not exactly Wayne Gretzky."

With Sather behind the bench and Dave Dryden in goal, the Oilers took to the Chicago Stadium ice on Oct. 10, 1979, for Edmonton's first regular season NHL game. They went on the power play trailing 2-0 when, at 9:49 of the first period, 20-year-old Lowe fired a puck past Tony Esposito, the Oilers' first goal in the National Hockey League.

"I shot it and one of the 'Hawks — I think it was Bob Murray — deflected the puck," said Lowe, whose goal was assisted by Gretzky and Brett Callighen. "The first thing I thought of as I went to the bench was that I wished my mother had been here (from Montreal) to see it. Then it dawned on me ... it was the Oilers' first NHL goal.

"I guess I'm in the Oiler record book for all time."

Lowe took his first NHL game in stride. "It didn't seem that much different," he said. "It wasn't any tougher, I didn't think. I was in a little bit of a daze at the start because I couldn't believe I was actually playing in the league ... but that wore off."

The starting lineup for the Oilers' first game had Lowe and Lee Fogolin on defence, Dryden in goal and the checking line of Stan Weir, Dave Hunter and Dave Lumley up front. "We weren't sure what to expect in our first NHL game," said Lowe, who went on to score 84 regular season NHL goals and play in 1,254 regular season games.

Edmonton lost 4-2, but Chicago coach Eddie Johnston said: "I heard they were the best of the four new teams and I have to believe it now."

It wouldn't always be obvious. The Oilers started off with a 3-12-6 record and were a dismal 9-22-9 at the mid-season mark. With the Oilers in the midst of a losing skid in which they would win only once in 11 games, the *Edmonton Journal*'s mercurial columnist Terry Jones wrote that he would eat his words if the Oilers made the playoffs "with a sauce of bitter lemon, sour grapes and sauerkraut topped with sour cream."

Lo and behold, the little team that couldn't in the first half of the season, actually *could* in the second half. Sather made a number of moves, getting Don Ashby for Bobby Schmautz, Don Murdoch for Cam Connor and goalie Ron Low for Ron Chipperfield.

With the changes, the club began making a most improbable run at a playoff spot.

Led by the amazing Gretzky, who was fighting Los Angeles Kings' Marcel Dionne for the league scoring title, the Oilers earned eight wins and a tie in their final 11 games, finishing with a 28-39-13 record, nailing down the 16th and final playoff position and leaving Jones a date with a dinner plate in the Oilers' dressing room before the playoffs.

"When you've been there, you know how to get there," said Gretzky, of

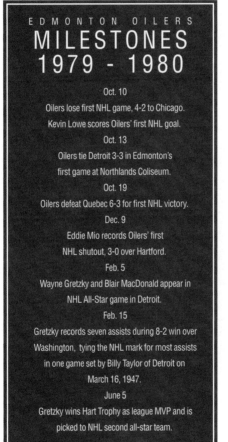

EDMONTON OILERS
MILESTONES
1979 - 1980

Oct. 10
Oilers lose first NHL game, 4-2 to Chicago.
Kevin Lowe scores Oilers' first NHL goal.

Oct. 13
Oilers tie Detroit 3-3 in Edmonton's
first game at Northlands Coliseum.

Oct. 19
Oilers defeat Quebec 6-3 for first NHL victory.

Dec. 9
Eddie Mio records Oilers' first
NHL shutout, 3-0 over Hartford.

Feb. 5
Wayne Gretzky and Blair MacDonald appear in
NHL All-Star game in Detroit.

Feb. 15
Gretzky records seven assists during 8-2 win over
Washington, tying the NHL mark for most assists
in one game set by Billy Taylor of Detroit on
March 16, 1947.

June 5
Gretzky wins Hart Trophy as league MVP and is
picked to NHL second all-star team.

1979 -1980
FIFTEEN MINUTES
OF FAME

Jim Grant was a 20-year-old business administration student and goaltender with the NAIT Ooks when he got a 2 p.m. phone call on Jan. 27, 1980. Edmonton Oilers netminder Eddie Mio had sprained his ankle and the Oilers wanted Grant to back up Jim Corsi at the Coliseum that night against the Philadelphia Flyers, who were in the midst of a NHL record 35-game undefeated streak.

"I've never even played Junior A or Tier 2," said Grant, after the 5-2 win by Philadelphia. "On the one hand, I was hoping nothing would happen to Corsi. But still, it would have been something to write home about if I'd just got into a game for a few minutes."

Grant, who wore No. 33, was paid $100 for his evening of cheerleading. "I'm just thrilled that I got a chance," he said. "I would have worked for free, but they paid me anyway. My girlfriend got a ticket to the game, too. And I got to keep the goalsticks I taped."

Grant has since become a certified financial planner with HSBC in Edmonton. "I remember saying to Mark Messier in the dressing room, 'This is just like the big time,'" recalled Grant in June of 2003. "He said, 'Jim, this is the big time.'"

And Wendy, the girlfriend who used that ticket, became Grant's wife.

making the playoffs. "We won't be like Colorado and maybe Washington. They've never been there. We won't have to go through that."

The teenaged Gretzky finished the regular season with a whopping 51 goals and 137 points, and hoped it was enough to hold off Dionne for the Art Ross Trophy during the final weekend of play. "Sure, I'm apprehensive," said Gretzky, with a two-point lead and fingers crossed. "Who knows, I may never get this close to a scoring championship again."

Dionne ended up with the same 137 points as Gretzky, but Dionne was awarded the Art Ross on the basis of scoring 53 goals to Gretzky's 51.

No matter. The important thing was that the Oilers

The Flyers celebrate a goal on Oilers netminder Ron Low, while Oiler Brett Callighen watches.

"All they need is a couple of key drafts and a trade or two and, I'll tell

you what, they're going to be there."

— Flyers goaltending coach Jacques Plante

EDMONTON OILERS
1979-1980

had squeaked into the playoffs. In the best-of-five first round, 16th-place Edmonton faced the Philadelphia Flyers, the overall first-place finishers. Edmonton lost the opener 4-3 on Bobby Clarke's overtime goal, the second game 5-1 and the third 3-2 on Ken Linseman's goal in double-overtime.

After the final game, Flyers goaltending coach Jacques Plante, a onetime WHA Oiler, made an eerie prediction about his former club. "All they need is a couple of key drafts and a trade or two and, I'll tell you what, they're going to be there," said Plante. "In five years, they could be playing for the Stanley Cup in the final series. And when they get there, with the talented youth they have, they'll be around for a long, long time."

Handshake heartbreak: Oilers captain Blair MacDonald (left), along with Don Ashby and Brett Callighen wish the Flyers luck.

"In five years, they could be playing for the Stanley Cup in the final series. And when they get there, with the talented youth they have, they'll be around for a long, long time."

— Jacques Plante

Edmonton Oilers 1979-80 Results & Statistics

REGULAR SEASON

COACH	GP	W	L	T	PTS	GF	GA
Glen Sather	80	28	39	13	69	301	32

4th Smythe Division, 16th Overall.

Playoffs:
Lost Preliminary Round 3-0 vs Philadelphia.

REGULAR SEASON

PLAYER	GP	G	A	PTS	PIM
Wayne Gretzky	79	51	86	137	2
Blair MacDonald	80	46	48	94	
Stan Weir	79	33	33	66	4
Brett Callighen	59	23	35	58	72
Dave Lumley	80	20	38	58	138
Don Murdoch (NYR)	56	23	19	42	1
Don Murdoch (EDM)	10	5	2	7	
Don Murdoch (TOT)	66	28	21	49	2
Dave Hunter	80	12	31	43	10
Doug Hicks	78	9	31	40	5
Ron Chipperfield	67	18	19	37	2
Risto Siltanen	64	6	29	35	26
Mark Messier	75	12	21	33	12
Pat Price	75	11	21	32	13
Kevin Lowe	64	2	19	21	7
Don Ashby (COL)	11	0	1	1	
Don Ashby (EDM)	18	10	9	19	
Don Ashby (TOT)	29	10	10	20	
Cam Connor	38	7	13	20	130
Al Hamilton	31	4	15	19	2
Lee Fogolin	80	5	10	15	10
Dave Semenko	67	6	7	13	135
Colin Campbell	72	2	11	13	19
Bill Flett	20	5	2	7	
Peter Driscoll	39	1	5	6	5
Dan Newman	10	3	1	4	
Kari Makkonen	9	2	2	4	
Ron Low (QUE)	15	0	2	2	
Ron Low (EDM)	11	0	1	1	
Ron Low (TOT)	26	0	3	3	
Jim Corsi	26	0	3	3	
Ed Mio	34	0	1	1	
John Bednarski	1	0	0	0	
Bob Dupuis	1	0	0	0	
Ron Carter	2	0	0	0	
Mike Forbes	2	0	0	0	
Bryon Baltimore	2	0	0	0	
Jim Harrison	3	0	0	0	
Mike Toal	3	0	0	0	
Ron Areshenkoff	4	0	0	0	
Alex Tidey	5	0	0	0	8
Don Cutts	6	0	0	0	
Poul Popiel	10	0	0	0	
Wayne Bianchin	11	0	0	0	
Dave Dryden	14	0	0	0	

REGULAR SEASON

GOALTENDER	GP	MINS	GA	SO	GAA.	W
Ron Low (QUE)	15	828	51	0	3.70	5
Ron Low (EDM)	11	650	37	0	3.42	8
Ron Low (TOT)	26	1478	88	0	3.57	13
Don Cutts	6	269	16	0	3.57	1
Jim Corsi	26	1366	83	0	3.65	8-1
Bob Dupuis	1	60	4	0	4.00	0
Ed Mio	34	1711	120	1	4.21	9-1
Dave Dryden	14	744	53	0	4.27	2

DAVID SLAYS GOLIATH

They chose as their theme song for the 1980-81 playoffs *The Impossible Dream*, from the 1965 Broadway musical *The Man of La Mancha*.

In truth, more than fighting unbeatable foes and reaching unreachable stars, it seemed more like mere wishful thinking that the Edmonton Oilers were engaged in when they met the Montreal Canadiens in the first round of the Stanley Cup playoffs.

But it was to be perhaps one of the finest moments in the first 25 years of the Oilers' NHL history. By sweeping the omnipotent Canadiens three straight, led by a cherub named Andy Moog in goal, the Oilers announced to the hockey world that their day would soon be at hand.

"The most important thing we did was create a winning attitude here," said Wayne Gretzky, after the team took the defending Stanley Cup champion New York Islanders to six games in the second playoff round (New York went on to defend its title). "We lost the series, but hopefully we also lost forever the droopy kind of attitude and we'll start to show a lot more in the regular season from now on.

"Now when a player comes to this team, he'll have to adopt the attitude that is here."

It had been a season that started with new looks everywhere. The Coliseum had been expanded by 2,051 seats. In the front office, general manager Larry Gordon left to become the owner of the Oilers' new farm club in Kansas, the Wichita Wind. Glen Sather surrendered the Oilers' coaching reins to serve as general manager. Bryan Watson took over Sather's position behind the bench.

There were also changes in player personnel. Defenceman Al Hamilton became the first Oiler to have his sweater retired. Goalie Peter LoPresti, defenceman Paul Coffey and forwards Matti Hagman, Jari Kurri and Glenn Anderson became the newest players to don the Oiler orange and blue. Kurri, a 20-year-old, fourth-round draft pick from Finland, replaced injured Brett Callighen on the line with Gretzky and captain Blair MacDonald.

But the team stumbled out of the starting gate under Watson's inexperienced leadership and, after just four wins in the first 18 games, Sather fired his longtime buddy and resumed coaching himself. "It was awful, maybe the second hardest thing I've had to do," said Sather. "The only thing harder might have been telling Ron Chipperfield he was traded last March while his mother was dying."

Soon after, the Oilers drubbed the powerhouse Montreal Canadiens 9-1 in Edmonton in what a local columnist described as the most impressive win in the team's short history.

The Oilers made some late season moves in March of 1981, trading Pat Price and captain Blair MacDonald, who had scored 46 goals the year before. Sather explained the latter move with his infamous quote: "Even a fire hydrant could score 40 goals playing with Gretzky."

It would take more than a fire hydrant to cool off the kid known as the Great One. At the tender age of 20, Gretzky took aim at Phil Esposito's NHL record for the most points in a season. He passed Esposito's mark on March 30, 1981, assisting on a Mark Messier goal in Pittsburgh to give him 153 points.

The next period, Gretzky's 102nd assist on a Kurri goal tied Bobby Orr's 1970-71 single-season record for assists.

"Gretzky has far more ability than I have ... had," said Esposito. "I got my points because I was with one helluva hockey team. Gretzky gets his because he *is* the Edmonton Oilers."

With 55 goals and 164 points, Gretzky became the youngest player to ever win the Art Ross Trophy for most points, at 20 years and two months. The youngest previous winner was left winger Harvey "Busher" Jackson of the Toronto Maple Leafs, who won it at age 21 in 1931-32.

Gretzky, who again won the Hart Trophy and made the first all-star team, carried the Oilers into 14th place and the playoffs for the second season in a row.

Despite 99's heroics, no one could have predicted what happened next as the young Oilers faced the mighty Canadiens in the first round of the best-of-five Stanley Cup playoffs — except maybe, the Oilers themselves.

"Maybe we're so young that we're naive," suggested Oilers captain Lee Fogolin before the series started.

Shockingly, Edmonton swept the Habs 6-3 and 3-1 in Montreal, then 6-2 in Edmonton.

The hero was pint-sized Andy Moog, who had started the season as the club's No. 4 goalie on the depth chart, and orchestrated what *Edmonton Journal* columnist Terry Jones called "perhaps the greatest single sporting thrill in Edmonton history."

The Oilers then fell in six hard-fought games to the Islanders in Round 2, but gained the eventual champion's respect.

"It was all based on emotion and desire," said Islanders captain Denis Potvin, of the series. "It was so tough to play them. They were all over the ice. They made it so frustrating."

The Oilers drew great confidence from their magical playoff.

"We proved to ourselves that you don't have to be 30 years old before you can win," said Coffey. "We're not going to spend 10 years' apprenticeship before we're winners now. This was a tremendous learning experience.

"If we can't learn great gobs from this, we can't learn anything."

EDMONTON OILERS
MILESTONES
1980 - 1981

Oct. 12
Glenn Anderson scores his first NHL goal on Colorado goaltender Al Smith.

Oct. 18
Jari Kurri beats Billy Smith of the New York Islanders for his first NHL goal.

Oct. 22
Paul Coffey scores his first NHL goal as Oilers post their first NHL win over the Calgary Flames.

Feb. 18
Wayne Gretzky has his second seven-point night — five goals and two assists — in a 9-2 win over St. Louis. Four goals within seven minutes and 58 seconds set the record for fastest four individual goals, and ties the record for most goals by an individual in one period.

Mar. 30
Gretzky breaks Phil Esposito's record for most points in a season, with 153, and ties Bobby Orr's record for most assists in a season, with 102.

April 11
Oilers beat the Montreal Canadiens 6-2 for the franchise's first NHL playoff round win, 3-0 in games.

June 9
Gretzky wins the Hart Trophy as MVP and makes the first all-star team.

Opposite: Unbelievable! The neophyte Oilers knock off the vaunted Montreal Canadiens in three straight games, thanks largely to the efforts of goaltender Andy Moog. Moog shakes hands with his counterpart from the Montreal Canadiens, Richard Sevigny, after the improbable Oilers' sweep.

1980 - 1981
TRAGEDY IN THE OILERS' FAMILY

Don Ashby, who scored six points on a line with Wayne Gretzky one night during the 1980-81 season, died on May 30, 1981, when his 1977 BMW collided with a truck just north of Penticton, B.C. "He was so easy-going, such a nice guy," said Gretzky.

Ashby, 26, was on his way home to Kamloops from Wichita, Kan., where he finished third in Central Hockey League scoring with the Edmonton Oilers farm club.

A first-round draft pick of the Toronto Maple Leafs, Ashby moved to the Colorado Rockies and was traded to Edmonton for Bobby Schmautz in February of 1980. He played seven games with the Oilers.

Andy Moog was amazing against the mighty Montreal Canadiens, blocking this shot off his shoulder in the third and deciding game of Edmonton-Montreal first-round series. Moog and the Oilers knocked off the powerful Habs for the Oilers' first-ever NHL playoff series win.

Wayne Gretzky gets the worst of this collision with Montreal Canadiens defenceman Rod Langway. The Oilers' Brett Callighen waits in the wings.

EDMONTON OILERS
1980-1981

*Public nemesis No. 1 — Islanders goalie Billy Smith. Smith threatens Wayne Gretzky with his goal stick,
while the Great One has a few choice words of his own for the Islanders' puckstopper.*

Kamikaze Glenn Anderson sweeps in on Smith, as New York captain Denis Potvin tries to clear Anderson from the front of Battlin' Billy.

Edmonton Oilers
1980-81
Results & Statistics

COACH	GP	W	L	T	PTS	GF	GA
Bryan Watson (4-9-5) & Glen Sather (25-26-11)							
	80	29	35	16	74	328	327

4th Smythe Division, 14th Overall.

Playoffs: Won Preliminary Round 3-0 vs Montreal, Lost
Quarter-Final 4-2 vs NY Islanders.

REGULAR SEASON

PLAYER	GP	G	A	PTS	PIM
Wayne Gretzky	80	55	109	164	28
Jari Kurri	75	32	43	75	40
Mark Messier	72	23	40	63	102
Brett Callighen	55	25	35	60	32
Glenn Anderson	58	30	23	53	24
Matti Hagman	75	20	33	53	16
Risto Siltanen	79	17	36	53	54
Blair MacDonald	51	19	24	43	27
Kevin Lowe	79	10	24	34	94
Stan Weir	70	12	20	32	40
Paul Coffey	74	9	23	32	130
Pat Price	59	8	24	32	193
Lee Fogolin	80	13	17	30	137
Dave Hunter	78	12	16	28	98
Doug Hicks	59	5	16	21	76
Garry Unger (LA)	58	10	10	20	40
Garry Unger (EDM)	13	0	0	0	6
Garry Unger (TOT)	71	10	10	20	46
Dave Semenko	58	11	8	19	80
Don Murdoch	40	10	9	19	18
Pat Hughes (PIT)	58	10	9	19	161
Pat Hughes (EDM)	2	0	0	0	0
Pat Hughes (TOT)	60	10	9	19	161
Garry Lariviere (QUE)	52	3	13	16	50
Garry Lariviere (EDM)	13	0	2	2	6
Garry Lariviere (TOT)	65	3	15	18	56
Dave Lumley	53	7	9	16	74
Curt Brackenbury	58	2	7	9	153
Charlie Huddy	12	2	5	7	6
Don Ashby	6	2	3	5	2
Peter Driscoll	21	2	3	5	43
Eddie Mio	43	0	5	5	6
John Hughes	18	0	3	3	18
Ron Low	24	0	3	3	0
Tom Roulston	11	1	1	2	2
Gary Edwards	15	0	2	2	0
Roy Sommer	3	1	0	1	7
Andy Moog	7	0	1	1	0
Tom Bladon	1	0	0	0	0
Peter LoPresti	2	0	0	0	0

REGULAR SEASON

GOALTENDER	GP	MINS	GA	SO	GAA.	W-L-T
Gary Edwards	15	729	44	0	3.62	5-3-4
Andy Moog	7	313	20	0	3.83	3-3-0
Eddie Mio	43	2393	155	0	3.89	16-15-9
Ron Low	24	1260	93	0	4.43	5-13-3
Peter LoPresti	2	105	8	0	4.57	0-1-0

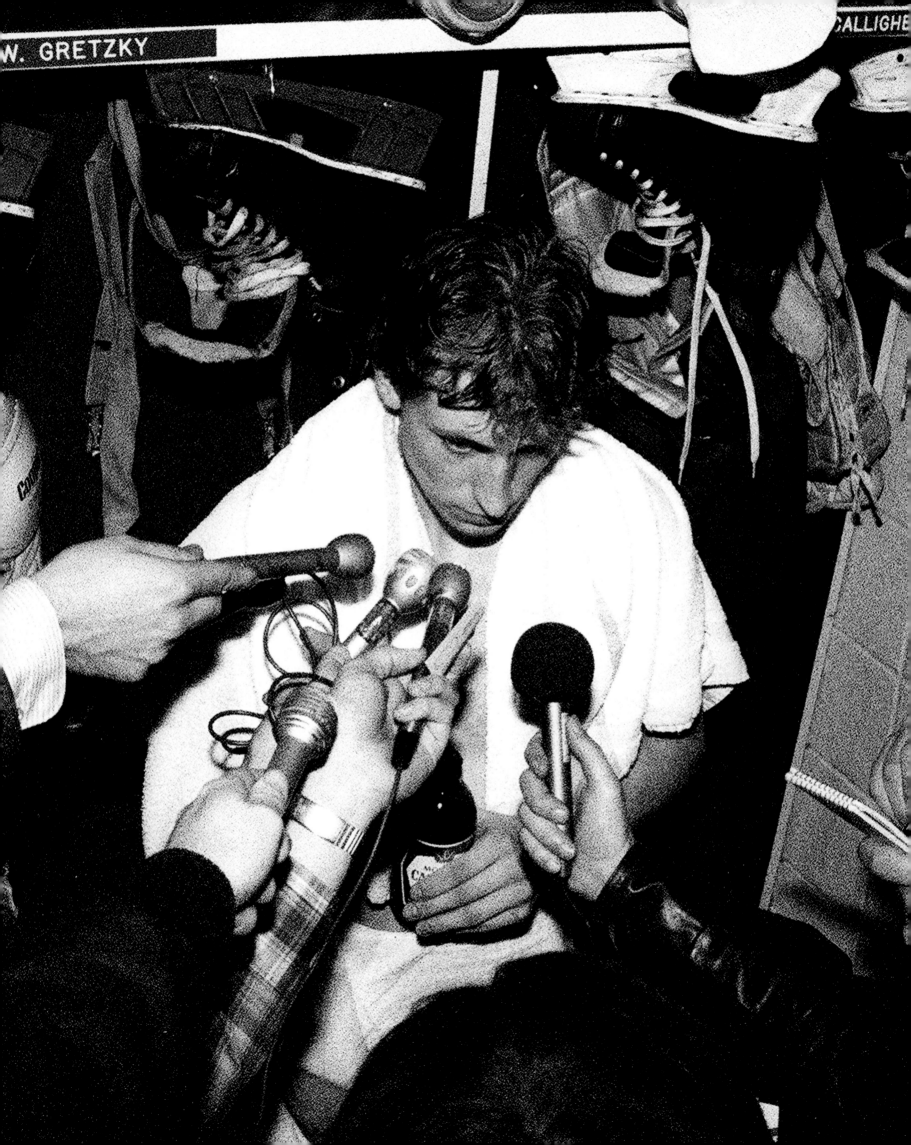

EDMONTON OILERS
1981-1982
PRIME-TIME PRETENDERS?

They began the season as destiny's darlings, the killers of the Montreal Canadiens the year before, but the Edmonton Oilers finished 1981-82 as The Not Quite Ready For Prime-Time Players.

In fact, after blowing leads of 4-1 and 5-0 and dropping the best-of-five first playoff round to the Los Angeles Kings, the Oilers were pilloried in the press. Wrote *Edmonton Journal* columnist Terry Jones: "From today until they've won a playoff series again, they are weak-kneed wimps who thought they were God's Gift To The National Hockey League but found out that they were nothing but Adolescent, Front-Running Goodtime Charlies who couldn't handle any adversity."

Ahem.

The Oilers indeed entered the season sensing they were about to knock on the door of greatness. One of the final cogs was put in place when they managed to get a Spruce Grove youngster, goaltender Grant Fuhr, as the eighth pick overall in the 1981 NHL entry draft.

"He's the best pro prospect since Bernie Parent," said Oilers chief scout Barry Fraser.

"To be honest, I didn't think there was any way Grant would still be there when we picked," said coach Glen Sather. "When you get a chance to draft somebody like him, you just can't pass."

"Edmonton is my home town," said Fuhr, in a laid-back style that would become his trademark. "There may be a little added pressure because I'm from there, but I don't mind. It's a good place to play."

Sather also added Ted Green as an assistant coach, despite his absence of pro coaching experience. Green, best known for having recovered from a near fatal brain injury that resulted in a plate being put in his head, would instil a ferocity within the young Oilers that would eventually serve them well in Stanley Cup encounters with the battle-hardened New York Islanders and especially the Philadelphia Flyers.

"Our hockey club doesn't have the winning heritage," said Sather. "We need somebody to tell the kids what it takes, the sacrifices that have to be made in order to win."

Sather and Scotty Bowman in Buffalo were the only people to hold both general manager and coaching titles at the time. "With the Oilers, it's like watching a family grow up, as corny as that sounds," said Sather. "Until they come of age, I'm going to stick with it. I've thought about quitting lots of times, usually after a loss, but I've gone through too much adversity to take the easy way out and just be a GM."

During the summer, the rumours started that two-time Hart Trophy winner Wayne Gretzky, who had made $150,000 in salary plus $125,000 in bonuses the previous year, would be requesting $500,000 for the upcoming season. Six months later, the ante was reportedly up to $10 million over 10 years. In early December, he received the first of many major media honours, becoming the first hockey player to be named *Sporting News* Man of the Year.

Then came Dec. 30, 1981.

Maurice "The Rocket" Richard of the Montreal Canadiens had set the NHL record of 50 goals in 50 games during the 1944-45 season. Mike Bossy of the New York Islanders had tied it in 1980-81.

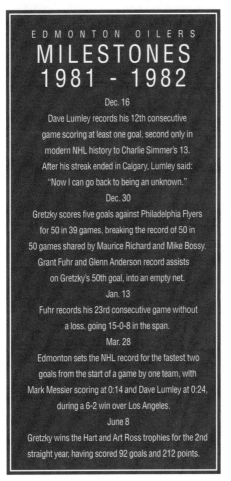

EDMONTON OILERS
MILESTONES
1981 - 1982

Dec. 16
Dave Lumley records his 12th consecutive game scoring at least one goal, second only in modern NHL history to Charlie Simmer's 13. After his streak ended in Calgary, Lumley said: "Now I can go back to being an unknown."

Dec. 30
Gretzky scores five goals against Philadelphia Flyers for 50 in 39 games, breaking the record of 50 in 50 games shared by Maurice Richard and Mike Bossy. Grant Fuhr and Glenn Anderson record assists on Gretzky's 50th goal, into an empty net.

Jan. 13
Fuhr records his 23rd consecutive game without a loss, going 15-0-8 in the span.

Mar. 28
Edmonton sets the NHL record for the fastest two goals from the start of a game by one team, with Mark Messier scoring at 0:14 and Dave Lumley at 0:24, during a 6-2 win over Los Angeles.

June 8
Gretzky wins the Hart and Art Ross trophies for the 2nd straight year, having scored 92 goals and 212 points.

Dec. 30 was Gretzky's 39th game of the season. The Oilers were playing Philadelphia at the Coliseum. Gretzky already had 45 goals.

Then he went to work. A five-footer from the edge of the crease. A howitzer from 35 feet. A breakaway 25-footer off goalie Pete Peeters' chest. A 30-footer over Peeters' shoulder. And finally, a 30-footer along the ice with Peeters on the bench for an extra attacker with three seconds left in the game.

Fifty goals, 39 games.

"It's the second-best feeling I've ever had — it's not quite as thrilling as beating Montreal in the playoffs last year," said Gretzky.

Two weeks later, Gretzky was on an eastern road trip that would include Edmonton's only game in Toronto that season. He had 132 interview requests, in addition to a two-hour media conference in Toronto to handle all the demands there.

"I know I don't have his patience," said Sather. "But Wayne still answers everyone. He is still willing to accept it all as part of the game. I don't know how much longer he can remain the way he is."

Turns out he didn't remain the same for too much longer, at least financially.

On Jan. 20, 1982, it was announced that Gretzky's 21-year contract signed in 1979 had been replaced by a new 21-year pact — nine years plus two six-year options. The first 15 years of the deal were said to be worth $20 million — a starting yearly base salary of $650,000 plus incentives — plus a shopping centre to be named in 1988 as part of a tax strategy. "It's hard to believe — after all I'm just a farm boy," said Gretzky.

But the Great One was making believers out of everyone else, gobbling up records faster than Jethro devoured a bowl of cereal.

On Feb. 24, 1982, in Buffalo, Gretzky snared a loose puck inside the Sabres zone, took about three strides, shook off a desperate Richie Dunn check, and sent a soft 20-footer past Buffalo netminder Don Edwards at 13:24 of the third period.

His first of three goals on the night gave him 77 for the year, smashing the record of 76 Phil Esposito had set 11 years earlier. The 77th goal came in Gretzky's 64th game, 14 fewer than Esposito took for 76. "When it went in, the first thing that went through my head was, 'Well, that puts us ahead 4-3,'" said Gretzky. "It was only when I made my turn that there was a sense of relief."

He wound up with 92 goals, 110 assists and 212 points.

The season ended with the Oilers in second place overall in the NHL with 111 points, yet assistant coach Billy Harris offered a bit of foreshadowing: "It could turn out to be that we might never be as good as we are right now. Things like that can happen."

Just in time for the playoffs, Edmonton signed University of Alberta product Randy Gregg, a six-foot-four defenceman who had toiled for two seasons with the Kokudo Bunnies in Japan, en route to earning his medical degree. "I worried that his skills and timing had slowed down playing in Japan," said Sather. "I wasn't sure he would be aggressive enough, either. But here, he just has to take his body and get in the road. He doesn't have to fight."

Opposite: The sting of defeat. A disconsolate Wayne Gretzky explains what went wrong after Los Angeles upset the heavily favoured Oilers in the first round of the playoffs.

EDMONTON OILERS
1981-1982

1981 - 1982
THE GREAT (GRETZKY) DEBATE

It was inevitable that someone would soon try to boost their own profile by taking a run at Wayne Gretzky's. In an *Edmonton Journal* exclusive during February of 1982, veteran New York hockey author Stan Fischler picked up the cue and stomped soundly on The Great One.

"It is a travesty of hockey history to discuss Gretzky in the same breath as Maurice (The Rocket) Richard, Howie Morenz, Gordie Howe or Jean Beliveau," wrote Fischler. "I roar with laughter when I read Michael Farber in the *Montreal Gazette* eulogize Gretzky at the expense of The Rocket or Howe. Farber and his ilk write in ignorance."

But for every tirade like Fischler's, there was a story like that of Theresa Heise, a student at M.E. LaZerte high school in Edmonton, who every night before going to bed took a gold-framed picture of Gretzky and placed it on her desk as she did her homework. Every newspaper clipping, magazine article, picture, poster, book and item of clothing that featured Gretzky covered the walls and doors of her room.

"He's just the biggest idol I've ever had," said Heise, 16. "There's just something about his personality. He doesn't show that he's a superstar — like Burt Reynolds. Wayne's not a show-off."

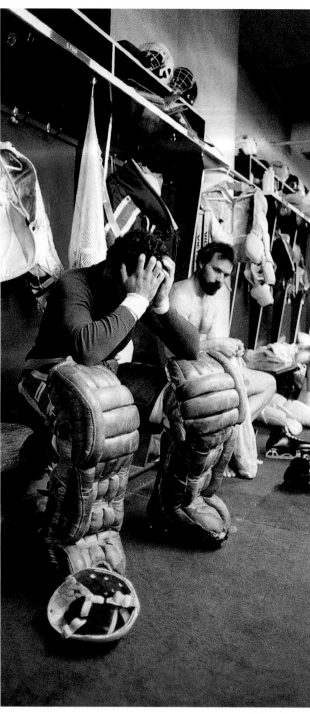

Top middle: Jay Wells and his jubilant Los Angeles Kings' teammates celebrate their upset win over the Oilers in the preliminary round playoff series. Oilers goalie Grant Fuhr, at left, and forward Stan Weir, at right, take the loss hard.

Facing the 17th-place Los Angeles Kings in the first round of the playoffs, the Oilers led the first game 4-1, but lost 10-8. A 5-0 Game 3 lead evaporated, the Kings winning 6-5 on Daryl Evans' goal at 2:35 of overtime in what has been chronicled as the most amazing comeback against the Oilers ever — the Miracle on Manchester.

"I've never seen a comeback like that in 30 years of hockey and I never dreamed you'd ever see anything like that in the Stanley Cup playoffs," said Kings coach Don Perry. "Miracles happen. They really do."

In the fifth and deciding game in Edmonton, where the Oilers had lost only six of 42 games during the season, Los

Top right: Mark Messier bows his head in shame, while the Kings' Charlie Simmer (at left) celebrates a goal against the Oilers.

Edmonton Oilers 1981-82 Results & Statistics

COACH	REGULAR SEASON						
	GP	W	L	T	PTS	GF	GA
Glen Sather	80	48	17	15	111	417	295

1st Smythe Division, 2nd Overall. Playoffs: Lost Smythe Division Semifinal 3-2 vs Los Angeles.

PLAYER	REGULAR SEASON				
	GP	G	A	PTS	PIM
Wayne Gretzky	80	92	120	212	26
Glenn Anderson	80	38	67	105	71
Paul Coffey	80	29	60	89	106
Mark Messier	78	50	38	88	119
Jari Kurri	71	32	54	86	32
Dave Lumley	66	32	42	74	96
Risto Siltanen	63	15	48	63	24
Matti Hagman	72	21	38	59	18
Pat Hughes	68	24	22	46	99
Kevin Lowe	80	9	31	40	63
Dave Hunter	63	16	22	38	63
Laurie Boschman (TOR)	54	9	19	28	150
Laurie Boschman (EDM)	11	2	3	5	37
Laurie Boschman (TOT)	65	11	22	33	187
Lee Fogolin	80	4	25	29	154
Brett Callighen	46	8	19	27	28
Dave Semenko	59	12	12	24	194
Doug Hicks	49	3	20	23	55
Garry Lariviere	62	1	21	22	41
Garry Unger	46	7	13	20	69
Stan Weir	51	3	13	16	13
Charlie Huddy	41	4	11	15	48
Tom Roulston	35	11	3	14	22
Mike Forbes	16	1	7	8	26
Grant Fuhr	48	0	6	6	6
Ken Berry	15	2	3	5	9
Marc Habscheid	7	1	3	4	2
Lance Nethery (NYR)	5	0	0	0	0
Lance Nethery (EDM)	3	0	2	2	2
Lance Nethery (TOT)	8	0	2	2	2
Curt Brackenbury	14	0	2	2	12
Andy Moog	8	0	1	1	2
Todd Strueby	3	0	0	0	0
Walt Poddubny	4	0	0	0	0
Don Jackson	8	0	0	0	18
Ron Low	29	0	0	0	2
Randy Gregg	-	-	-	-	-

GOALTENDER	REGULAR SEASON					
	GP	MINS	GA	SO	GAA.	W-L-T
Grant Fuhr	48	2847	157	0	3.31	28-5-14
Ron Low	29	1554	100	0	3.86	17-7-1
Andy Moog	8	399	32	0	4.81	3-5-0

Angeles won 7-4. After the game, hanging in the Los Angeles dressing room was an Oiler doll constructed by the Kings using an oil can, with a noose around its neck. Several Kings delighted in taking turns choking it.

"The pressure, which we've never really had to deal with until the start of the playoffs this year, really caught up to a lot of guys," said Sather. Later, during the summer, he would add: "I knew we were in trouble before the playoffs, when blood tests on four players showed they were anemic. Wayne Gretzky, Mark Messier, Kevin Lowe and Dave Semenko were worn out."

They would have a long summer to rest.

1982-1983
ON THE VERGE OF GREATNESS

Stung by the weak-kneed wimp label from the previous playoffs, the Edmonton Oilers responded the best way they knew how. They earned 106 points during the 1982-83 season, second only to the Boston Bruins' 110.

And they shrugged off the albatross of playoffs past when they won three straight series to reach the Stanley Cup final against the three-time defending champion New York Islanders.

If the Oilers were badly in need of a lightning rod to focus their energy during the finals, the *Edmonton Journal* provided it with a front-page bullet-riddled poster of Islanders goalie Billy Smith, dubbing him "Public Enemy Number One."

Smith, who had slashed Oiler Glenn Anderson in the latest of many affronts on opponents, was so overwhelmed by the outcry of hostility against him that he won the Conn Smythe Trophy as best playoff performer in a four-game sweep of the finals.

Something about sleeping dogs.

Coach Glen Sather had gone into the 1982-83 season vowing to concentrate more on team achievement, even at the expense of individual goals, even those of Wayne Gretzky.

"I know next year he is definitely not playing as much," said Sather, during the summer of '82. "He will not have the kind of year he just had. He may want to play a lot, but I'm not going to let him. I'll use him killing penalties, but less on the power play."

Gretzky had been subject of a hot rumour, that the New York Rangers had offered Edmonton owner Peter Pocklington $20 million for the Great One, which caused Sather to respond: "I'd say that if anyone offered $20 million, they'd be a bit short."

"There's a tremendous amount of pressure to out-do what I've accomplished," said Gretzky. "Everything went just the right way last season. I got to play 80 games. There were no slumps, no nagging injuries or colds hanging on. It was the first time since I was 10, I think, where I broke out with a lot of goals. Usually my assists are double."

John Muckler replaced Bill Harris as assistant coach, and Sather acquired forwards Ken "The Rat" Linseman from the Philadelphia Flyers and Jaroslav Pouzar from the Czechoslovakian national team.

While the Oilers romped to a 47-21-12 record, there were reminders that this was still a team in its infancy, still finding its way in the world, still experiencing growing pains.

During a short but memorable conversation in October, Gretzky and linemate Jari Kurri talked about goals:

"Going for 50?" asked Gretzky.

Kurri shook his head.

"Why?" asked Gretzky.

"I'm a two-way player," said Kurri.

Kurri was right. He scored only 45 that season. He'd wait a year before notching 52.

One memorable growing pain came the night of Jan. 9, 1983, when the Oilers outshot the Detroit Red Wings 32-20, yet lost to the 19th-best team in the league. Halfway through the second period, the 17,498 fans in the Coliseum started taunting sophomore goalie Grant Fuhr, giving him the raspberry cheer for a save on an easy shot.

"I've given up on them (the fans)," said Fuhr after the game. "They're totally horse (bleep). They're jerks."

It was mentioned that once his words became public, the fans' affection for him could diminish even more. "I could care less what they want to do," said Fuhr, just 20 at the time. "They're a bunch of jerks."

Two weeks later, just one year after being named the Campbell Conference starting goalie in the NHL all-star game, Fuhr was demoted to the minor league Moncton Alpines to regain his form and confidence. Until then, he and Mike Liut in St. Louis had been the only two NHL goalies without a minute's experience in the minors.

Fuhr played 10 games with Moncton, and came back in time to help the Oilers roar into the playoffs with a 16-3-2 record during their final 21 regular season games.

As the calendar year wound down, Wayne Gretzky was named athlete of the year by everyone from ABC TV's *Wide World of Sports* to the *Chicago Tribune*. He was the first three-in-a-row winner of the Canadian Press athlete of the year award.

But Gretzky felt the most prestigious award was becoming only the third hockey player or team — after Bobby Orr in 1970 and the U.S. Olympic hockey team in 1980 — to ever receive the *Sports Illustrated* Sportsman of the Year Award.

"I took a look at the list of people and I'm in the same group of people as Jack Nicklaus and Mickey Mantle," said Gretzky. "I think it was harder to win the *Sports Illustrated* award because hockey isn't really one of the major sports. There's baseball and football, golf, tennis. From what I understand, I beat out Hershel Walker, Alexis Arguello and Robin Yount. I think Jimmy Connors was fifth."

One sign that the Oilers were aging nicely came when one of Gretzky's records was broken — by a teammate. Pat Hughes scored two short-handed goals in 25 seconds during a 7-5 win over St. Louis on Jan. 11, snapping the NHL mark of 27 seconds set by Gretzky the previous March. "Hell, I don't mind," said Gretzky. "It's super for Patty, and not just because he's my backgammon buddy."

Oilers defenceman Don Jackson, who had been in the penalty box, said: "I stood up after the second goal and asked if they wanted me to stay in longer."

When the playoffs came, 1,500 of the 17,000 Oilers' season ticket holders didn't pick up their option for playoff tickets. Said fan John Livingstone: "They wanted $17. No bloody way."

For the Oilers, the lesson of the previous year's playoffs, that inglorious blowing of two huge leads and the ultimate first-round defeat to the lowly Los Angeles Kings, was not forgotten this time around.

Edmonton took out the Winnipeg Jets in three straight, the Calgary Flames in five — including a 10-2 romp in Cowtown — and swept the Chicago Black Hawks in four games.

During the latter series, an 8-2 defeat had so flummoxed 'Hawks coach Orval Tessier, that Mount Orval blew his top: "We'll probably call Mayo Clinic for about 18 heart transplants before the next game. I don't know if we can get them done in time, though. There's usually a waiting list for those sorts of things."

Thus the Oilers went into the Stanley Cup final for the first time, against a formidable foe, the champion Islanders. "Any way you look at it, it'll be another

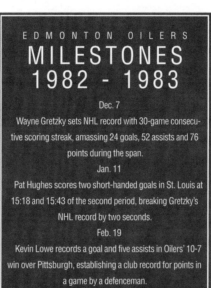

EDMONTON OILERS
MILESTONES
1982 - 1983

Dec. 7
Wayne Gretzky sets NHL record with 30-game consecutive scoring streak, amassing 24 goals, 52 assists and 76 points during the span.

Jan. 11
Pat Hughes scores two short-handed goals in St. Louis at 15:18 and 15:43 of the second period, breaking Gretzky's NHL record by two seconds.

Feb. 19
Kevin Lowe records a goal and five assists in Oilers' 10-7 win over Pittsburgh, establishing a club record for points in a game by a defenceman.

June 7
Mark Messier joins Gretzky on the first all-star team.

Opposite: Wayne Gretzky followed up his record-smashing 1981-82 season with an equally impressive '82-83 campaign.

1982-1983
LET'S GET READY
TO RUMBLE ...

It wasn't exactly the Thrilla' in Manilla or the Rumble in the Jungle. But three rounds of exhibition boxing during the summer of 1983 between Muhammad Ali, the oft-crowned heavyweight boxing champ of the world, and Dave Semenko, the uncrowned heavyweight champ of the National Hockey League, drew 6,000 fans at $40 a pop to the Coliseum.

The charity exhibition was the brainchild of Oiler forward Mark Messier's uncle Larry Messier, who had worked his way into Ali's entourage by merchandising coins and other Ali mementoes.

Ali, who had fought a couple of five-round exhibitions in the since-demolished Edmonton Gardens more than a decade earlier, had been slowed considerably since then by a variety of ailments from the few blows he hadn't deflected over the ages. He spoke softly and seldomly, and his attention wandered.

At the fight, Semenko entered to the theme of *Rocky*, wearing a bathrobe of some description. Ali entered with longtime cornerman Bundini Brown, and never took his sweatsuit top off during the fight.

Semenko opened the first round with a left jab to the head. The rest of the round was well-choreographed with few punches traded. Every round featured a little Ali Shuffle, the back-and-forth movement of his feet, albeit much slower than what the likes of George Foreman and Joe Frazier had encountered.

In the end, the fight was declared a draw.

There was no demand for a rematch.

growing period for us ... if we win or lose," said Sather before the series began.

With Billy Smith heroic and histrionic, the Islanders won the Cup in four straight games. But the cherubic Oilers had

learned from the seasoned pros.

"Their composure, their stamina," bemoaned an envious Gretzky.

"We've come a long way, yet we've got a long way to go by

Hail the plumbers. Tom Roulston (right), Dave Semenko (centre) and Dave Lumley celebrate a goal.

their standards. They don't get very exuberant when they get up, or overly down when they lose."

Jackson marvelled at the Islanders' discipline. Kevin Lowe noted their ability to score first every game.

And Andy Moog chalked it up to intelligence, "doing the right thing at the right time."

It was a lesson that Edmonton would absorb well during the next 12 months.

Here's a celebration from a more conventional source: Wayne Gretzky is congratulated for one of his 71 goals in 1982-83.

Edmonton Oilers 1982-83 Results & Statistics

COACH	GP	W	L	T	PTS	GF	GA
Glen Sather	80	47	21	12	106	424	315

REGULAR SEASON

1st Smythe Division, 3rd Overall. Playoffs: Stanley Cup Finalists; Won Smythe Division Semifinal 3-0 vs Winnipeg, Won Smythe Division Final 4-1 vs Calgary, Won Campbell Conference Final 4-0 vs Chicago, Lost Stanley Cup Final 4-0 vs NY Islanders.

REGULAR SEASON

PLAYER	GP	G	A	PTS	PIM
Wayne Gretzky	80	71	125	196	59
Mark Messier	77	48	58	106	72
Glenn Anderson	72	48	56	104	70
Jari Kurri	80	45	59	104	22
Paul Coffey	80	29	67	96	87
Ken Linseman	72	33	42	75	181
Charlie Huddy	76	20	37	57	58
Willy Lindstrom (WPG)	63	20	25	45	8
Willy Lindstrom (EDM)	10	6	5	11	2
Willy Lindstrom (TOT)	73	26	30	56	10
Pat Hughes	80	25	20	45	85
Tom Roulston	67	19	21	40	24
Kevin Lowe	80	6	34	40	43
Dave Lumley	72	13	24	37	158
Jaroslav Pouzar	74	15	18	33	57
Dave Hunter	80	13	18	31	120
Randy Gregg	80	6	22	28	54
Dave Semenko	75	12	15	27	141
Laurie Boschman	62	8	12	20	183
Lee Fogolin	72	0	18	18	92
Marc Habscheid	32	3	10	13	14
Don Jackson	71	2	8	10	136
Andy Moog	50	0	4	4	16
John Blum	5	0	3	3	24
Garry Unger	16	2	0	2	8
Garry Lariviere	17	0	2	2	14
L. Middlebrook (NJ)	9	0	1	1	2
L. Middlebrook (EDM)	1	0	0	0	0
L. Middlebrook (TOT)	10	0	1	1	2
Todd Strueby	1	0	0	0	0
Ron Low	3	0	0	0	0
Don Nachbaur	4	0	0	0	17
Grant Fuhr	32	0	0	0	6
Ray Cote	-	-	-	-	-

REGULAR SEASON

GOALTENDER	GP	MINS	GA	SO	GAA.	W-L-T
L. Middlebrook	1	60	3	0	3.00	1-0-0
Andy Moog	50	2833	167	1	3.54	33-8-7
Grant Fuhr	32	1803	129	0	4.29	13-12-5
Ron Low	3	104	10	0	5.77	0-1-0

1983-1984
A DREAM REALIZED

Despite being swept in the previous Stanley Cup final, most of the pieces were in place for the Edmonton Oilers, and coach Glen Sather knew it was a matter of not messing with the team's chemistry.

Solidification of personnel included defenceman Kevin Lowe signing a four-year contract worth a reported $600,000, while Sather himself agreed to a new long-term deal from owner Peter Pocklington to coach and manage the club.

"I like to have one guy in charge and I think Glen Sather has done a good job," said Pocklington. "He's grown from a novice to the best in the business, as far as I'm concerned."

The only changes of note came when ironman Garry Unger (914 consecutive games) retired after 17 years, hard-nosed winger Kevin McClelland was picked up from Pittsburgh, the club agreed to practise at West Edmonton Mall on regular occasions and Wayne Gretzky became the team's fourth NHL captain.

It was an outward sign that Gretzky had gone from pimple-faced teenager to a leader of men at age 22, after Lee Fogolin abdicated the role he knew Gretzky was now ready to handle.

"I wasn't the captain for my statistics," said Fogolin. "I've just gone out to do my best and be a good disciplined player.

"I led by example, hoping it would rub off."

Gretzky hadn't worn a captain's 'C' permanently since bantam. He termed it "a great honour" and noted that NHL officials could no longer ignore his debating skills. "I was told by every one of them to get lost."

The other notable change was in the waistline of goalie Grant Fuhr. He was down to 182 pounds, hoping to recover from the sophomore jinx, when his goals-against average inflated by a full goal per game.

"It wasn't the second helping but the third that hurt me the year before," said Fuhr.

Edmonton opened the season with a seven-game winning streak, including a 4-3 victory over the Flames to christen the new $100-million Olympic Saddledome in Calgary.

Soon after, the Oilers broke the backs of coaches Tom Watt of the Winnipeg Jets and Billy MacMillan of the New Jersey Devils.

An 8-5 victory by Edmonton over Winnipeg, on the strength of a seven-point night by Gretzky, caused Watt to say: "We were beaten by a team led by the single greatest athlete in the world. He played a magnificent game. I've seen enough of him to last me for a long, long time."

The next day Watt was fired.

Then in mid-November, the Oilers blasted the Devils 13-4 and Gretzky delivered one of his most famous soliloquies: "I feel darn sorry for their goalies,

Ronnie (Low) and Chico (Resch). It got to the point where it wasn't funny. I mean we didn't have (Dave) Semenko, (Ken) Linseman, (Mark) Messier. If we'd had them, we might have scored 20. It's not a question of New Jersey not working, it's a question of talent. They better stop running a Mickey Mouse operation and start putting somebody on the ice. That franchise has been looking that way for nine years. It's not funny, it's disappointing. It happened in Colorado where the franchise folded. We could lose another franchise if they don't get their act together."

Two days later, Gretzky apologized. But MacMillan was soon fired, Tommy McVie was brought in to coach and the club was overhauled.

When Edmonton won a January game 12-8 over the Minnesota North Stars, one shy of the 64-year old NHL record of 21 total goals in a game, Oilers coach John Muckler mused: "We're in the entertainment business and tonight was Fan Appreciation Night."

A January road trip brought Gretzky to New Jersey, where he faced the rabble after his Mickey Mouse comments. Devils fans wore Mouseketeer headgear, but as *The Journal*'s Jim Matheson reported: "When Gretzky got three points, they were forced to lend him their ears."

In January, Gretzky missed a couple of practices in Detroit due to a fibrous growth on his ankle.

Oilers surgeon Dr. Gordon Cameron said it caused Gretzky some difficulty because it was "bothersome in terms of his skating stride." The growth would be removed after the playoffs, when dye checks testing for malignancy were negative.

With Gretzky and Kurri injured in February, Pat Hughes scored five goals in a game as the team finished a run of 18-2-2. But that was followed by a five-game losing streak, climaxed by an 11-0 loss in Hartford. The Whalers scored four power-play goals while McClelland was serving a major for belting Sylvain Turgeon.

But Gretzky and Kurri returned and the team got back on track. Gretzky had back-to-back four-goal games, with one goal that so incensed St. Louis coach Jacques Demers that he stormed off the bench after referee Ron Fournier and threw his glasses on the ice.

Late in the season, Glenn Anderson scored four goals against Hartford including his 50th of the season, en route to 54.

"I lost both my contact lenses when I fell into the boards in the second period," said Anderson, who still seemed to be able to find the net.

With Edmonton setting NHL single season records of 446 goals and 36 short-handed goals, they were prepared for the run that would give them their first Stanley Cup victory.

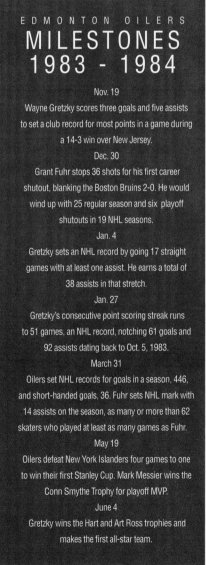

EDMONTON OILERS
MILESTONES
1983 - 1984

Nov. 19
Wayne Gretzky scores three goals and five assists to set a club record for most points in a game during a 14-3 win over New Jersey.

Dec. 30
Grant Fuhr stops 36 shots for his first career shutout, blanking the Boston Bruins 2-0. He would wind up with 25 regular season and six playoff shutouts in 19 NHL seasons.

Jan. 4
Gretzky sets an NHL record by going 17 straight games with at least one assist. He earns a total of 38 assists in that stretch.

Jan. 27
Gretzky's consecutive point scoring streak runs to 51 games, an NHL record, notching 61 goals and 92 assists dating back to Oct. 5, 1983.

March 31
Oilers set NHL records for goals in a season, 446, and short-handed goals, 36. Fuhr sets NHL mark with 14 assists on the season, as many or more than 62 skaters who played at least as many games as Fuhr.

May 19
Oilers defeat New York Islanders four games to one to win their first Stanley Cup. Mark Messier wins the Conn Smythe Trophy for playoff MVP.

June 4
Gretzky wins the Hart and Art Ross trophies and makes the first all-star team.

Opposite: Oilers win! Oilers win! Oilers win! The players rush goaltender Andy Moog after knocking off the four-time defending champion Islanders 5-2 in Game 5 of the final, capturing their first Stanley Cup.

1983-1984

The Edmonton Oilers rode the dying wishes of a 12-year-old boy along the path to the club's Stanley Cup victory in 1984.

Todd Kryzanowski had been diagnosed with leukemia in November, was hospitalized, but hoped it would go into remission so he could receive a bone marrow transplant from his sister.

It never did.

Kryzanowski was a good friend of the eldest son of Oilers coach Glen Sather, who told the team of the youngster's situation during the playoffs. "We were all touched and moved by Todd," said Sather, who along with wife Ann visited Todd in hospital. "He meant a great deal to my family."

"He was an Oiler fan, there's no question," said Todd's father Mac Kryzanowski. "He was a very sensitive boy and didn't like the violence of the game, but he loved to watch."

Before a series-ending win against the Calgary Flames, Todd told his mother Lil: "Tell Mr. Sather for the Oilers to win because I'll be watching them from heaven."

He died April 21, and the Oilers dedicated the seventh game of the series to him, a 7-4 victory. "One of his last wishes was for the Oilers to win the Stanley Cup," said Mac Kryzanowski. "He kept asking my wife and oldest daughter the score right to the end. I don't think they've ever played a better game."

Oilers defenceman Randy Gregg said Todd's last wishes "certainly hit home to a lot of players."

A month later, Edmonton won its first Stanley Cup.

Above: Wayne Gretzky shakes off a hook from Islander winger Bob Nystrom to get a shot off against Billy Smith. Below: Willy Lindstrom (19) is congratulated by teammates, including Charlie Huddy, after beating Smith.

EDMONTON OILERS
1983-1984

Above: Andy Moog robs Butch Goring on a breakaway. Left: Isles goalie Billy Smith wilts under a barrage from the Oilers after stoning them the year before in the playoffs. Below: Smith is down and out on another Oiler goal in the Stanley Cup final. Below left: New York coach Al Arbour (second from left) and some of his troops contemplate what went wrong against the mighty Oilers, who upset the Islanders' plans for a fifth straight Stanley Cup.

Edmonton Oilers
1983-84
Results & Statistics

	REGULAR SEASON						
COACH	GP	W	L	T	PTS	GF	GA
Glen Sather	80	57	18	5	119	446	314

STANLEY CUP CHAMPIONS,
1st Smythe Division, 1st Overall. Playoffs: Won Smythe Division Semifinal 3-0 vs Winnipeg, Won Smythe Division Final 4-3 vs Calgary, Won Campbell Conference Final 4-0 vs Minnesota, Won Stanley Cup Final 4-1 vs NY Islanders.

	REGULAR SEASON				
PLAYER	GP	G	A	PTS	PIM
Wayne Gretzky	74	87	118	205	39
Paul Coffey	80	40	86	126	104
Jari Kurri	64	52	61	113	14
Mark Messier	73	37	64	101	165
Glenn Anderson	80	54	45	99	65
Ken Linseman	72	18	49	67	119
Pat Hughes	77	27	28	56	61
Dave Hunter	80	22	26	48	90
Kevin Lowe	80	4	42	46	59
Charlie Huddy	75	8	34	42	43
Randy Gregg	80	13	27	40	56
Willy Lindstrom	73	22	16	38	38
Kevin McClelland (PIT)	24	2	4	6	62
Kevin McClelland (EDM)	52	8	20	28	127
Kevin McClelland (TOT)	76	10	24	34	189
Jaroslav Pouzar	67	13	19	32	44
Dave Lumley	56	6	15	21	68
Lee Fogolin	80	5	16	21	125
Don Jackson	64	8	12	20	120
Dave Semenko	52	6	11	17	118
Grant Fuhr	45	0	14	14	6
Tom Roulston	24	5	7	12	16
Pat Conacher	45	2	8	10	31
Rick Chartraw (NYR)	4	0	0	0	4
Rick Chartraw (EDM)	24	2	6	8	21
Rick Chartraw (TOT)	28	2	6	8	25
Ken Berry	13	2	3	5	10
Raimo Summanen	2	1	4	5	2
Kari Jalonen (CGY)	9	0	3	3	0
Kari Jalonen (EDM)	3	0	0	0	0
Kari Jalonen (TOT)	12	0	3	3	0
Jim Playfair	2	1	1	2	2
Tom Gorence	12	1	1	2	0
Gord Sherven	2	1	0	1	0
Marc Habscheid	9	1	0	1	6
Todd Strueby	1	0	1	1	2
John Blum	4	0	1	1	2
Andy Moog	38	0	1	1	4
Dean Clark	1	0	0	0	0
Steve Graves	2	0	0	0	0
Reg Kerr	3	0	0	0	0
Ray Cote	13	0	0	0	2
Larry Melnyk	-	-	-	-	-

	REGULAR SEASON					
GOALTENDER	GP	MINS	GA	SO	GAA.	W-L-T
Andy Moog	38	2212	139	1	3.77	27-8-1
Grant Fuhr	45	2625	171	1	3.91	30-10-4

If there was any pressure for the 1984-85 Edmonton Oilers to repeat as Stanley Cup champions, it was only because the darn thing had historically been won in bunches.

The New York Islanders had won four straight before Edmonton ended their streak. The Montreal Canadiens had taken four in a row before that. In fact, you had to go back to the 1961 Chicago Blackhawks and the 1940 New York Rangers to find a team that didn't win a medley of Cups after first achieving success. Fear of being perceived as one-year wonders was very much in the back of Oiler minds.

They needn't have worried. The Oilers polished off the Philadelphia Flyers in five games — including a convincing 8-3 coffin closer — to keep the Cup in Edmonton a second year.

"We have gotten a reputation for being arrogant and a flash in the pan," said Wayne Gretzky after the final game. "We wanted to show people we aren't. We wanted a second one more than the first."

Gretzky nipped high-scoring, smooth-skating defenceman Paul Coffey for the Conn Smythe Trophy as best playoff performer, not that Coffey minded one bit.

"It's sweeter this time," said Coffey. "When you're the biggest team on the block, people want to beat you. We went through a lot of adversity this year. We had a lull in the final four to six weeks of the regular season. Some people said we wouldn't beat Winnipeg because they were going so hot. We proved them wrong."

The Oilers had three new players on the roster when they embarked on their journey in search of a second Stanley Cup. Mike Krushelnyski had come over from Boston in a trade for Ken Linseman. Bill Carroll was picked up in the waiver draft after three seasons with the New York Islanders. And Gord Sherven was a product of the Canadian Olympic team and University of North Dakota.

Perhaps more importantly, Glen Sather had signed the core of his stars to long-term contracts. Gretzky was inked until 1999, Glenn Anderson signed for eight years, Coffey and Mark Messier for five years each, and goalie Grant Fuhr's contract was extended three years, keeping him under wraps for four more seasons in total.

The season got off to an eventful start. A combination of events — losing the Norris Trophy as best defenceman to Rod Langway and becoming a key player for Canada in the Canada Cup international hockey tournament — caused Coffey to take a new-found sense of pride in his defensive play. Then Messier was lost for six weeks due to a badly sprained knee. Through it all, the Oilers set an NHL record, going 15 games from the start of the season without a loss, posting a 12-0-3 record. That beat the previous best of 11-0-3 by the Montreal Canadiens in 1943-44. "We don't want to be known just as a team that won the Stanley Cup," said Coffey. "A chance to set a league record that stood for 40-odd years is a chance to do something very special."

"It's one of the oldest records there is and it means a lot for the players because they got it together," said coach Sather.

When Gretzky scored his 1,000th point on Dec. 19, 1984, it was his first milestone of longevity, and particularly meaningful because he expected his dread of flying would limit his career. "I remember what some high-profile people said

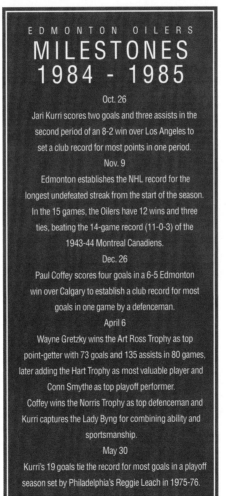

EDMONTON OILERS
MILESTONES
1984 - 1985

Oct. 26
Jari Kurri scores two goals and three assists in the second period of an 8-2 win over Los Angeles to set a club record for most points in one period.

Nov. 9
Edmonton establishes the NHL record for the longest undefeated streak from the start of the season. In the 15 games, the Oilers have 12 wins and three ties, beating the 14-game record (11-0-3) of the 1943-44 Montreal Canadiens.

Dec. 26
Paul Coffey scores four goals in a 6-5 Edmonton win over Calgary to establish a club record for most goals in one game by a defenceman.

April 6
Wayne Gretzky wins the Art Ross Trophy as top point-getter with 73 goals and 135 assists in 80 games, later adding the Hart Trophy as most valuable player and Conn Smythe as top playoff performer. Coffey wins the Norris Trophy as top defenceman and Kurri captures the Lady Byng for combining ability and sportsmanship.

May 30
Kurri's 19 goals tie the record for most goals in a playoff season set by Philadelphia's Reggie Leach in 1975-76.

when I first broke in — that I was too small, too slow," said Gretzky. "I felt if I kept playing the way I did, then, over a period of time, I would prove them wrong."

By assisting on Krushelnyski's goalmouth tap-in during a 7-3 win over Los Angeles, Gretzky reached the 1,000-point plateau in just 424 games, nearly four seasons (296 games) quicker than Guy Lafleur had taken to hit 1,000 points back in 1981.

"You take it for granted now, the things he does," said father Walter Gretzky, who was on hand for the occasion in Edmonton, along with wife Phyllis and son Brent.

"The game was anticlimactic to the wonderful achievement," said Kings superstar Marcel Dionne, who himself had hit 1,000 points in 740 games. "What Gordie Howe said about him is just the way it is. He's a marvel to watch."

Refusing to compare Gretzky to other 1,000-point getters, Dionne just mused: "All I'll say is the guy could have played anytime. He has such quick hands."

Reflecting on Howe's 1,850 points in 26 years, the 23-year-old Gretzky said: "I've played seven years of hockey. I'm in the second half of my career. How much longer I can play I don't know. I know I won't break Gordie's playing for 30 years (including the WHA). I don't think anybody will beat his 800 goals either. If I get to 1,500 points, well ..."

As the season continued, Messier came back from his injury, but on Boxing Day he knocked out Calgary's Jamie Macoun, imparting a broken cheekbone and bruised nerve to the Flames' defenceman. Messier was given a 10-game suspension.

In January, the Oilers acquired Mark Napier from the Minnesota North Stars for Sherven and Terry Martin. Sather planned on uniting Napier with Messier and Anderson, to ease some of the scoring pressure on the Gretzky-Kurri-Krushelnyski line.

Meanwhile, the story came out that owner Peter Pocklington was using Gretzky's 21-year personal services contract as collateral on a bank loan "for no more than $20 million" with Alberta Treasury Branch, later to be called ATB Financial. "I'm in danger of selling the Oilers or Wayne," said Pocklington. "I have had two offers on Wayne, both about two years ago. I won't say which teams, but it wasn't $18 million, the figure I keep reading."

As the season ended, it became obvious a shift had taken place in the *modus operandi* of the Oilers. Finishing with a 49-20-11 record, 10 points fewer than in the previous season, Edmonton scored its fewest goals (401) in four seasons, but also gave up the second fewest (298) in the club's NHL history.

Gretzky increased his total of NHL records owned and shared to 37, as he boosted his NHL single-season assists record to 135. He finished with 73 goals and Kurri had 71, the first European to score more than 70 in the NHL. Adding credence to Sather's line that "I'd probably be going for my 500th goal if I was playing with him (Gretzky)," Krushelnyski established personal bests with 43 goals, 45 assists and 88 points.

That set the stage for the playoff run.

Opposite: Jari Kurri, who tied an NHL record for most goals in the playoffs with 19, celebrates one of them against the Chicago Blackhawks.

31

1984 - 1985
THE GREAT ONE'S
GREATEST FEAR

Hockey did not come without at least one drawback for Wayne Gretzky.

He has a fear of flying. Not your everyday rumbling tummy fear, but the white-knuckle variety that comes with every takeoff, landing and bump in the night. And playing for a team based on the Canadian prairies, thousands of miles away from most opponents, the fear was much more than a minor inconvenience.

He would see a hypnotist about it, but the benefits would soon wear off. "I don't have claustrophobia on planes ... it's not like a closed-in feeling," said Gretzky. "I just can't take the bumpy rides. Maybe I'm afraid of heights. I just know I'm scared.

"I may be the only guy in the NHL who wants to go back to the days of the six-team NHL. Remember, they rode trains."

Gretzky was not alone in his fear of flying, joining other athletes such as former National Football League coach John Madden and Boston Red Sox baseball star Jackie Jensen, the latter having quit the game because of it.

Eventually, Gretzky derived relief by going into the cockpit during flights, explaining that seeing the plane respond to levers and toggles gave him a comforting sense of control. His price of admission to the cockpit was usually autographed pictures for the entire flight crew.

But regulations kept him out of cockpits during takeoffs and landings and during flights over American airspace.

Ho hum — just another great day at the office for the defending Stanley Cup champion Oilers.

The Oilers find the net against Philadelphia's Bob Froese in the Stanley Cup finals.

Oiler puckstopper Grant Fuhr was his acrobatic best against the Flyers.

EDMONTON OILERS
1984-1985

Oiler Willy Lindstrom beats Froese yet again.

A shell-shocked Froese replaced an injured Pelle Lindbergh in the Flyers net, without much success.

Edmonton Oilers
1984-85
Results & Statistics

COACH	GP	W	L	T	PTS	GF	GA
			REGULAR SEASON				
Glen Sather	80	49	20	11	109	401	298

STANLEY CUP CHAMPIONS,
1st Smythe Division, 2nd Overall. Playoffs: Won Smythe Division Semifinal 3-0 vs Los Angeles, Won Smythe Division Final 4-0 vs Winnipeg, Won Campbell Conference Final 4-2 vs Chicago, Won Stanley Cup Final 4-1 vs Philadelphia.

REGULAR SEASON

	GP	G	A	Pts	PIM
Wayne Gretzky	80	73	135	208	52
Jari Kurri	73	71	64	135	30
Paul Coffey	80	37	84	121	97
Mike Krushelnyski	80	43	45	88	60
Glenn Anderson	80	42	39	81	69
Mark Napier (MIN)	39	10	18	28	2
Mark Napier (EDM)	33	9	26	35	19
Mark Napier (TOT)	72	19	44	63	21
Mark Messier	55	23	31	54	57
Charlie Huddy	80	7	44	51	46
Dave Hunter	80	17	19	36	122
Willy Lindstrom	80	12	20	32	18
Dave Lumley (HTF)	48	8	20	28	98
Dave Lumley (EDM)	12	1	3	4	13
Dave Lumley (TOT)	60	9	23	32	111
Pat Hughes	73	12	13	25	85
Kevin Lowe	80	4	21	25	104
Kevin McClelland	62	8	15	23	212
Randy Gregg	57	3	20	23	32
Don Jackson	78	3	17	20	141
Dave Semenko	69	6	12	18	167
Bill Carroll	65	8	9	17	22
Lee Fogolin	79	4	13	17	126
Gord Sherven	37	9	7	16	10
Jaroslav Pouzar	33	4	8	12	28
Larry Melnyk	28	0	11	11	25
Marc Habscheid	26	5	3	8	4
Raimo Summanen	9	0	4	4	0
Grant Fuhr	46	0	3	3	6
Marco Baron	1	0	0	0	0
Daryl Reaugh	1	0	0	0	0
Ray Cote	2	0	0	0	2
Steve Smith	2	0	0	0	2
Mike Zanier	3	0	0	0	0
Andy Moog	39	0	0	0	8
Esa Tikkanen	–	–	–	–	–

REGULAR SEASON

GOALTENDER	GP	MINS	GA	SO	GAA.	W-L-T
Andy Moog	39	2019	111	1	3.30	22-9-3
Marco Baron	1	33	2	0	3.64	0-1-0
Grant Fuhr	46	2559	165	1	3.87	26-8-7
Mike Zanier	3	185	12	0	3.89	1-1-1
Daryl Reaugh	1	60	5	0	5.00	0-1-0

A BUMP IN THE ROAD

The 30th of April in 1986 had already figured to be a memorable day in the life of Edmonton Oiler defenceman Steve Smith.

Born in Glasgow, Scotland, the six-foot-four rookie was celebrating his 23rd birthday, with the promise of many years of greatness ahead of him. And, if all went well, the night would be spent celebrating a Game 7 victory over the Calgary Flames in the second round of the Oilers' quest for a third straight Stanley Cup.

Well, all didn't go well.

Playing in front of 17,498 fans at Northlands Coliseum, the Oilers had battled back from a 2-0 deficit to tie the Flames 2-2. At 3:14 of the third period, Smith moved from behind his own net to start an attack with a long pass towards centre ice.

It never got there.

The puck hit the left calf of Oiler goalie Grant Fuhr, standing high at the top of his crease, and rebounded back into the Edmonton net for a 3-2 Calgary lead.

The bewildered throng in the stands asked, "What happened?" And Smith fell to his hands and knees in remorse — a freeze frame of the Oilers' entire 1985-86 season, and what would be the everlasting moment of infamy in the history of the franchise.

As the teams shook hands after the 3-2 Calgary win, Flames bad man Nick Fotiu hugged Smith and said: "Keep your head up, you'll be back here soon." Smith smashed his stick over the boards as he left the ice, then went to the Edmonton dressing room, where he was one of the few players to sit at his cubicle, awaiting the inevitable media inquisition.

Kevin Lowe emerged from a back room to yell at the reporters: "It's pretty obvious what happened!"

It was telling that Smith would come out to face the music, when most of his teammates were hiding their despair in an area of the dressing room off limits to reporters.

"Sooner or later I've got to face it," said Smith, who aged much more than one birthday that night. "It was human error — I guess I've just got to live with it."

So he explained what happened. When he had seen the Flames' Lanny McDonald bearing down on him, Smith had tried to pass to an Oiler forward — "there were two of them circling" — but Fuhr had moved in the way. "I got good wood on it. I thought the puck went in fast," said Smith, managing a faint laugh during the post-mortem.

"He (Smith) is going to be a great defenceman," said Wayne Gretzky. "It was an unfortunate incident, one that will probably be remembered for a while."

Smith would go on to spend 15 NHL seasons with Edmonton, Chicago and ironically Calgary, where he would also serve as an assistant coach. During 134 playoff games, he would score 11 times into opposition nets, but it was the goal into his own net that would haunt him.

The loss to the Flames was an abrupt end to a season that had started with John Muckler being named co-coach, while assistant Ted Green left the team to

devote full time to his businesses, primarily marketing a coin-operated skate-sharpening machine. He was replaced by Bob McCammon, fired by the Philadelphia Flyers, who still paid out part of his contract after he joined Edmonton. During a road trip with the Oilers into Vancouver, McCammon was greeted with his regular paycheque from the Flyers, and deadpanned: "They're playing so well, I'm thinking of asking for a raise."

The summer before the season started was an eventful one. Tennis star Martina Navratilova wrote in her autobiography that she wanted to have a child with Gretzky. Scott Metcalfe, who would play two games with the Oilers, was drafted in the first round, while Kelly Buchberger, a future captain, was taken in the ninth. And general manager Glen Sather continued his tradition of reaching out to players who had fallen on tough times, as he signed former Boston Bruin Craig MacTavish, who had served a one-year jail term for vehicular homicide outside Boston.

"I really didn't think this day was going to come," said MacTavish, upon his release.

He would earn 23 goals and 47 points in 74 games, which earned the team's nomination for the Bill Masterton Trophy, recognizing sportsmanship, perseverance, skills and dedication to the game.

"It's the comeback of the century," said Sather. "It's a Cinderella story that a guy can get his life back together after what he went through."

MacTavish would become a four-time Stanley Cup winner (three with the Oilers), Edmonton team captain and, eventually, head coach.

It was during the 1985 exhibition season that Gretzky faced off against his brother Keith, who had joined the Buffalo Sabres. "I didn't look at him and I don't think he looked at me, either," said Keith, who lost the draw to big brother, as parents Walter and Phyllis were among the 9,549 fans at the sold-out Metro Centre in Halifax. In fact, it would be Keith's brother Brent who would make regular season appearances in the NHL, playing 13 games and scoring one goal with the Tampa Bay Lightning in the mid-1990s.

With Gretzky taking a night off in the last pre-season game, the captain's 'C' was worn by Dave Semenko, who doubted it was a fixture on his sweater and "should come off in the wash."

Gretzky was back on duty during the season, notching seven assists for the second time in a 12-9 shootout over the Chicago Black Hawks, which earned him an appearance with *Larry King Live* on CNN.

King anointed Gretzky "the greatest offensive player in the history of team sports."

In February, Dave Hunter, who had proven his value as a rugged checker in previous Stanley Cup finals, was sentenced to 28 days in jail for a drunk driving offence 13 months earlier.

Despite the distraction, the Oilers finished with 119 points, first overall and

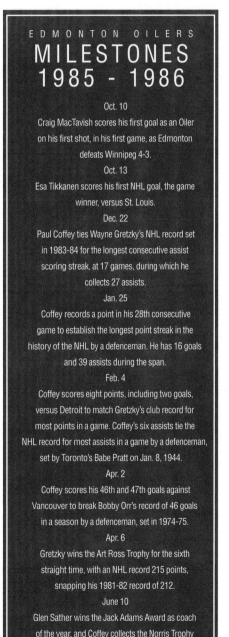

E D M O N T O N   O I L E R S
MILESTONES
1985 - 1986

Oct. 10
Craig MacTavish scores his first goal as an Oiler on his first shot, in his first game, as Edmonton defeats Winnipeg 4-3.

Oct. 13
Esa Tikkanen scores his first NHL goal, the game winner, versus St. Louis.

Dec. 22
Paul Coffey ties Wayne Gretzky's NHL record set in 1983-84 for the longest consecutive assist scoring streak, at 17 games, during which he collects 27 assists.

Jan. 25
Coffey records a point in his 28th consecutive game to establish the longest point streak in the history of the NHL by a defenceman. He has 16 goals and 39 assists during the span.

Feb. 4
Coffey scores eight points, including two goals, versus Detroit to match Gretzky's club record for most points in a game. Coffey's six assists tie the NHL record for most assists in a game by a defenceman, set by Toronto's Babe Pratt on Jan. 8, 1944.

Apr. 2
Coffey scores his 46th and 47th goals against Vancouver to break Bobby Orr's record of 46 goals in a season by a defenceman, set in 1974-75.

Apr. 6
Gretzky wins the Art Ross Trophy for the sixth straight time, with an NHL record 215 points, snapping his 1981-82 record of 212.

June 10
Glen Sather wins the Jack Adams Award as coach of the year, and Coffey collects the Norris Trophy as top defender for the second straight year.

Opposite: Oiler defenceman Steve Smith is devastated after his gaffe against the Calgary Flames cost the Oilers a shot at a third Stanley Cup.

35

1985 - 1986
COFFEY SURPASSES IDOL ORR

Paul Coffey had only met Bobby Orr once, at a Wayne Gretzky celebrity tennis tournament, but Coffey had a full grasp of the history he wrote the night of April 2, 1986.

With two goals on Vancouver Canucks rookie netminder Wendel Young — bouncing one off Vancouver defenceman Doug Lidster and later finishing off an end-to-end rush — Coffey broke Orr's 11-year-old record of 46 goals in a season by a defenceman.

"I don't care if somebody gets 150 points some day and beats me, to me he's the greatest defenceman who ever played," said Coffey, of Orr. "There was (Doug) Harvey and (Eddie) Shore before him, but Orr came into the league in 1966 and revolutionized the game. Myself and Ray Bourque and others, we're all just followers."

Orr, his greatness curtailed by knee injuries that left its magnitude a cause of wonder, sent a telegram from the Nabisco Dinah Shore golf tournament in Palm Springs.

"Please accept my congratulations to you for your outstanding accomplishments," wrote Orr. "You have been a credit to the game, both on and off the ice, and I'm pleased that a person of your calibre has succeeded me in the record books. Warmest regards."

Coffey, who earlier in the season set the NHL record for defencemen going 28 straight games with at least one point, concluded the season with 48 goals, also a record that still holds. He ended his 21-year career with 396 regular season goals.

Wayne Gretzky is dumped by Flames defenceman Gary Suter.

Flames forward Perry Berezan rifles one off goalie Grant Fuhr's shoulder.

tying their 1983-84 points record, and swept the Vancouver Canucks three straight in the playoffs before being stunned by Calgary in the second round on Smith's gaffe.

At the traditional post-season team photo session, dressing room attendant Joey Moss took his place sitting on the ice in front of the first row of players. That caused his buddy Gretzky to muse: "Last year we had the Stanley Cup in the middle of the picture, this year we've got Joey."

The shock of the playoff loss was magnified a week later when *Sports Illustrated* magazine came out with a cover story quoting unnamed sources as saying several members of the Oilers had been involved with cocaine and other illegal drugs. Sather dismissed the story as being rife with "inaccuracies, misquotes and innuendo," but confessed: "I certainly have to think this is

Oilers defenceman Steve Smith crumples to the ice in horror after banking a shot off Grant Fuhr's leg and into his own net.

Kevin Lowe clears the Flames' Tim Hunter away from Fuhr.

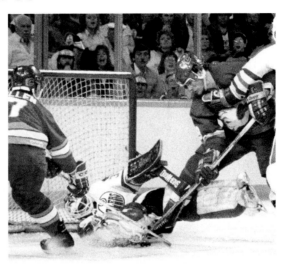

Two Calgary Flames are thwarted by Fuhr in close.

one of the lowest points I've had in hockey."

The good news was that Steve Smith spent the summer at his home in London, Ont., receiving bags and bags of mail to cheer him up. Included were more than 450 letters from readers of the *Edmonton Journal*'s Brunch section, which invited people to pen Smith their wishes or whines.

"I'd say there were more than 1,000 letters," said Smith.

"Some were from businesses and a lot were from school kids. They'd say funny things like, 'I scored on my own net in soccer.' 'I know you feel down.' 'Why don't I tell you a joke?'"

Among the empathetic was one youngster who wrote Smith that his ball hockey team could use a defenceman. And Candace Chwakel, a 12-year-old from Camrose, sent $10 to help him "pay off the $2 million you owe Peter Pocklington."

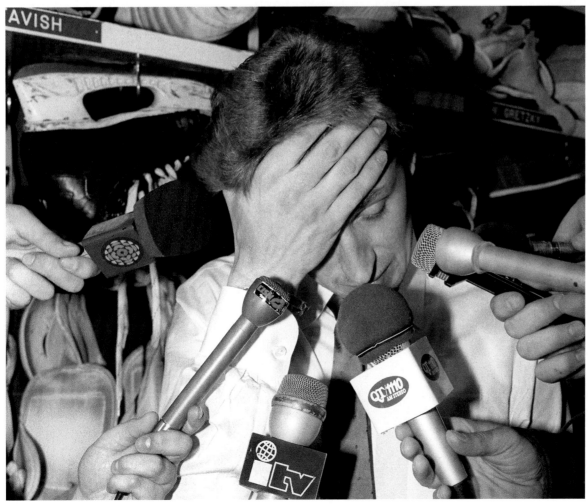

After the game, Gretzky talks to reporters about what derailed the Oilers' efforts to win a third straight Stanley Cup.

Edmonton Oilers 1985-86 Results & Statistics

COACH	REGULAR SEASON						
	GP	W	L	T	PTS	GF	GA
Glen Sather	80	56	17	7	119	426	310

1st Smythe Division, 1st Overall. Playoffs: Won Smythe Division Semifinal 3-0 vs Vancouver, Lost Smythe Division Final 4-3 vs Calgary.

	REGULAR SEASON				
PLAYER	GP	G	A	PTS	PIM
Wayne Gretzky	80	52	163	215	46
Paul Coffey	79	48	90	138	120
Jari Kurri	78	68	63	131	22
Glenn Anderson	72	54	48	102	90
Mark Messier	63	35	49	84	68
Mark Napier	80	24	32	56	14
Craig MacTavish	74	23	24	47	70
Charlie Huddy	76	6	35	41	55
Mike Krushelnyski	54	16	24	40	22
Raimo Summanen	73	19	18	37	16
Dave Hunter	62	15	22	37	77
Kevin McClelland	79	11	25	36	266
Randy Gregg	64	2	26	28	47
Lee Fogolin	80	4	22	26	129
Steve Smith	55	4	20	24	166
Marty McSorley	59	11	12	23	265
Dave Lumley	46	11	9	20	35
Dave Semenko	69	6	12	18	141
Kevin Lowe	74	2	16	18	90
Esa Tikkanen	35	7	6	13	28
Don Jackson	45	2	8	10	93
Mike Rogers (NYR)	9	1	3	4	2
Mike Rogers (EDM)	8	1	0	1	0
Mike Rogers (TOT)	17	2	3	5	2
Gord Sherven (MIN)	13	0	2	2	11
Gord Sherven (EDM)	5	1	1	2	4
Gord Sherven (TOT)	18	1	3	4	15
Risto Jalo	3	0	3	3	0
Grant Fuhr	40	0	2	2	0
Andy Moog	47	0	2	2	8
Ken Solheim	6	1	0	1	5
Jeff Brubaker (TOR)	21	0	0	0	67
Jeff Brubaker (EDM)	4	1	0	1	12
Jeff Brubaker (TOT)	25	1	0	1	79
Dean Hopkins	1	0	0	0	0
Mike Moller	1	0	0	0	0
Selmar Odelein	4	0	0	0	0
Jeff Beukeboom	-	-	-	-	-

	REGULAR SEASON					
GOALTENDER	GP	MINS	GA	SO	GAA.	W-L-T
Andy Moog	47	2664	164	1	3.69	27-9-7
Grant Fuhr	40	2184	143	0	3.93	29-8-0

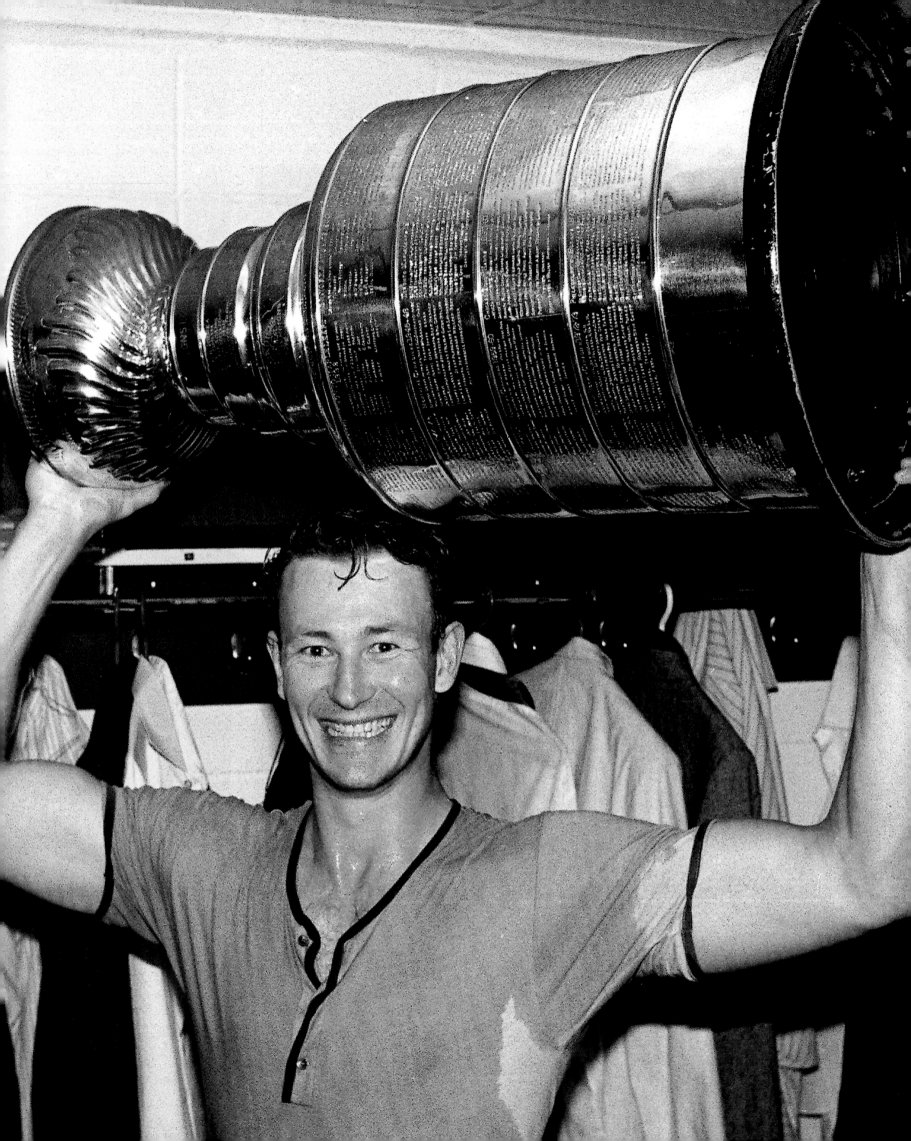

WELCOME BACK, STANLEY

The theme for the Edmonton Oilers during the 1987 Stanley Cup finals was the Orleans hit *Still The One*:

"We're still having fun,

"And you're still the one."

The implications were many — that the Oilers were still the best National Hockey League team, and that despite the shocking exit at the hands of the Calgary Flames the previous playoffs, the Oilers were still No. 1 in the hearts of Edmonton fans.

But when Murray Craven scored after just 74 seconds to give the Philadelphia Flyers the lead in the seventh game of the 1987 finals, *Toronto Star* Hall of Fame hockey writer Frank Orr pointed to the pair of Stanley Cup banners hanging from the Coliseum rafters and mused: "The theme might be Still The Two."

However, the Oilers came back with one goal in each period to defeat the Flyers 3-1.

And in a gesture of class and empathy, after Wayne Gretzky took the Cup from NHL president John Ziegler for the celebratory victory lap around the ice, the first person Gretzky handed it to for the next leg of the relay was Steve Smith.

It had been Smith's errant bank shot off the leg of goalie Grant Fuhr into the Oiler net that had prematurely ended Edmonton's Cup run against Calgary the previous playoffs, causing an elongated summer of discontent.

"It was such a long, tough summer, and a long two years getting it back," said Gretzky. "But it was worth the wait."

"It's like losing your house, then working hard enough to get the money to get it back," said defenceman Charlie Huddy.

"I guess maybe you have to lose the Cup to really appreciate it," said forward Mike Krushelnyski.

It turned out the *Sports Illustrated* story of drug use among the Oilers that surfaced after the Calgary loss may have helped deaden that blow.

"As bad as it was, maybe the drug story made it easier for us," said defenceman Kevin Lowe. "There were two questions asked instead of one. It deflected some of the talk about our loss."

The Oilers didn't want to be remembered as clones of the Boston Bruins of the 1970s, a team loaded with talent like Phil Esposito, Johnny Bucyk and Bobby Orr, yet winning only two Stanley Cups.

"When you're the champion, everybody is trying to beat you, trying to find new things that work," said coach John Muckler. "Calgary finally found the right formula. With video, there are no secrets. The champion tends to stay the same and doesn't change. Now that we've lost, it's going to force us to rethink things."

Randy Gregg ended his six-week retirement and the Oilers acquired the rights to defenceman Reijo Ruotsalainen from the New York Rangers (he had been playing in Switzerland) for Don Jackson.

Edmonton stumbled to an 11-8-1 start, causing coach Glen Sather to say: "I think it's a combination of insecurity coming from losing last year and not adapting to it well."

Then came a shot in the arm. On Nov. 23, 1986, Gretzky scored three goals in a

5-2 win over the Vancouver Canucks and the third one — a 100-footer with 19-year-old Canuck goalie Troy Gamble on the bench in his NHL debut — made Gretzky the fastest player to record 500 NHL goals. It took him just 575 games, beating the previous fastest, Mike Bossy of the New York Islanders, who did it in 647 games.

"I give almost everything to my father (Walter)," said Gretzky, of the milestone stick and puck. "I kid him about keeping all these things, but when I go home (to Brantford, Ont.) he catches me looking at them."

Gretzky said the only mementoes he had in his own residence were the *Sports Illustrated* sportsman of the year and ABC *Wide World of Sport* trophies.

Gretzky had won 14 cars to that point in his career, including one after an all-star game that he gave to his bodyguard, Dave Semenko. Alas, when the Oilers traded Semenko to the Hartford Whalers, he didn't ask how the Edmonton fans were taking it. "I don't think it will be as bad as it was in Montreal when the fans rioted over Rocket Richard not playing," said Semenko.

Assistant equipment manager Lyle Kulchisky moved Paul Coffey into Semenko's stall in the Oilers' dressing room, explaining: "Gotta be at least a five-year vet to get into the shrine."

In February, Gretzky moved past Stan Mikita into fourth spot in career NHL points, with 1,468 in his eighth season, causing Mikita to wonder: "What took him so long? When you start counting by 200s every year, it adds up pretty fast."

That same month, Sather attached a revolving door to the Oilers' lineup. Jaroslav Pouzar, who was playing in Germany after three years with the Oilers, returned. As a line of media approached his dressing room stall after his first game back, Pouzar became a museum guide: "Gretzky is this way. Here is 35-year-old man."

Former captain Lee Fogolin, who nurtured defence partner Kevin Lowe for seven seasons, was traded back to the Buffalo Sabres along with Mark Napier for Norm Lacombe and Wayne Van Dorp.

"I'll never forget what Fogey did for me my first year ... only 18 and battling for the scoring title with Marcel (Dionne)," said Gretzky. "We were playing in Detroit and Dennis Polonich was on against my line. As we lined up for the first faceoff, Fogey called time. He skated over to Polonich and said if he laid a hand on me, he'd break Polonich in half.

"I couldn't believe it."

And before the March trade deadline, Kent Nilsson was acquired from Minnesota for a future draft pick.

During March, owner Peter Pocklington proposed to the NHL board of directors that he do a public share offering of the club. "Sports is too much of a business to be a sport," said Pocklington, who would remain majority owner under the plan.

Fortune magazine listed the Oiler franchise as worth $35 million at the time, but reports were that the New York Rangers had offered $15 million for Wayne Gretzky alone.

The team roared down the stretch with a 12-4-1 record — including a

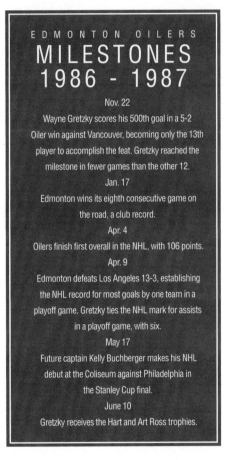

E D M O N T O N   O I L E R S

MILESTONES
1986 - 1987

Nov. 22

Wayne Gretzky scores his 500th goal in a 5-2 Oiler win against Vancouver, becoming only the 13th player to accomplish the feat. Gretzky reached the milestone in fewer games than the other 12.

Jan. 17

Edmonton wins its eighth consecutive game on the road, a club record.

Apr. 4

Oilers finish first overall in the NHL, with 106 points.

Apr. 9

Edmonton defeats Los Angeles 13-3, establishing the NHL record for most goals by one team in a playoff game. Gretzky ties the NHL mark for assists in a playoff game, with six.

May 17

Future captain Kelly Buchberger makes his NHL debut at the Coliseum against Philadelphia in the Stanley Cup final.

June 10

Gretzky receives the Hart and Art Ross trophies.

The Edmonton Oilers blasted the Los Angeles Kings 9-3 on March 6 of 1987, but the best shooter that night was Edmonton Mayor Laurence Decore.

Rick Hansen had brought his around-the-world Man in Motion Tour to the Coliseum, raising money for spinal cord research, and Decore took to centre ice to fire pucks at an empty net for a minute. Edmonton would give $5,000 for every goal he scored to Hansen's cause.

Wayne Gretzky and teammates watched in amazement as Decore fired 18 of 26 shots into the net, donating $90,000. "That's why he's mayor, I guess — he can do everything," said Gretzky. "I thought he'd make one or two shots."

Later, the secret to Decore's success emerged. During practice, he had been taught to aim at the point of the oil drop in the Oilers' logo at centre ice.

Decore, who served as mayor from 1983 to 1988, then became provincial Liberal leader. He died of cancer in 1999, at age 59.

seven-game winning streak — for 106 points, finishing first overall in the NHL for the third time in four years.

When they started the playoffs, the lineup included six newcomers who had come aboard since the previous year — Van Dorp, Lacombe, Nilsson, Moe Lemay from Vancouver and Craig Muni, a free agent from Toronto. Gone were Fogolin and Napier to Buffalo, Semenko to Hartford, Jackson to the Rangers and Raimo Summanen to Vancouver.

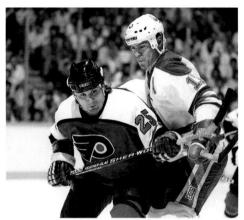

Above: Flyers goalie Ron Hextall was heroic against the Oilers, earning him a Conn Smythe trophy for top playoff performer. But the Oilers got the best of him in Game 7 of the Stanley Cup final. Top right: Mark Messier ties up the Flyers' Peter Zezel. Right: Oiler Kevin McClelland fights for position in front of Hextall. Below: the Flyers catch their breath at the bench, knowing that they've fallen just short against the powerful Oilers in the seventh and deciding game.

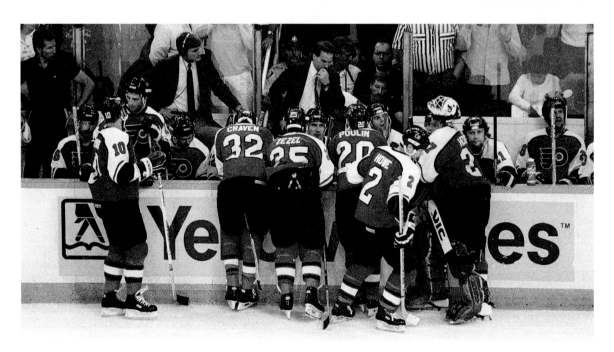

As well, Dave Lumley had retired.

"I think we've got a better hockey club now, but we lost some character people," said Sather. "This team is a lot more aware of what is ahead.

"I think we fooled ourselves last year. There were a lot of games where we didn't play very well and still won.

"This year the league is better and we had to play stronger to win."

Edmonton Oilers
1986-87
Results & Statistics

COACH	GP	W	L	T	PTS	GF	GA
				REGULAR SEASON			
Glen Sather	80	50	24	6	106	372	284

STANLEY CUP CHAMPIONS,
1st Smythe Division, 1st Overall. Playoffs: Won Smythe Division Semifinal 4-1 vs Los Angeles, Won Smythe Division Final 4-0 vs Winnipeg, Won Campbell Conference Final 4-1 vs Detroit, Won Stanley Cup Final 4-3 vs Philadelphia.

Top left: Glenn Anderson is skewered by a Flyer henchman during the Stanley Cup final. Left: Jari Kurri beats Ron Hextall with what turned out to be the Stanley Cup winning goal in Game 7 against the Flyers. Above: Anderson gets a hug from Wayne Gretzky after scoring the insurance marker late in the third period in Game 7, as the Northlands Coliseum faithful explode with emotion. Below: the Oilers explode off the bench as the buzzer sounds and they are crowned Stanley Cup champions once more.

REGULAR SEASON

PLAYER	GP	G	A	PTS	PIM
Wayne Gretzky	79	62	121	183	28
Jari Kurri	79	54	54	108	41
Mark Messier	77	37	70	107	73
Esa Tikkanen	76	34	44	78	120
Glenn Anderson	80	35	38	73	65
Paul Coffey	59	17	50	67	49
Kent Nilsson (MIN)	44	13	33	46	12
Kent Nilsson (EDM)	17	5	12	17	4
Kent Nilsson (TOT)	61	18	45	63	16
Mike Krushelnyski	80	16	35	51	67
Craig MacTavish	79	20	19	39	55
Kevin Lowe	77	8	29	37	94
Moe Lemay (VAN)	52	9	17	26	128
Moe Lemay (EDM)	10	1	2	3	36
Moe Lemay (TOT)	62	10	19	29	164
Craig Muni	79	7	22	29	85
Kevin McClelland	72	12	13	25	238
Randy Gregg	52	8	16	24	42
Steve Smith	62	7	15	22	165
Mark Napier	62	8	13	21	2
Charlie Huddy	58	4	15	19	35
Raimo Summanen	48	10	7	17	15
Dave Hunter	77	6	9	15	75
Reijo Ruotsalainen	16	5	8	13	6
Normand Lacombe (BUF)	39	4	7	11	8
Normand Lacombe (EDM)	1	0	0	0	2
Normand Lacombe (TOT)	40	4	7	11	10
Jeff Beukeboom	44	3	8	11	124
Marty McSorley	41	2	4	6	159
Jaroslav Pouzar	12	2	3	5	6
Stu Kulak	23	3	1	4	41
Danny Gare	18	1	3	4	6
Lee Fogolin	35	1	3	4	17
Mike Moller	6	2	1	3	0
Steve Graves	12	2	0	2	0
Grant Fuhr	44	0	2	2	6
Andy Moog	46	0	2	2	8
Dave Lumley	1	0	0	0	0
Wayne Van Dorp	3	0	0	0	25
Dave Semenko	5	0	0	0	6
Kelly Buchberger	-	-	-	-	-

REGULAR SEASON

GOALTENDER	GP	MINS	GA	SO	GAA.	W-L-T
Grant Fuhr	44	2388	137	0	3.44	22-13-3
Andy Moog	46	2461	144	0	3.51	28-11-3

WALTZING TO CUP NO. 4

The analogy had been made that the 1987-88 Edmonton Oilers, in the autumn of their reign, were like aging boxer Muhammad Ali after his legs had lost their snap. That's when Ali proved how great he was, observers said, winning flat-footed, without his dance.

"Nice analogy, except for two things," wrote *Edmonton Journal* sports columnist Cam Cole, after the Oilers won their fourth Stanley Cup in five years in May of 1988. "This ain't autumn, and the Oilers can still dance a bit. People will call it a waltz, perhaps, this fourth Stanley Cup, because that's how the champions made it look — sweeping the Boston Bruins in four games, more or less, running their playoff record to 16-2."

"I think people were shocked and bewildered how we won this time around," said Kevin Lowe, referring to a litany of player moves and labour troubles that disrupted the entire season.

The difference from the previous year was the departure of so many players, namely Paul Coffey, Kent Nilsson, Reijo Ruotsalainen and Andy Moog.

"But it just shows you that the game is bigger than any individuals," said coach Glen Sather. "I think this is a big compliment to (Wayne) Gretzky, (Mark) Messier, (Glenn) Anderson, (Jari) Kurri and (Grant) Fuhr ... they've stayed here and they've been here for all the new people."

Sather said comparing Cup wins was like trying to pit one of your children against another.

"This club has a lot of ability, but a lot of discipline, too," the Oilers' general manager said. "We played as a real strong team. Last year's club played with individual talent. I don't think it's fair to say this team is better than last year's though, or that our first Stanley Cup team that beat the Islanders was No. 1. Every team has its own characters and own people that make things different. Each team had its own personality. They've all been great. And all have been winners."

The problem that faced Sather as the Oilers entered the 1987-88 season was that after three Cup wins in four years, keeping established players entering the prime of their earning years would be difficult. The 1987 Canada Cup tournament allowed Messier and Coffey to find out what Boston's Ray Bourque was making. And, with the 1988 Olympics in Calgary now open to pros, players had another option.

Before the season started, Nilsson and Ruotsalainen decided to return to play in Italy and Sweden respectively. Moog and Randy Gregg joined the Canadian Olympic team, although Gregg would return to the Oilers after the Games. Among preseason holdouts Coffey, Messier and Mike Krushelnyski, only Coffey would be a casualty, eventually traded to Pittsburgh.

It was the same type of fate that dogged New York Islanders general manager Bill Torrey near the end of his club's reign. "I went up to Bill to congratulate him after they beat us (Vancouver) in the '82 finals," said former Canucks coach Harry Neale. "And I remember him saying, 'There's nothing like winning the Cup, but it sure screws up your summer something terrible with salary demands.' "

"In the long run this could make us stronger," said Sather. "The team could be much better because we've given young guys (Norm Lacombe, Kelly Buchberger, Jim Ennis, Darryl Reaugh) a chance to develop."

The team also lost Bob McCammon, who served as assistant coach one year and then as director of player development after Ted Green rejoined the coaching crew. McCammon said his new deal as Vancouver head coach was for "about 100 years, it's one of those no-yell-at, no-fire contracts."

On Nov. 7, the Oilers presented Gretzky with a silver stick in honour of 1,000 assists, engraved with the names of all the goal scorers he had assisted.

Gretzky had also moved into a tie with Edmonton product Johnny Bucyk for sixth place with 556 career goals. But as for Gordie Howe's record 801 goals, Gretzky said: "I think Gordie's pretty safe."

The Coffey trade finally happened in late November, as he, Dave Hunter and Wayne Van Dorp went to the Penguins for forwards Craig Simpson and Dave Hannan plus defencemen Moe Mantha and Chris Joseph.

"I'm not here to work miracles," said Coffey, 27, in Pittsburgh. "But I have six to eight good years left in me and the first thing I want to do is help Pittsburgh get in the playoffs."

Just the previous week, Penguins superstar Mario Lemieux had tabbed Simpson, 20, as a future 50-goal scorer. It would happen sooner than expected.

On Dec. 11, Gretzky assisted on a goal by Kurri to move ahead of Phil Esposito into third spot among NHL scorers with 1,591 points, in just 662 games.

At the halfway mark in the season, the Oilers had 48 points in 40 games, with attention being drawn by defence partners Steve Smith and Jeff Beukeboom, both six-feet-four, who had been dubbed "The Twin Towers."

Then on Jan. 12, Gretzky announced that his girlfriend of seven months, actress-dancer Janet Jones, had accepted his proposal of marriage. Said Gretzky's mother Phyllis: "I'm very excited. It's about time."

Both Wayne and Janet turned 27 that month.

This engagement thing was catchy. The next month, Craig MacTavish announced that he would marry Debbie Andrews, the daughter of auto magnate and former nightclub owner Denny Andrews.

With Gregg slated to return to the Oilers after the Olympics, Sather traded defender Mantha to Minnesota for fiery centre Keith Acton.

And soon after the Games, Moog was traded to Boston for winger Geoff Courtnall, the Bruins' second-leading scorer, and a 20-year-old goalie named Bill Ranford, who was on the farm in Maine.

Late in the season, the Oilers went through a 3-4-1 stretch, and the *Journal*'s Cole wrote: "For perhaps the first time in their professional lives, hockey's magnificent whiz kids have felt the cold breath of mortality blowing down on them."

On the Ides of March, 21-year-old Simpson fulfilled the prophesy espoused by former teammate Lemieux at the beginning of the season by scoring his 50th goal on Jacques Cloutier. Only Gretzky, at 19 years and two months, and Pierre Larouche, at 20 years and five months, had performed the feat at a younger age.

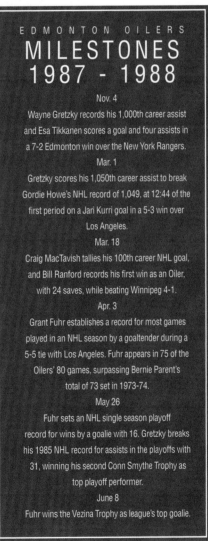

EDMONTON OILERS
MILESTONES
1987 - 1988

Nov. 4
Wayne Gretzky records his 1,000th career assist and Esa Tikkanen scores a goal and four assists in a 7-2 Edmonton win over the New York Rangers.

Mar. 1
Gretzky scores his 1,050th career assist to break Gordie Howe's NHL record of 1,049, at 12:44 of the first period on a Jari Kurri goal in a 5-3 win over Los Angeles.

Mar. 18
Craig MacTavish tallies his 100th career NHL goal, and Bill Ranford records his first win as an Oiler, with 24 saves, while beating Winnipeg 4-1.

Apr. 3
Grant Fuhr establishes a record for most games played in an NHL season by a goaltender during a 5-5 tie with Los Angeles. Fuhr appears in 75 of the Oilers' 80 games, surpassing Bernie Parent's total of 73 set in 1973-74.

May 26
Fuhr sets an NHL single season playoff record for wins by a goalie with 16. Gretzky breaks his 1985 NHL record for assists in the playoffs with 31, winning his second Conn Smythe Trophy as top playoff performer.

June 8
Fuhr wins the Vezina Trophy as league's top goalie.

Opposite: Mark Messier, right, jaws with Calgary Flames behemoth Joel Otto.
No upsets this time around, as Edmonton swept the Flames in the Smythe Division final.

1987 - 1988
NUGENT, MORETTO AND 99

A pre-season game in Indianapolis between the Edmonton Oilers and St. Louis Blues on Sept. 25, 1987, brought Wayne Gretzky back to the city where he turned pro.

He had been just 17 and didn't have a credit card when he signed his first pro contract with Nelson Skalbania for $1.75 million in 1978.

Gretzky's linemates for his eight games with the Indianapolis Racers (three goals, three assists) had been Kevin Nugent and Angelo Moretto.

Nugent, a product of Notre Dame, had been drafted by the Boston Bruins in 1975. He had two goals and 10 points in 25 games with the Racers that season and went on to work on Wall Street.

Moretto, who attended the University of Michigan, had been drafted by California in 1973 and played five NHL games with the Cleveland Barons in 1976-77. With Indianapolis, he had three goals and four points in 18 games.

"The Twin Towers," Gretzky had dubbed them, in deference to their six-foot-three stature.

Gretzky, Eddie Mio and Peter Driscoll then were sold by Skalbania to Edmonton.

"Peter and I would drive by the Steak and Shake on a Friday night and there would be Gretz, holding court with the high school kids in his new Trans-Am," said Mio, recalling those days in Indianapolis. "That was about the only time he seemed his age."

Only 5,591 fans turned out for Gretzky's return to Indianapolis in 1987, watching him earn three assists in Edmonton's 4-1 win over St. Louis. "I was a little rusty and had new skates on," said Gretzky.

Bruins goaltender Andy Moog, right, wards off the Oilers' attack.

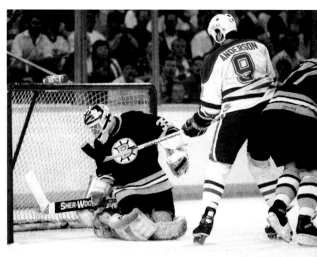

Glenn Anderson slips past Ray Bourque and shovels the puck toward the Boston net ...

"Now I've got to go out and do it again," said Simpson, who wound up with 56 goals on the season.

However, he never hit the 50-goal mark again in his 10-year NHL career.

When the regular season was done, the Oilers didn't win the Smythe Division, they finished with fewer than 100 points for the first time since 1981 and Wayne Gretzky didn't win or tie as top league scorer for the first time in nine years.

Overconfidence was not a fear at playoff time. And that turned out to be a good thing.

Above: the fearless Glenn Anderson sets a screen in front of Andy Moog.
At right: Wayne Gretzky celebrates after slipping one past Moog.

EDMONTON OILERS
1987-1988

... and scores against Bruins netminder Moog.

Grant Fuhr stands on guard, along with defenceman Craig Muni,
while two Bruins try unsuccessfully to bat the puck into the net.

"This club has a lot of ability, but a lot of discipline, too.
We played as a real strong team."

Oilers coach Glen Sather

Four and counting: Grant Fuhr, left, congratulates ex-teammate Moog
after Fuhr's Oilers beat Moog's Bruins four straight to capture Cup No. 4.

Edmonton Oilers
1987-88
Results & Statistics

COACH	GP	W	L	T	PTS	GF	GA
Glen Sather	80	44	25	11	99	363	288

STANLEY CUP CHAMPIONS,
2nd Smythe Division, 3rd Overall. Playoffs: Won Division Semifinal 4-1 vs Winnipeg, Won Division Final 4-0 vs Calgary, Won Campbell Conf. Final 4-1 vs Detroit, Won Stanley Cup Final Boston.

REGULAR SEASON

PLAYER	GP	G	A	PTS	PIM
Wayne Gretzky	64	40	109	149	24
Mark Messier	77	37	74	111	103
Jari Kurri	80	43	53	96	30
Craig Simpson (PIT)	21	13	13	26	34
Craig Simpson (EDM)	59	43	21	64	43
Craig Simpson (TOT)	80	56	34	90	77
Glenn Anderson	80	38	50	88	58
Esa Tikkanen	80	23	51	74	153
Geoff Courtnall (BOS)	62	32	26	58	108
Geoff Courtnall (EDM)	12	4	4	8	15
Geoff Courtnall (TOT)	74	36	30	66	123
Steve Smith	79	12	43	55	286
Mike Krushelnyski	76	20	27	47	64
Charlie Huddy	77	13	28	41	77
Craig MacTavish	80	15	17	32	47
Keith Acton (MIN)	46	8	11	19	74
Keith Acton (EDM)	26	3	6	9	21
Keith Acton (TOT)	72	11	17	28	95
Dave Hannan (PIT)	21	4	3	7	24
Dave Hannan (EDM)	51	9	11	20	43
Dave Hannan (TOT)	72	13	14	27	67
Marty McSorley	60	9	17	26	223
Jeff Beukeboom	73	5	20	25	201
Kevin Lowe	70	9	15	24	89
Craig Muni	72	4	15	19	77
Normand Lacombe	53	8	9	17	36
Kevin McClelland	74	10	6	16	281
Chris Joseph (PIT)	17	0	4	4	12
Chris Joseph (EDM)	7	0	4	4	8
Chris Joseph (TOT)	24	0	8	8	18
Grant Fuhr	75	0	8	8	16
Steve Graves	21	3	4	7	10
Steve Dykstra (BUF)	27	1	1	2	99
Steve Dykstra (EDM)	15	2	3	5	39
Steve Dykstra (TOT)	42	3	4	7	130
Dave Hunter	21	3	3	6	30
Moe Mantha	25	0	6	6	26
Tom McMurchy	9	4	1	5	9
John Miner	14	2	3	5	18
Ron Shudra	10	0	5	5	6
Randy Gregg	15	1	2	3	8
Bill Ranford	6	0	2	2	0
Selmar Odelein	12	0	2	2	30
Jim Ennis	5	1	0	1	10
Kelly Buchberger	19	1	0	1	81
Scott Metcalfe	2	0	0	0	
Warren Skorodenski	3	0	0	0	
Moe Lemay	4	0	0	0	
Dave Donnelly	4	0	0	0	
Daryl Reaugh	6	0	0	0	

REGULAR SEASON

GOALTENDER	GP	MINS	GA	SO	GAA	W
Bill Ranford	6	325	16	0	2.95	3
Grant Fuhr	75	4304	246	4	3.43	40-2
Daryl Reaugh	6	176	14	0	4.77	1
W. Skorodenski	3	61	7	0	6.89	0

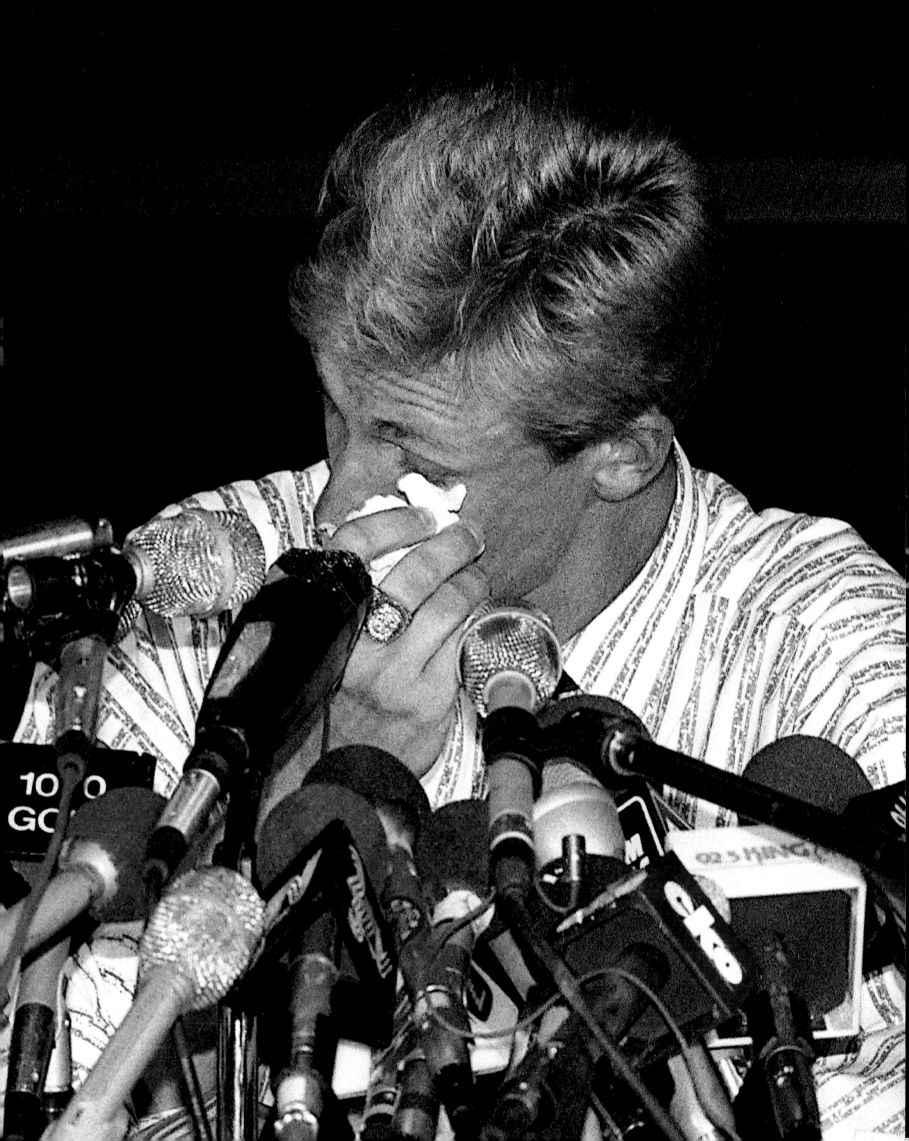

There had always been rumours, but they began heating up in early August of 1988.

Wayne Gretzky was going to be traded. Day by day, pieces of a possible trade to Los Angeles came to light in newspapers in L.A., Montreal and Edmonton.

Then finally, on Aug. 9, the bombshell exploded.

Gretzky, Marty McSorley and Mike Krushelnyski were sent to the Los Angeles Kings for Jimmy Carson, Martin Gelinas, three first-round draft picks and $15 million US ($20 million Cdn).

One day, the Great One had been contemplating buying and moving into the house of Pat Bowlen, owner of the National Football League's Denver Broncos, overlooking the North Saskatchewan River. The next day, Gretzky was in Los Angeles, tugging on a newly designed black-and-silver Kings jersey with a pair of nines on the back.

"I'm disappointed leaving Edmonton. I really admire all the fans and respect everyone over the years, but ... ," said Gretzky, before breaking into tears at the news conference.

The Oilers opened their 1988-89 training camp facing the stark reality that Gretzky's dressing room stall was now inhabited by Craig Simpson.

Gretzky himself had told equipment man Lyle Kulchisky, "Why don't you move in Simmer?" — anointing his own heir apparent.

"Right from the beginning I felt he was helping me along as much as he could," said Simpson, who had scored 56 goals the previous year. "He was giving me advice, showing me how you act and the responsibilities of being a leader, especially on a great NHL team like the Edmonton Oilers."

The pressure to somehow make up for the departure of the greatest hockey player ever was shared by Carson, who had scored 55 goals as a teenager with the Los Angeles Kings.

"I'd watch him do something and the next day in practice I'd try it," said Carson, of Gretzky. "You can't make comparisons to Wayne. But there's a lot of pressure and I'd like to get off to a good start."

Inheriting Gretzky's 'C' as captain was Mark Messier, who said: "As players, we have a responsibility to ourselves, our teammates and the city of Edmonton to do the best we can under the circumstances given to us. That's the bottom line."

"We won't have the same charisma without Gretzky," said assistant coach Ted Green. "Wayne had the ability to break open any part of the game. Other teams had fear when Wayne was there.

"But Wayne played a lot; with him gone a lot of players will get to play more, we'll get into a more regular rotation of lines."

Along with Gretzky, McSorley and Krushelnyski, gone from the Oilers' Stanley Cup lineup were Geoff Courtnall and Steve Dykstra. That left only two players from the Oilers' 1979 opening night lineup in the NHL — Messier and Kevin Lowe — with 129 players having worn the orange and blue uniforms during the span in between.

Newcomers this time around included Carson, Gelinas, Greg Adams and Doug Smith.

"We're on trial, no question about it," said co-coach John Muckler. "There's

people out there who want their pound of flesh."

The heat was also on Jari Kurri to perform without Gretzky at his side. Muckler thought it might be the other way around. "I think people should ask Wayne if he'll miss Jari. To me, he's one of the most complete players in the NHL."

The regular season opener at Northlands Coliseum had everything — dry-ice fog, a Stanley Cup banner being raised and then the Cup itself appearing.

Everything but Gretzky.

But when Carson scored two goals in a 5-1 Edmonton win over the New York Islanders, the pain lessened. "You could hear tonight that the crowd was excited, that they were happy for Jimmy Carson and Martin Gelinas and Chris Joseph," said Lowe. "I think there's a freshness about the team that the crowd senses."

When Gretzky made his return as a King on Oct. 19, Coliseum fans wore T-shirts reading: "We're mad as hell and we're not going to ticket anymore."

CBC televised its first mid-week regular season *Hockey Night in Canada* game since the Vancouver Canucks joined the NHL in 1970. Tim Feehan, the Edmonton-come-Los Angeles crooner who three months earlier sang at Gretzky's wedding, sang the national anthem for his return.

Wrote *Edmonton Journal* columnist Cam Cole: "The fact is, Gretzky didn't get much of an ovation. (Oilers owner Peter) Pocklington didn't get much of a protest. And what everyone else got was ... well, the seventh game of the regular season."

The Oilers won it 8-6.

The team churned out a respectable 22-14-4 record during the first half of the season, which Carson thought was amazing. "Maybe it looks different to a Kevin Lowe or a Mark Messier — guys who've seen the team when it was boom-boom-boom, 10 wins in a row, then a loss, then 10 more wins," said Carson. "But for me, this is unbelievable."

However, the Oilers stumbled badly during the second half of the season, with a 16-20-4 record. General manager Glen Sather reacquired Dave Hunter from the Winnipeg Jets' waiver list to add some spunk and picked up heavyweight Dave Brown from the Philadelphia Flyers.

"Whether it's new people or injuries or we're tired or whatever, you still have to work hard to do the fundamentals of the game," said a somewhat-exasperated Sather, during the doldrums.

The team fell from 99 points to 84, their lowest total since they had 74 in 1980-81, and seventh place overall. "I guess when you consider how inconsistent and poorly we played, maybe seventh isn't too bad," said Green. "We just never got on any rolls. We only had one winning streak (seven games) all season.

"It has been a very, very tough season mentally — it has for all the guys," said Carson. "For me, with the Gretzky trade hanging there and all the rumours ... I feel like there's a big, black cloud sitting right there."

As coincidence had it, the opening round of the playoffs pitted Edmonton against the Gretzky-led Kings. Former U.S. president Ronald Reagan, who once appeared in a hockey movie called *The Duke of West Point*, sent a letter to the Kings exhorting them to "Win one for the Gipper!"

The Oilers took a 3-1 lead in the series, but the Kings came back with wins of

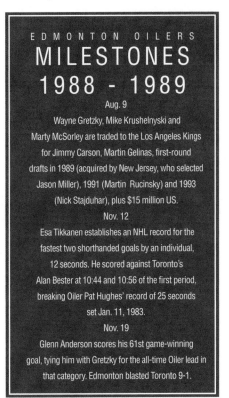

EDMONTON OILERS
MILESTONES
1988 - 1989
Aug. 9
Wayne Gretzky, Mike Krushelnyski and Marty McSorley are traded to the Los Angeles Kings for Jimmy Carson, Martin Gelinas, first-round drafts in 1989 (acquired by New Jersey, who selected Jason Miller), 1991 (Martin Rucinsky) and 1993 (Nick Stajduhar), plus $15 million US.

Nov. 12
Esa Tikkanen establishes an NHL record for the fastest two shorthanded goals by an individual, 12 seconds. He scored against Toronto's Alan Bester at 10:44 and 10:56 of the first period, breaking Oiler Pat Hughes' record of 25 seconds set Jan. 11, 1983.

Nov. 19
Glenn Anderson scores his 61st game-winning goal, tying him with Gretzky for the all-time Oiler lead in that category. Edmonton blasted Toronto 9-1.

Opposite: Aug. 9, 1988. Wayne Gretzky struggles to hold his emotions at a press conference to announce his trade to the Los Angeles Kings.

47

1988-1989 ALL-STAR REUNION

The 40th NHL All-Star game was held in Edmonton on Feb. 7, 1989, with the Campbell Conference thumping the Wales Conference 9-5.

Amid the sellout of 17,503 people were Wayne Gretzky's wife, Janet, and baby daughter, Paulina, who watched him score once and assist twice. Gretzky won a car as game MVP, the 14th car he'd won during his NHL career. Eddie Mio, the best man at Gretzky's wedding, joked: "Maybe he'll let me drive it until Paulina is 16."

But Wayne had another plan for the auto.

"This one's for a guy who did a lot for me and didn't get much credit," said Gretzky. "This is for Dave Semenko."

Calgary's Joey Mullen had two goals and an assist for the winners, while Oiler Jari Kurri chipped in three points.

"It was nice to see him (Gretzky) in our room again, and in the training room," said former housemate Kevin Lowe. "He always used to go in there between periods and watch the intermissions on TV. I forgot what that was like."

4-2, 4-1 and then 6-3 in Los Angeles to become the sixth team in league history to come back from such a deficit.

"I didn't enjoy playing against friends," said Gretzky, who had 13 points in the series.

"I'm happy for the players in L.A. I'm happy for the city of Los Angeles, I'm happy for the coaches and Mr. (Bruce)

Glenn Anderson finds the back of the net on Kings goalie Kelly Hrudey.

The Kings' Mike Allison finds the five-hole on Grant Fuhr.

Wayne Gretzky, now a King, comes back to haunt his old teammates.

EDMONTON OILERS
1988-1989

McNall, who's been tremendous to myself and my family.

"But on the other side, nobody takes losing worse than Mark Messier and Kevin Lowe."

"Nobody stays at the top forever," said Green. "We've had a great kick at the cat for a young organization. You can name a whole bunch who haven't won a thing."

Esa Tikkanen, the Grate One, at his pesky best.

Craig Simpson and Mark Messier celebrate another goal.

Anderson manages to beat Hrudey once more, although the Gretzky-led Kings came back to knock the Oilers out of the playoffs in Game 7.

Edmonton Oilers
1988-89
Results & Statistics

			REGULAR SEASON				
COACH	GP	W	L	T	PTS	GF	GA
Glen Sather	80	38	34	8	84	325	306

3rd Smythe Division, 7th Overall. Playoffs: Lost Smythe Division Semifinal 4-3 vs Los Angeles.

		REGULAR SEASON			
PLAYER	GP	G	A	PTS	PIM
Jari Kurri	76	44	58	102	69
Jimmy Carson	80	49	51	100	36
Mark Messier	72	33	61	94	130
Esa Tikkanen	67	31	47	78	92
Craig Simpson	66	35	41	76	80
Glenn Anderson	79	16	48	64	93
Craig MacTavish	80	21	31	52	55
Charlie Huddy	76	11	33	44	52
Tomas Jonsson (NYI)	53	9	23	32	34
Tomas Jonsson (EDM)	20	1	10	11	22
Tomas Jonsson (TOT)	73	10	33	43	56
Normand Lacombe	64	17	11	28	57
Keith Acton	46	11	15	26	47
Miroslav Frycer (DET)	23	7	8	15	47
Miroslav Frycer (EDM)	14	5	5	10	18
Miroslav Frycer (TOT)	37	12	13	25	65
Kevin Lowe	76	7	18	25	98
Steve Smith	35	3	19	22	97
Kevin McClelland	79	6	14	20	161
Craig Muni	69	5	13	18	71
Randy Gregg	57	3	15	18	28
Kelly Buchberger	66	5	9	14	234
Craig Redmond	21	3	10	13	12
Dave Hunter (WPG)	34	3	1	4	61
Dave Hunter (EDM)	32	3	5	8	22
Dave Hunter (TOT)	66	6	6	12	83
Mark Lamb	20	2	8	10	14
Chris Joseph	44	4	5	9	54
Greg Adams	49	4	5	9	72
Reed Larson	10	2	7	9	15
Doug Halward (DET)	18	0	1	1	36
Doug Halward (EDM)	24	0	7	7	25
Doug Halward (TOT)	42	0	8	8	61
Jeff Beukeboom	36	0	5	5	94
Dave Brown (PHI)	50	0	3	3	100
Dave Brown (EDM)	22	0	2	2	66
Dave Brown (TOT)	72	0	5	5	166
Martin Gelinas	6	1	2	3	0
Doug Smith	19	1	1	2	9
John LeBlanc	2	1	0	1	0
Alan May	3	1	0	1	7
Mike Ware	2	0	1	1	11
Ken Hammond	5	0	1	1	8
Grant Fuhr	59	0	1	1	6
Nick Fotiu	1	0	0	0	0
Francois Leroux	2	0	0	0	0
Selmar Odelein	2	0	0	0	2
Kim Issel	4	0	0	0	0
Glen Cochrane (CHI)	6	0	0	0	13
Glen Cochrane (EDM)	12	0	0	0	52
Glen Cochrane (TOT)	18	0	0	0	65
Bill Ranford	29	0	0	0	2

		REGULAR SEASON				
GOALTENDER	GP	MINS	GA	SO	GAA.	W-L-T
Bill Ranford	29	1509	88	1	3.50	15-8-2
Grant Fuhr	59	3341	213	1	3.83	23-26-6

SURPRISE! CUP NO. 5

Nobody expected the Edmonton Oilers would wind up with hockey's version of a "baker's dozen," a fifth Stanley Cup thrown in for good measure after four had been won with Wayne Gretzky.

But when the Oilers beat the Boston Bruins 4-1 to win the 1990 Cup finals, *Edmonton Journal* hockey writer Jim Matheson wrote: "On Aug. 9, 1988, it was minus 99 in Edmonton. Today, it's plus five. The icy chill that was there when Wayne Gretzky blew town has been replaced by a warm-all-over feeling."

It was the Oilers' fifth Cup in seven years, and certainly the least expected. How surprising was it? The City of Edmonton hadn't even planned a parade for the team, like the four previous times. Wrote *Edmonton Journal* columnist Cam Cole: "On Aug. 9, 1988, this moment was never going to happen ... not in a million years."

"Nobody expected us to be back this soon," offered winger Craig Simpson, who led everyone with 16 playoff goals. "I don't think anybody expected us to be sitting where we are today."

"We wanted it for the young guys — it's so great to see the joy in their faces," said Kevin Lowe. "But Mess (Mark Messier) and I looked at each other and said: 'This one's for the G-man (Gretzky), because he's still such a big part of our team.'"

"I think after last year we had to prove we were still a character team and a great hockey team," said Craig MacTavish. "This year really helped us out. We all miss Gretz and wish he was here, but you go on. We certainly didn't want to win this as one-upmanship on Wayne Gretzky. He's still a big part of this hockey team in our hearts, the job he's done for us. It's certainly not any sweeter because he's not here."

The season had started after a somewhat bizarre summer in 1989. Tomas Jonsson, who had joined the team from the New York Islanders, decided to return to play in Sweden.

Glen Sather, who had been hinting for years he might retire as coach, finally did. He would concentrate on general manager duties, John Muckler would be the coach, Ted Green would move up to co-coach and, soon after, Ron Low would be brought in as an assistant coach.

With 442 wins at the time, Sather felt he could hand over the reins after the team went a year without Gretzky. "It's time to make a change," said Sather. "Our great players are getting a little older and it's time to let the kids develop."

But it was goalie Grant Fuhr who was in for the strangest summer, which would be a prelude to an unimaginable season. Fuhr announced his retirement on a golf cart on June 8, came out of retirement on Aug. 25, fired his agent Rich Winter on Sept. 26 and soon after was sued for breach of contract by Winter. It was all over a $500,000 offer Fuhr had to wear Pepsi on his goal pads, which the National Hockey League disallowed.

He missed the beginning of the season with appendicitis, he smashed up his

Jaguar, he split up with his wife and then came shoulder surgery that caused him to miss another two months.

The man who two years earlier played 94 league and playoff games would play only 21 this season.

The 1989-90 season was a landmark one for the NHL, with the arrival of eight Russians and a Latvian on the scene, courtesy of Soviet leader Mikhail Gorbachev's policy of glasnost, or openness. Among those wiping their feet on the welcome mat were Igor Larionov, who once traded some caviar for a Wayne Gretzky hockey stick, and a flashy kid named Alexander Mogilny, who learned English in six weeks.

The Oilers started the season with Glenn Anderson bouncing back from a woeful 16-goal season, rookie Martin Gelinas now ready for prime time and life without Gretzky no longer a novelty.

"We've got a young hockey club, we're in a transition period," said Muckler.

But the club was rocked just four games into the season when Jimmy Carson quit the team, citing "tremendous negative vibes" in Edmonton.

"I went from being really wanted by the Kings to being brought to the Oilers in a set of circumstances (the Gretzky trade)," said Carson later. "They'd lost the greatest player in the world and the fans weren't happy."

After trying to make a trade all summer, Sather finalized one in November — Carson, Kevin McClelland and a fifth-round draft pick to the Detroit Red Wings for Petr Klima, Joe Murphy, Jeff Sharples and Adam Graves. It was an impossible trade to evaluate.

Klima had a history of personal problems, Murphy had been a No. 1 overall draft pick, Sharples had suffered the sophomore jinx and Graves was described as "a nonentity, so far."

By mid-November, the Oilers were 6-9-5, but with the Carson deal done, the team went 15-2-2 before the new year.

In January, Sather dealt Norm Lacombe to Philadelphia, brought in Czech star Vladimir Ruzicka and recycled Reijo Ruotsalainen from New Jersey in exchange for Sharples.

The team ended with 90 points, six more than the previous year, and fifth best overall. Perhaps the most pleasant surprise was goalie Bill Ranford, forced to play 56 games given Fuhr's various injuries and holdouts, as the team gave up 23 fewer goals than the season before.

The Carson trade had been the turning point. "I don't think we'd have finished in second place (in the Smythe Division) without that deal being made," said Muckler. "It's no knock on him, but if Jimmy Carson was still here, I don't think we'd have been second.

"We filled a lot of positions. We got three guys who can play."

And when the playoffs came, play they did.

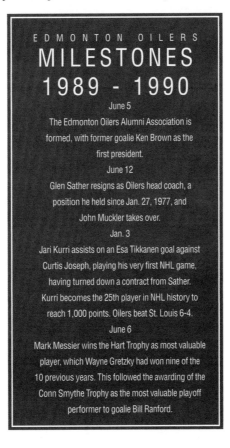

E D M O N T O N   O I L E R S
MILESTONES
1989 - 1990

June 5
The Edmonton Oilers Alumni Association is formed, with former goalie Ken Brown as the first president.

June 12
Glen Sather resigns as Oilers head coach, a position he held since Jan. 27, 1977, and John Muckler takes over.

Jan. 3
Jari Kurri assists on an Esa Tikkanen goal against Curtis Joseph, playing his very first NHL game, having turned down a contract from Sather. Kurri becomes the 25th player in NHL history to reach 1,000 points. Oilers beat St. Louis 6-4.

June 6
Mark Messier wins the Hart Trophy as most valuable player, which Wayne Gretzky had won nine of the 10 previous years. This followed the awarding of the Conn Smythe Trophy as the most valuable playoff performer to goalie Bill Ranford.

Opposite: High-fives all around — Glenn Anderson, Craig Simpson, Craig Muni et al celebrate a goal on the way to a most surprising fifth Stanley Cup win against the Boston Bruins in Game 5 of the final in the Boston Garden.

1989-1990
IMMORTALIZED
IN BRONZE

The idea of a statue in his honour kind of spooked Wayne Gretzky. "It gives you a funny feeling, thinking about that," said Gretzky, before the unveiling of the bronze tribute to him on Aug. 27, 1989.

"But it'll probably feel funnier when I walk past it myself. I mean, you're not supposed to be still alive, are you? I think I'd be lying if I said I wasn't a little embarrassed. I'm still only 28 years old."

Molson Breweries paid $75,000 for former Edmontonian John Weaver, who had moved to Hope, B.C., to design and make the life-size impression of Gretzky holding the Stanley Cup over his head, with his trademark sweater half-tucked in his pants.

More than 14,000 people bought 99-cent tickets for the event at the Coliseum, to welcome Gretzky, wife Janet, and eight-month-old daughter, Paulina.

Gretzky also received the key to the city, a permanent Molson Cup for three-star selections (he won it nine times), a photo album of his career highlights (including a shot of him facing off against Cincinnati Stinger Mark Messier) and a painting by local artist Joan Healey titled *The Parting*. It showed three kids in Oiler jerseys at an outdoor rink with the Edmonton skyline in the background, the kid wearing No. 99 waving goodbye to the kids wearing No. 4 and No. 11. Los Angeles singer Tim Feehan, formerly of Edmonton, composed a special song for the occasion, *The Memories Will Last Forever.*

"Honestly, I was more nervous in the morning than I can ever recall," said Gretzky. "I was nervous when I got married, I was nervous in the Stanley Cup finals, I was nervous when I did *Saturday Night Live.* But nothing like this. I was a wreck."

The statue was then moved to its permanent home outside the north side of the Coliseum, standing 15 feet high on its base.

As he is wont to do, Oiler grinder Kelly Buchberger mixes it up with the Boston Bruins during the Stanley Cup final series in Boston. Above, he's sandwiched between Bruin defenceman Glen Wesley (left) and Dave Christian. At left, Buchberger plows into Bruins defenceman Don Sweeney.

Below, Glenn Anderson swoops in and scores a crucial goal on Boston goalie Andy Moog.

EDMONTON OILERS
1989-1990

Top: A member of the Oilers' Kid Line, Adam Graves, tries to meander past Allen Pedersen and Ray Bourque, but gets a faceful of leather for his efforts. Right: Steve Smith shows his appreciation for Mark Messier's goal.

Below: the Oilers' bench senses another Cup win late in Game 5 of the team's five-game finals victory over Boston.

Edmonton Oilers 1989-90 Results & Statistics

REGULAR SEASON

COACH	GP	W	L	T	PTS	GF	GA
John Muckler	80	38	28	14	90	315	283

STANLEY CUP CHAMPIONS, 2nd Smythe Division, 5th Overall. Playoffs: Won Smythe Division Semifinal 4-3 vs Winnipeg, Won Smythe Division Final 4-0 vs Los Angeles, Won Campbell Conference Final 4-2 vs Chicago, Won Stanley Cup Final 4-1 vs. Boston.

REGULAR SEASON

PLAYER	GP	G	A	PTS	PIM
Mark Messier	79	45	84	129	79
Jari Kurri	78	33	60	93	48
Glenn Anderson	73	34	38	72	107
Petr Klima (PIT)	13	5	5	10	6
Petr Klima (EDM)	63	25	28	53	66
Petr Klima (TOT)	76	30	33	63	72
Esa Tikkanen	79	30	33	63	161
Craig Simpson	80	29	32	61	180
Craig MacTavish	80	21	22	43	89
Steve Smith	75	7	34	41	171
Kevin Lowe	78	7	26	33	140
Joe Murphy (DET)	9	3	1	4	4
Joe Murphy (EDM)	62	7	18	25	56
Joe Murphy (TOT)	71	10	19	29	60
Mark Lamb	58	12	16	28	42
Martin Gelinas	46	17	8	25	30
Randy Gregg	48	4	20	24	42
Charlie Huddy	70	1	23	24	56
Adam Graves (DET)	13	0	1	1	13
Adam Graves (EDM)	63	9	12	21	123
Adam Graves (TOT)	76	9	13	22	136
Vladimir Ruzicka	25	11	6	17	10
Craig Muni	71	5	12	17	81
Geoff Smith	74	4	11	15	52
Reijo Ruotsalainen (NJ)	31	2	5	7	14
Reijo Ruotsalainen (EDM)	10	1	7	8	6
Reijo Ruotsalainen (TOT)	41	3	12	15	20
Jeff Beukeboom	46	1	12	13	86
Kelly Buchberger	55	2	6	8	168
Normand Lacombe	15	5	2	7	21
Peter Eriksson	20	3	3	6	24
Dave Brown	60	0	6	6	145
Jimmy Carson	4	1	2	3	0
Kevin McClelland	10	1	1	2	13
Chris Joseph	4	0	2	2	2
Bill Ranford	56	0	2	2	18
Mike Greenlay	2	0	1	1	0
Francois Leroux	3	0	1	1	0
Trevor Sim	3	0	1	1	2
Bruce Bell	1	0	0	0	0
Randy Exelby	1	0	0	0	0
Tom Lehmann	1	0	0	0	0
Norm Maciver	1	0	0	0	0
Mike Ware	3	0	0	0	4
Eldon Reddick	11	0	0	0	0
Grant Fuhr	21	0	0	0	2
Anatoli Semenov	-	-	-	-	-

REGULAR SEASON

GOALTENDER	GP	MINS	GA	SO	GAA.	W-L-T
Eldon Reddick	11	604	31	0	2.08	5-4-2
Bill Ranford	56	3107	165	1	3.19	24-16-9
Grant Fuhr	21	1081	70	1	3.89	9-7-3
Randy Exelby	1	60	5	0	5.00	0-1-0
Mike Greenlay	1	20	4	0	12.00	0-0-0

1990-1991

THE LAST HURRAH

In many ways, the 1990-91 season turned out to be a last hurrah for the Edmonton Oilers as fans had known them.

Paul Coffey and Wayne Gretzky were already gone. Jari Kurri followed suit before the season began. Mark Messier, Grant Fuhr and Glenn Anderson would depart after it ended.

It took an overtime tie and an overtime win, both against the Calgary Flames, plus a 6-3 win over the Winnipeg Jets in the last three regular season games, to give Edmonton a .500 record. Their 80 points were the club's fewest in a decade.

They made it to the third round of the playoffs, but looking tired, beaten up and old, fell to the Minnesota North Stars in five games. "I can't say enough about this team — it showed more guts and grit than any team I've ever played on ... and I'm very proud of all our guys," said Messier.

The roller-coaster season had been very closely tied to the Oilers' captain.

To be sure, the team dearly missed Jari Kurri, who spent the season playing for the Milan Devils in Italy. And they also suffered when a drug suspension limited Fuhr to 13 regular season appearances.

But it was injuries to Messier, first a sprained knee and then a broken left thumb, that proved most telling. He dressed for only 53 games. The team played .566 hockey (28-21-4) with him in the lineup, and .370 (9-16-2) without him.

As was becoming routine with a franchise growing older, the summer of 1990 had some ominous moments.

Gainers Inc. filed a $7.75-million suit against Oilers owner Peter Pocklington, bringing Gainers' total claim against its former owner to $12.15 million.

Pocklington then said his impending $100-million sale of Palm Dairies had him thinking of building his own arena, and vacating Northlands Coliseum in two years. Northlands general manager Colin Forbes countered with a $70-million offer from Northlands to buy the Oilers, saying: "I'm as serious as Mr. Pocklington is in building his own building."

Then came the departure of Kurri, who admitted that the Oilers offered him more money to stay, but Milan's short season would allow him to play for Finland in the world championship that was going to be staged in his homeland.

"We're losing the best right winger in the game, no question," said coach John Muckler.

The Oilers also lost their former trainer, John Blackwell, who became assistant general manager of the Philadelphia Flyers.

The Oilers played four pre-season games in Dusseldorf, West Germany, plus Munich and Graz, Austria. Upon their return, defenceman Randy Gregg was lost in the waiver draft to the Vancouver Canucks and he declared his retirement.

When the season opener came and they raised the fifth Stanley Cup banner, *Edmonton Journal* columnist Cam Cole sensed it was "as much invocation as celebration."

Wrote Cole: "All of it was not only for the fans, but for them. The players. The survivors.

"It has been an off-season to shake the foundation of any franchise, however strong, however resilient. Jari Kurri's defection to Italy. Grant Fuhr's 59-game drug suspension. Randy Gregg's retirement. Glenn Anderson's sudden holdout/retirement. Mark Messier's quest for a $2-million annual salary, termed 'out of the question' by general manager Glen Sather. And eight Oilers, including some current and future stars, playing out their option."

Anderson returned after a six-game contract holdout. But soon after coming out of the gate, the Oilers ran off nine straight losses, a club record at the time, and their overall record of 2-11-2 was dead last among 21 teams in the NHL.

That put the Oilers in the running for the Eric Lindros sweepstakes, namely the first pick in the 1991 Entry Draft, a prospect that caused Messier to say: "That's a farce. I'll guarantee you we won't be staying in last place for long."

The Oilers tried to forget their woes by playing golf with former U.S. president Gerald Ford in Palm Desert, Calif., and looking forward to Messier's return to the lineup.

Both proved effective cures of their woes.

The Oilers went through a torrid 25-11-1 run through the middle of the schedule, before tailing off with a 10-15-3 finish.

Fuhr's suspension was reduced to 59 games and he returned to the Oilers after five months on the sidelines, posting a 4-0 shutout of the New Jersey Devils on Feb. 18 in New Jersey. "Nervous? Yes I was," said Fuhr. "I thought I was shaky at the start. Not like the first game I ever played, against Winnipeg, but close."

The topsy-turvy Oilers' lineup resulted in them finishing the season with only 272 goals, compared to their previous low of 301 in 1979-80. Top scorer Esa Tikkanen had 69 points, fewer than Mark Recchi, John Cullen and Brian Leetch had assists.

"From what we did this season, we can't rank too high on anybody's list," said Oiler Craig MacTavish, of the club's playoff chances. "We're not going to make excuses ... we had a bad season. It was a year where we were constantly climbing uphill.

"But with what we've done in the past ... you can't count us out."

"I don't know if we can do it again," said coach John Muckler. "But I'll tell you one thing, whatever we've got, we'll give. I don't have any doubt of that."

Defenceman Kevin Lowe reflected on how the core of great players had shrunk during the past four years — Coffey, Gretzky and Kurri having departed. "The game has really changed in the sense of contracts," said Lowe. "And in the future, I think it might be hard to keep teams together for a long time."

Anderson recalled how shocked he had been as a rookie when Blair MacDonald was traded to Vancouver in March of 1981. "He was our team captain, and I thought he was the core and a big strong point of our hockey club," said Anderson. "And they not only traded him, they compared him to a fire hydrant."

(Sather's infamous quote after that trade: "Even a fire hydrant could score 40 goals playing with Gretzky.")

And Messier, perhaps knowing he would be playing his last playoffs as an

---

E D M O N T O N   O I L E R S

MILESTONES

1990 - 1991

July 30

Jari Kurri signs a two-year contract to play with the Milan Devils in Italy.

Nov. 10

The Oilers run their losing streak to nine games with a 7-4 loss in Los Angeles, having erased their previous losing record of six games set in February and March of 1980.

Jan. 13

During a 5-3 win over Philadelphia, Mark Messier records his 1,000th career NHL point and Glenn Anderson hits the 400-goal mark. There were only 28 players with 1,000 points and 31 with 400 goals.

Feb. 20

Oilers tie the NHL record for fewest shots on goal, one period, with zero against Minnesota.

Feb. 28

Oilers set the NHL record for most penalties in one game, 44 (26 minors, 7 majors, 6 misconducts, 4 game misconducts and 1 match penalty). Oilers and Kings set the record for most penalties, both teams, one game, with 85.

Opposite: The jig is up. The Oilers watch a jubilant bunch of Minnesota North Stars charge the ice after beating Edmonton in the Campbell Conference final.

On Aug. 31, 1990, *Edmonton Journal* reporters Tom Barrett and David Staples broke the front page news that Oiler goalie Grant Fuhr had been a cocaine user for about seven years.

In late September, Fuhr was suspended for one year by NHL president John Ziegler, but could ask for reinstatement on Jan. 15, 1991, and be back in action Feb. 18. It was the longest NHL drug suspension to date, with Don Murdoch's year-long suspension having been commuted to 40 games.

In mid-January, Fuhr bared his soul in a 90-minute interview with *The Journal.* He was under supervision of personal trainer Susan Bell, playing shinny hockey — often forward — twice a week, seeing sports psychologist Murray Smith and being tested for drugs in his system every week.

"I read the papers to see what day it is," said Fuhr, who estimated losing $1 million in salary and endorsements. "It's been hard. Hard to figure out, hard to justify. Game days are hardest. I still have tough times game days, I don't like coming to the games, but you go anyway. I don't like sitting in the stands."

On Feb. 4, Fuhr's suspension was commuted to 59 games, and he spent a week with the Oilers' Cape Breton farm team. His NHL return after five months was the stuff of dreams, a 4-0 shutout of the New Jersey Devils on Feb. 18 in New Jersey.

"This one was a long time coming," said Fuhr, who stopped 27 shots. "I've been looking forward to it for months. How does it feel? Very good."

Fuhr went on to play 17 games in the playoffs that season, with a 3.00 goals-against average.

Oiler, said: "I don't think there's ever going to be an easy way to end everything we've had. It's not possible to end it real smooth or real great.

"There's a lot of hockey left to be played ... it just might not be together."

Wrote Cam Cole: "The Last Hurrah for the Oilers, as we have known them? It may be."

In the first playoff round, the Oilers led the Calgary Flames 3-1 in games, but Calgary rebounded with wins of 5-3 and 2-1 — the latter on Theoren Fleury's marker at 4:40 of overtime — to force a seventh game.

In that, Esa Tikkanen scored three times, including the

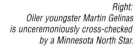
Right:
Oiler youngster Martin Gelinas is unceremoniously cross-checked by a Minnesota North Star.

Bottom:
Super pest Esa Tikkanen consoles goalie Grant Fuhr after the Oilers fell to the Stars.

EDMONTON OILERS
1990-1991

winner at 6:58 of overtime, a screened 40-foot wrist shot over Calgary goalie Mike Vernon's shoulder.

"This is one of the finest wins, and one of the greatest series we've played," said Sather.

In the second round against the Los Angeles Kings, four of the six games went into overtime and all ended 4-3, with Petr Klima scoring the winner in the second game, Tikkanen in the third and Craig MacTavish in the sixth.

But the Oilers' roll ended in the third round against the 16th-place Minnesota North Stars. The Oilers lost the series after five games.

The last hurrah was over.

Left:
Esa Tikkanen and Craig Simpson fight in front of the Minnesota net.
Bottom left:
Players on the Oilers bench hang their heads, realizing that they won't be defending their Stanley Cup title.

Below:
Tikkanen suffers the indignity of having to watch the North Stars' celebration.

COMPLETE CHANGING OF THE GUARD

The first glory era of the Edmonton Oilers was laid to rest before the 1991-92 season with the departure of Mark Messier, Grant Fuhr and Glenn Anderson, but the body had one last twitch in it.

The club finished with 82 points, two better than the previous season, and made it to three rounds of the Stanley Cup playoffs before falling four straight to the Chicago Blackhawks.

"I'm as proud of this team as any I've ever been with," said general manager Glen Sather. "They worked very hard and they deserve to be proud of themselves for as far as they got."

"From where we came (in January) when we were fifth in our division, in danger of missing the playoffs ... to be here ... ," said defenceman Kevin Lowe. "Hey, there's 18 other teams who didn't get this far."

Lowe wound up the season as the lone Oiler remaining from their first NHL season in 1979, as well as from their original Stanley Cup win in 1984, as Sather faced a flood of free agents and almost totally dismantled his team.

Before the season had started, he engineered a three-way deal that sent Jari Kurri (who had played the previous year in Italy) to Los Angeles and Dave Brown and Corey Foster to Philadelphia. Coming to Edmonton were Scott Mellanby, Craig Berube and Craig Fisher.

Then coach John Muckler went to the Buffalo Sabres as director of hockey operations, Ted Green replaced him at the Oiler helm and former University of Alberta Golden Bear Kevin Primeau was later added as an assistant coach.

Adam Graves went to the New York Rangers as a free agent, getting $2.4 million US for five years. Judge Edward Houston, who as a lawyer 20 years earlier had represented Ted Green in his assault case after a horrendous stick-swinging incident with Wayne Maki, awarded the Oilers' Troy Mallette as compensation. (It was a decision that would haunt the Oilers' franchise for years. Mallette would play 306 further games in the NHL, adding just 26 more goals and 68 points. Graves would go on to play 935 more NHL games and counting, scoring 306 goals and 556 points during that time.)

But the overhaul didn't end there. Charlie Huddy went to Los Angeles as a free agent. Then it was Fuhr, Anderson and Berube to the Toronto Maple Leafs for Vincent Damphousse, Luke Richardson, Peter Ing, Scott Thornton and future considerations. Steve Smith was shipped to the Chicago Blackhawks for Dave Manson and a third-round draft choice. Ken Linseman went to Toronto for future considerations.

And finally came the long-awaited movement of Messier plus future considerations to the New York Rangers, for Bernie Nicholls, Steve Rice, Louie DeBrusk and $5 million. That deal would be consummated five weeks later with Jeff Beukeboom going to the Rangers for David Shaw.

"I had a fantastic 12 years in Edmonton, but I'm looking forward to the new challenge ahead of me in New York," said Messier, who had won five Stanley Cups, the 1984 Conn Smythe Trophy and 1990 Hart Trophy.

Lowe said the mass exodus had been inevitable, and necessary. "It used to be

players would come into the dressing room after a game and complain about losing," said Lowe. "But last year, they were mad about their contracts."

Said centreman Craig MacTavish: "We've gone through a lot of off-ice adversity. We've obviously had more name players come and go than other teams. But it's hardened us to the problems that go on. We're not at all discouraged."

With 10 newcomers who weren't on the roster the previous May, the Oilers had very quickly gone from one of the eldest teams in the National Hockey League to the second youngest — average age, 25 years, three months.

They opened with a 7-13-3 record, in 19th place in the 22-team league. They didn't have a single player among the top 45 in league scoring.

"If you're young and have talent like we do, it has to come to the top," said assistant coach Ron Low.

The team was on a roll with a seven-game undefeated streak when Nicholls, who had delayed reporting to the Oilers while his wife, Heather, went through a difficult pregnancy with twins, finally joined the team 10 weeks after the Messier trade.

"The high school team I'd been practising with was a little slower than the NHL," said Nicholls, upon his return to the league.

The team had given up 154 goals midway through the 80-game schedule, causing Green to say: "I don't think you can blame any one department, either. It's not just goaltending or the defence or the forwards. Blame the whole team."

On Jan. 23, 1992, Messier returned to the Coliseum for the first time since leaving the Oilers and had an assist and scored the winner in a 3-1 Ranger victory.

"By pure chance I looked up at the score clock while the anthems were on and I saw all the (Stanley Cup) banners," said Messier, who was greeted with a 90-second standing ovation.

"Seeing the banners brought back a lot of emotional feelings. I had to regroup pretty quickly."

As the team's record hit 18-24-7, Sather pleaded for patience. "It took us five years to get to the stage where we won," he said. "Even with all those players ... Gretzky, Messier, Kurri, Anderson, Coffey, Fuhr, it still took five years. They all had talent but they had to be nurtured. They had to be taught. It's never going to be the same. If we were in a market like New York or Chicago, maybe we could have kept these players for 10 years and they would have retired with 10 Stanley Cups. But it doesn't work that way."

The very next night, after a 5-2 loss to the expansion San Jose Sharks, Sather held a 20-minute closed door meeting with the players. The Oilers promptly roared down the stretch with an 18-9-3 record, which was interrupted by a 10-day strike as NHL players battled for better free agency and licensing.

The strong stretch run and rest during the strike set the scene for the playoffs, as the Oilers finished two games above .500, third in the Smythe Division and 12th overall.

Damphousse held up his end of the Fuhr trade, by leading the Oilers in goals with 38 — a career high to that point — and points with 89.

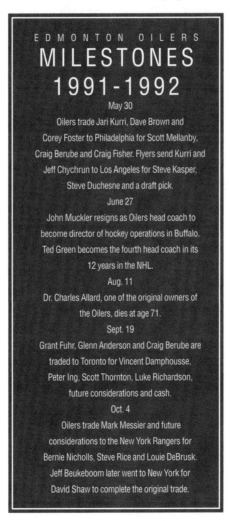

EDMONTON OILERS
MILESTONES
1991-1992

May 30
Oilers trade Jari Kurri, Dave Brown and Corey Foster to Philadelphia for Scott Mellanby, Craig Berube and Craig Fisher. Flyers send Kurri and Jeff Chychrun to Los Angeles for Steve Kasper, Steve Duchesne and a draft pick.

June 27
John Muckler resigns as Oilers head coach to become director of hockey operations in Buffalo. Ted Green becomes the fourth head coach in its 12 years in the NHL.

Aug. 11
Dr. Charles Allard, one of the original owners of the Oilers, dies at age 71.

Sept. 19
Grant Fuhr, Glenn Anderson and Craig Berube are traded to Toronto for Vincent Damphousse, Peter Ing, Scott Thornton, Luke Richardson, future considerations and cash.

Oct. 4
Oilers trade Mark Messier and future considerations to the New York Rangers for Bernie Nicholls, Steve Rice and Louie DeBrusk. Jeff Beukeboom later went to New York for David Shaw to complete the original trade.

Opposite: Oiler GM Glen Sather completely shuffled the deck, shipping away many key players. Left holding the fort are players like Craig MacTavish, Mark Lamb, Kelly Buchberger, Dave Manson, Brian Glynn and Bill Ranford.

1991 - 1992
SPUNK, GRIT AND DETERMINATION

The hiring of Ted Green as head coach of the Edmonton Oilers in 1991 was a crowning achievement for the former rugged defenceman.

In 1969, a helmetless Green had been felled by Wayne Maki in one of the most vicious stick-swinging incidents in hockey history, which left the Boston Bruins' defender with a synthetic plate in his head after three operations.

"Did I think I'd be a head coach in the NHL after Maki hit me?" said Green. "No, I was just trying to add two and two."

Green recovered to share in the Bruins' 1970 and 1972 Stanley Cup wins, as part of a defence ensemble that included Bobby Orr, Carol Vadnais and Dallas Smith. They were dubbed "Bob & Carol & Ted & Dallas," a play on words from the1969 movie *Bob & Carol & Ted & Alice*.

Green left Boston in 1972 and helped the Winnipeg Jets and New England Whalers win three World Hockey Association titles before retiring in 1979.

Oilers general manager Glen Sather hired Green as an assistant coach in 1981, for his grit. "He was a guy who fought back from a very serious injury, a guy who had to teach himself to write with his right instead of left hand (due to partial paralysis on his left side)," said Sather. "He had to rehabilitate himself; he's almost a scratch golfer again.

"When a guy with that determination and spunk is available, you go for him. You don't learn those things out of a book."

"No matter how you go into the playoffs, I think you reach a point during the first series where you either continue on, get over that hurdle and be real successful the rest of the way, or you come to a point where you can't better your game and you go the other way," said MacTavish.

Edmonton rolled over the Los Angeles Kings in six games during the opening round, which ended with a 3-0 shutout for Bill Ranford. It was the same script in Round 2, as the Oilers eliminated the Vancouver Canucks in six games, with Ranford once more earning a 3-0 shutout in the final meeting.

And the words of Ted Green on the day Messier had been traded were rekindled: "Don't worry about the passing of the

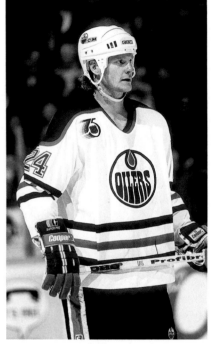

A new wave of Oilers. Peter Ing (left) arrived from Toronto as a backup to Bill Ranford, Dave Manson (centre) patrolled the blue-line and Scott Mellanby (right) added some toughness and scoring on the right side.

Troy Mallette (left) came to the Oilers as compensation for the Rangers' signing of free agent Adam Graves. Bernie Nicholls (centre) was part of the Mark Messier trade with New York, and Luke Richardson (right) arrived from the Maple Leafs in the deal that sent Grant Fuhr and Glenn Anderson to Toronto.

EDMONTON OILERS
1991-1992

Edmonton Oilers. There's only one way to kill this franchise ... that's with a wooden stake to the heart."

Green was praised for having moulded the newcomers in his image. But the magic finally ended in the third round, as the Oilers were swept by Chicago in four games.

Asked for the topic of his speech before Game 4, Green said

with a smile: "I just told them to play it like it was a seventh game ... only we have four of them."

Sather knew that starting over would be tough. "I find that part of it, taking a chance, exciting," said the general manager. "The groundwork is laid, the players are in place and there's a whole new era here."

Among those auditioning for a regular spot in the new-look lineup in 1991-92: Steven Rice (left), Scott Thornton (centre) and David Shaw (right).

Josef Beranek (left) was counted on to shore up an anemic offence, Vincent Damphousse (centre) led the team in scoring after arriving from Toronto, while big Louie DeBrusk (right), handled policeman duties while playing limited minutes for the Oilers.

EDMONTON OILERS
1992-1993
OUTSIDE THE PLAYOFFS LOOKING IN

The 1992-93 season for the Edmonton Oilers was symbolized quite nicely when the team held its skills competition in January.

The rapid fire accuracy shooting segment was won by assistant coach Ron Low, 42, who had been a goalie when he last played for a living, eight years earlier.

Edmonton Journal columnist Cam Cole pointed out that the Oilers of John Muckler in 1991 and Ted Green in 1992 were cumulatively two games over .500 in the regular season, but both teams rode the remnants of great leadership and terrific coaching to the conference final.

However, the chance for retribution in the playoffs didn't come in 1993, as the team missed post-season play for the first time in its 14-year National Hockey League history, with a 28-50-8 record, better than only the Hartford Whalers and three expansion teams.

Wrote Cole: "The fall was inevitable. The law of diminishing returns took over. Trade one great player for three lesser ones enough times and eventually you get a roster full of lesser ones. You get a team with four third lines. You get the Oilers.

"It may be as simple as this: goals cost money and the money isn't available."

Long before the season began, owner Peter Pocklington had said: "The players all want $1 million but reality is reality. The league isn't that nuts yet. No team can pay everybody that much."

General manager Glen Sather made a plea for fan support, as the season ticket base had fallen from 17,000 to 12,000. He said the team faced three options: increase revenues, control costs by trading high-priced players, or relocate.

A team that was once able to sign players to long-term deals now had no less than nine free agents, after having eight the summer before. The Oilers lost Mark Lamb and Anatoli Semenov in the expansion draft. Vincent Damphousse, who had led the team in goals with 38 and points with 89, was traded to the Montreal Canadiens for Shayne Corson, Brent Gilchrist and Vladimir Vujtek. Norm Maciver went to the Ottawa Senators in the waiver draft. And Joe Murphy held out for more money.

The regular season started with coach Ted Green saying: "I like the size of our team, our speed, our aggressiveness. But the question has been: can we score, because of the goals we gave up without Vinny (Damphousse) and Murphy?"

It would be a very telling question.

Kevin Lowe was also a holdout, so the captain's 'C' went to Craig MacTavish.

The Oilers got off to a 1-8-1 start, and MacTavish said: "You start losing and you kind of forget how to win. You lose confidence in yourself and start to stray from the things that have been successful in the past, and everybody goes to a more individual style."

Oiler concerns continued off the ice as well. Bernie Nicholls' wife, Heather, whose difficult pregnancy having twins the previous year delayed Bernie's arrival from New York, gave birth to a son, Jack, with Down syndrome.

One-quarter through the season, Edmonton was 20th among 24 teams in scoring and 21st in goals against.

"Compared to all the teams in the past, this is the worst offensive team we've

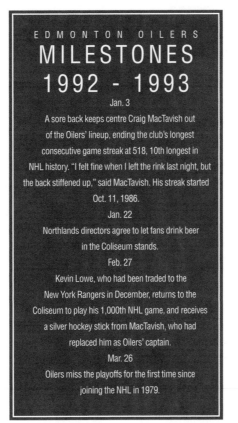

E D M O N T O N   O I L E R S
MILESTONES
1992 - 1993

Jan. 3

A sore back keeps centre Craig MacTavish out of the Oilers' lineup, ending the club's longest consecutive game streak at 518, 10th longest in NHL history. "I felt fine when I left the rink last night, but the back stiffened up," said MacTavish. His streak started Oct. 11, 1986.

Jan. 22

Northlands directors agree to let fans drink beer in the Coliseum stands.

Feb. 27

Kevin Lowe, who had been traded to the New York Rangers in December, returns to the Coliseum to play his 1,000th NHL game, and receives a silver hockey stick from MacTavish, who had replaced him as Oilers' captain.

Mar. 26

Oilers miss the playoffs for the first time since joining the NHL in 1979.

had," said Nicholls.

On Dec. 11, 1992, Lowe was traded to the New York Rangers. The last member from the Oilers' inaugural NHL season in 1979, and of the Oilers' first Stanley Cup win in 1984, was now gone. "I have nothing to say but: 13 great years, great experiences, great fun," said Lowe, 33. He added that he might return to Edmonton to live when his playing days were done and that a management job in the Oiler organization "is still a possibility."

"It's sad to think of all the fun we had with the great players, but you've got to start a new era, I guess," said Sather. "I thought Kevin might be the one guy who would be with us the whole way."

Pocklington mentioned that he might have to move the Oilers out of Edmonton, which caused Winnipeg Jets majority owner Barry Shenkarow to say it would be "a sad day" if Edmonton lost the Oilers. "If you don't get revenues from the building and you're paying rent and you're in a small market, there's not a chance you're going to survive," said Shenkarow. Indeed, in 1996, the Jets didn't.

In January, the Oilers traded Nicholls to the New Jersey Devils for Kevin Todd and Zdeno Ciger. "The only thing that's honestly going to bother me when I leave is that I didn't play my best for the fans in Edmonton," said Nicholls.

Days later, the Oilers acquired Edmonton product Brian Benning. Then in late February, the 63-game holdout by Murphy finally came to an end when he was traded to the Chicago Blackhawks for Igor Kravchuk and Dean McAmmond.

The Oilers also sent Gilchrist to the Minnesota North Stars for Todd Elik, whose father Bo had played for the old Edmonton Flyers pro team in 1962-63, with the likes of Mark Messier's dad, Doug.

And bigger news broke March 17 when Esa Tikkanen was traded to the Rangers for 22-year-old Doug Weight, just hours before the teams played each other in New York.

"You're told at 4 o'clock, then you go to a different dressing room with totally different guys," said Weight. "My family's coming tonight — they'll look down during the anthem and wonder what's going on. I think there's a winning attitude in Edmonton. I know (Mark) Messier is gone and (Wayne) Gretzky is gone, but it's in the city and they'll get back up there."

"I have lots of good friends there," said Tikkanen, of leaving Edmonton. "They were great teams there. Now I'm gone, too."

The revolving door continued on March 22 when Craig Muni, perhaps the finest practitioner of the old-fashioned hip check that the Oilers ever had, was sent to the Chicago Blackhawks for Mike Hudson.

But less than a week later the curtain fell. The team lost 4-1 to its unofficial alumni squad — Gretzky, Jari Kurri, Charlie Huddy and Marty McSorley with the L.A. Kings — and missed the playoffs for the first time since joining the NHL in 1979.

"I don't think anybody could have predicted that this team would miss the playoffs, five years ago," said Gretzky. "But they've basically given up everybody for young guys. The whole idea behind trading me, Mark Messier, Paul Coffey and everyone else was to keep from falling out of the playoffs. They didn't want

Opposite: With Kevin Lowe holding out and eventually traded to New York, Craig MacTavish became the Oilers' new captain.

63

1992 - 1993
KEVIN AND
CRAIG, PART 1

During the 1992-93 season, an irreversible bond was forged between Kevin Lowe and Craig MacTavish.

Lowe, who had been the Oilers' very first National Hockey League draft pick in 1979 and scored the club's first NHL goal that fall, was traded to the New York Rangers on Dec. 11, 1992.

He was the last member of the original 1979 NHL team and last member of Edmonton's first Stanley Cup winning team in 1984 to leave.

"Fans in Edmonton, the way they adopted the Oilers, their knowledge of hockey — that was all part of the success we had," said Lowe. "It's been a great, small-town atmosphere.

"Something funny happened. I took a wrong turn the day before yesterday, and drove past the very first house I was ever in in Edmonton. I'd never been back to that street in 13 years here and, for whatever reason, two days before I leave, I'm back on that street by accident."

His captain's 'C' was handed to MacTavish, who was in the process of setting the Oilers' record of 518 consecutive games played, while ironically becoming the last helmetless player in the NHL.

"Not in my wildest dreams did I think my career here would last as long as it has," said MacTavish. "When I first came here, I thought, 'If I could play three years here... .'"

Asked who his mentor was, MacTavish said: "Kevin Lowe. He's a great example, great leader. A great person. If there was one guy I learned the most from, it would be him."

The parade of players in and out of Edmonton continued unabated in 1992-93. Joining the team was Brent Gilchrist from Montreal (above), Mike Hudson from Chicago (below), and Brian Benning from Philadelphia (right).

to do what the Islanders did, but I guess only time will tell which way was the right way.

"They have some speed and size and young talent. If they're able to keep those players together over a period of time, they have a chance to be a very good hockey team again. But it's a different era now than it was with the young group of guys who were here together in the '80s. I don't know if it will ever be that easy again to keep a team together."

When the 1992-93 season ended, not one of the players from the Oilers' first Stanley Cup teams in 1984 and 1985 was still with the

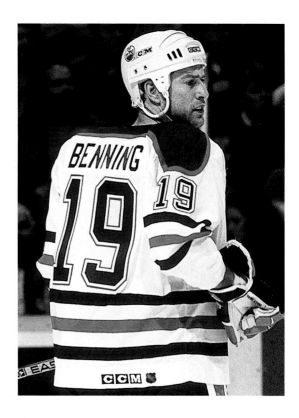

"You start losing and you kind of forget how to win. You lose confidence in yourself and start to stray from the things that have been successful in the past, and everybody goes to a more individual style."

— Craig MacTavish,
newly minted Oilers captain

EDMONTON OILERS
1992-1993

club. Only two remained, MacTavish and Kelly Buchberger, from the 1987 Cup crew. And three, including Craig Simpson, were left over from the 1988 Cup champs.

The troops left to coach Ted Green were termed Gang Green by the *Journal*'s Jim Matheson.

"We've had a good kick at the cat and you can't expect to be there every year," said Green.

"This game is a big wheel and you ride it up and hang on going down. You just hope that the wheel starts going back up and it doesn't take too long."

Joining Edmonton in mid-season from the New Jersey Devils were Kevin Todd (left) and Zdeno Ciger (below). Shayne Corson (above right) arrived in an off-season deal with Montreal in exchange for Vincent Damphousse.

"I don't think anybody could have predicted that this team would miss the playoffs, five years ago. But they've basically given up everybody for young guys. The whole idea behind trading me, Mark Messier, Paul Coffey and everyone else was to keep from falling out of the playoffs."

— Wayne Gretzky

HITTING ROCK BOTTOM

The nagging question before and during the 1993-94 season was where the Edmonton Oilers would end up. Owner Peter Pocklington would spend the entire season trying to hammer out a more favourable Coliseum leasing agreement with Edmonton Northlands and the City of Edmonton than the one he had until June of 1999.

Negotiations at various points hinted that the franchise would be moved to Hamilton or Minneapolis. National Hockey League commissioner Gary Bettman made a couple of trips to Edmonton to try smoothing out and fast-tracking the negotiations, with the expressed motive of keeping the team in the city.

Economic Development Edmonton chairman Rick LeLacheur, a former Edmonton Oil King junior whose family had a long history in the city's moving business, was brought in as a mediator.

The good news was that the team ended up in Edmonton.

The bad news was that they also ended up in 23rd place in the standings, with only 25 wins, the fewest in the club's NHL history, as the rebuilding program ramped up.

Petr Klima, the overtime hero of the Oilers' last Stanley Cup win in 1990, was dealt to the Tampa Bay Lightning for a third-round draft pick. Martin Gelinas, part of the Wayne Gretzky trade and a member of the Kid Line in the 1990 Stanley Cup win, was sent to the Quebec Nordiques for Scott Pearson. Goalie Ron Tugnutt and Scott Mellanby were lost to Anaheim and Florida respectively in the expansion draft.

Then on July 16, the San Jose Sharks tried using some sleight-of-hand to sign free agent Craig Simpson to a $130,000 contract, with a "reporting bonus" that would lift his annual salary for three years to more than $1 million. The ploy was that the Sharks wouldn't have to give up a draft pick for a player making less than $200,000, whereas signing a $1-million player would cost them two first-round picks.

Bettman called the deal "No Sale" on July 26, but five weeks later, Oilers general manager Glen Sather traded Simpson to the Buffalo Sabres for 18-year-old Slovakian winger Jozef Cierny.

As the 1993-94 season started, *Journal* writer Mark Spector profiled Sather as a mountain man, a Banff resident who had led the Oilers' successful assault on Mount NHL and come back down with them.

Said Sather: "If you're only around for the good times, I don't think it shows a lot of character."

Said Spector, slightly ahead of his time: "Forget all the players who have left the Oilers for greener pastures, the last and best acquisition left in the Edmonton Oiler fire sale is the GM."

The previous season had asked and answered the question of whether the Oilers could score enough goals — they scrounged only 2.88 per game. So when the team's two top scorers — Simpson and Klima — were traded, there was cause for concern.

But one light shone brightly. Oshawa centre Jason Arnott, who had been chosen seventh overall in the June entry draft, Edmonton's highest NHL draft pick since Paul Coffey went sixth overall in 1980, signed a three-year $2.1-million contract. At age 18, he became the second-youngest Oiler ever, with only Wayne Gretzky having started younger.

> ### EDMONTON OILERS
> ## MILESTONES
> ## 1993-1994
>
> **Nov. 9**
> Oilers end the longest winless streak in club history, 14 games, and longest losing streak in club history, 11 games, with a 4-2 win over the Detroit Red Wings, despite being outshot 48-20.
>
> **Nov. 24**
> Oilers lose 3-1 to the Chicago Blackhawks, setting an Oiler home losing record of nine straight games.
>
> **Apr. 13**
> Jason Arnott scores his 33rd goal of the season in a 2-2 tie with the San Jose Sharks, breaking Jari Kurri's Oiler team record of 32 goals by a rookie, set in 1980-81. Arnott ends up leading the team in scoring, and nets 68 points.

Even with Arnott, the team got off to its third brutal start in four seasons — two opening wins, then 14 winless games. The Oilers had a 5-21-5 record before they would again win two straight in mid-December.

Inside his private box, Pocklington paraded Dana Warg, executive director of the Target Centre in Minneapolis, as a warning that the Oilers could be moving. But Northlands got an interim court order halting any negotiations to shift the NHL franchise.

NHL referees, of all people, went on strike in mid-November for a 60-per-cent increase in starting salaries, compared to the 15 per cent offered by the league. Sixty minor pro and amateur refs and linesmen — including five from the Alberta Junior Hockey League — were summoned to a three-day training camp in Indianapolis as replacements.

The Oilers' 14-game winless steak and 11-game losing streak, both team records, came to an end on Nov. 9, 1993, with a 4-2 win over the Detroit Red Wings, despite being outshot 48-20.

"It gives you a whole new outlook on the rest of the season," said Craig MacTavish. "When you go as long as we did without winning a hockey game, it's like you're up against an insurmountable force."

The joy was short-lived. On Nov. 24, Edmonton set a club home losing record of nine straight games with a 3-1 defeat at the hands of the Chicago Blackhawks. The next day, with the club sporting a 3-18-3 record, Sather fired Ted Green as head coach and returned behind the bench himself.

"I've been treated extremely well by the organization," said Green. "Sometimes with kid gloves."

"I think it's my responsibility," said Sather, of trying to right a team gone wrong. "I don't think I could have put this on somebody else."

On Dec. 6, Sather unloaded defenceman Geoff Smith to the Florida Panthers and picked up Fredrik Olausson from the Winnipeg Jets in a three-way deal also involving draft picks.

On the ice, the Oilers responded briefly under Sather's return with a 10-6-3 showing, but then the losing ways returned as the team went 12-21-8 in the last half of the season.

"We've got a bunch of kids who fret and worry that they'll make a mistake; so the mistake happens," said Sather. "And then the mistakes multiply. It's become a confidence thing."

Wrote the *Journal*'s Cam Cole: "They are now 0-5 against the two first-year expansion teams — the Mighty Ducks of Anaheim (0-4) and the Mighty Panthers of Overtown (0-1) — and if you throw in their 0-2 against the very worst team in the history of professional hockey, the Mighty Bad Senators of Ottawa, it is difficult to escape the conclusion that the Oilers have hit rock bottom as a National Hockey League franchise."

Whereas Green could merely rearrange the deck furniture on the Titantic, Sather, as GM and coach, could chuck it out.

So Dave Manson went to Winnipeg for Boris Mironov, Mats Lindgren, plus first- and fourth-round draft picks. Brad Werenka went to Quebec for the rights to junior goalie Steve Passmore.

And, in an act of mercy, after nine years as an Oiler and 15 in the NHL, captain

Opposite: In a season of lows, one bright spot for the Oilers was the emergence of 18-year-old rookie Jason Arnott, who scored 33 goals, breaking the Oiler rookie scoring record held by Jari Kurri.

EDMONTON OILERS
1993-1994

Of dents and decals.

There exists in the Edmonton Oilers' dressing room a door like no others. It's big and heavy, made of hollow metal that's been banged in and, above all, it's ugly.

But it has a wonderful history and is itself a record book of the Edmonton Oilers' playoff success.

One night early in the Oilers' National Hockey League incarnation, the team gave fans stickers with the Oilers' logo on it. When the team won a playoff game, one of the decals was stuck on the metal door leading to the coaches' office. After each playoff win, another sticker went on the door.

A new row of stickers was started for each year's playoffs. And at the end of five of the rows was plastered a silver decal of the Stanley Cup.

Then there are the dents.

When Mark Messier was captain, he'd let the coaches know the players were ready to go by butt-ending the door with his stick, inflicting a dent. Esa Tikkanen later kept up the tradition. The result over time was three, huge circular indentations in the door.

The dressing room was later re-modelled, and the coaches' office was moved to the back of the locker-room. But the ugly door was preserved and now stands guarding the video room, near the dressing room entrance.

MacTavish was set free to join the New York Rangers in exchange for Todd Marchant.

"I have a lot of feelings for the guys in the locker-room here," said MacTavish, upon departing. "I can't say enough about how bright their futures are.

"Unfortunately for me, the clock is ticking and I probably wouldn't be here to see the fruition of it."

The season ended the way it had begun, with Arnott as the brightest light on the horizon, leading the team with 33 goals and scoring 68 points.

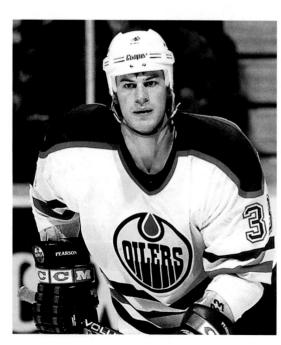

New to the Oilers in 1993-94 were Fredrik Olausson (top left) and Scott Pearson (bottom left). Pearson was traded from Quebec for Martin Gelinas. Above right: Jason Arnott (7) was still only a teenager, but played well beyond his years in his rookie season.

EDMONTON OILERS
1993-1994

"Seeing Jari Kurri play when I was a young kid — I never dreamed I'd be passing his rookie record," said Arnott, who bettered Kurri's 1980-81 team rookie mark of 32 goals.

Sather ended the season stating one of few certainties, namely that he would not be behind the bench the next year. But with two of the top-six first-round picks in the entry draft, he could see a slice of the Oilers of the early '80s.

"These kids are eager, anxious to please and they're developing," said Sather.

The Mountain Man was sensing another assault.

Also joining the team in 1993-94 were Vladimir Vujtek (top). Vujtek came from Montreal in the Damphousse trade. Doug Weight (above), wearing No. 42 when he first joined the Oilers, emerged as the team's leader and leading point-getter in 1993-94.

Edmonton Oilers
1993-94
Results & Statistics

	REGULAR SEASON					
COACH	GP	W	L	T	PTS	GF	GA

Ted Green (3-18-3) & Glen Sather (22-27-11)

| | 84 | 25 | 45 | 14 | 64 | 261 | 305 |

6th Pacific Division, 23rd Overall. Playoffs: Did not qualify.

	REGULAR SEASON				
PLAYER	GP	G	A	PTS	PIM
Doug Weight	84	24	50	74	47
Jason Arnott	78	33	35	68	104
Zdeno Ciger	84	22	35	57	8
Shayne Corson	64	25	29	54	118
Igor Kravchuk	81	12	38	50	16
Bob Beers (TB)	16	1	5	6	12
Bob Beers (EDM)	66	10	27	37	74
Bob Beers (TOT)	82	11	32	43	86
Scott Pearson	72	19	18	37	165
Fredrik Olausson (WPG)	18	2	5	7	10
Fredrik Olausson (EDM)	55	9	19	28	20
Fredrik Olausson (TOT)	73	11	24	35	30
Steven Rice	63	17	15	32	36
Boris Mironov (WPG)	65	7	22	29	96
Boris Mironov (EDM)	14	0	2	2	14
Boris Mironov (TOT)	79	7	24	31	110
Ilya Byakin	44	8	20	28	30
Dean McAmmond	45	6	21	27	16
Craig MacTavish	66	16	10	26	80
Mike Stapleton (WPG)	58	7	4	11	18
Mike Stapleton (EDM)	23	5	9	14	28
Mike Stapleton (TOT)	81	12	13	25	46
Kelly Buchberger	84	3	18	21	199
Kirk Maltby	68	11	8	19	74
Vladimir Vujtek	40	4	15	19	14
Brent Grieve (NYI)	3	0	0	0	7
Brent Grieve (EDM)	24	13	5	18	14
Brent Grieve (TOT)	27	13	5	18	21
Dave Manson	57	3	13	16	140
Scott Thornton	61	4	7	11	104
Louie DeBrusk	48	4	6	10	185
Adam Bennett	48	3	6	9	49
Peter White	26	3	5	8	2
Shjon Podein	28	3	5	8	8
Luke Richardson	69	2	6	8	131
Brad Werenka	15	0	4	4	14
Roman Oksiuta	10	1	2	3	4
Geoff Smith	21	0	3	3	12
Chris Joseph	10	1	1	2	28
Ian Herbers	22	0	2	2	32
Bill Ranford	71	0	2	2	2
Todd Marchant (NYR)	1	0	0	0	0
Todd Marchant (EDM)	3	0	1	1	2
Todd Marchant (TOT)	4	0	1	1	2
Gord Mark	12	0	1	1	43
Jozef Cierny	1	0	0	0	0
Wayne Cowley	1	0	0	0	0
Jeff Chychrun	2	0	0	0	0
Darcy Martini	2	0	0	0	0
Brad Zavisha	2	0	0	0	0
Todd Elik	4	0	0	0	6
Alexander Kerch	5	0	0	0	2
Tyler Wright	5	0	0	0	4
Marc Laforge	5	0	0	0	21
Fred Brathwaite	19	0	0	0	0

	REGULAR SEASON					
GOALTENDER	GP	MINS	GA	SO	GAA.	W-L-T
Wayne Cowley	1	57	3	0	3.16	0-1-0
Bill Ranford	71	4070	236	1	3.48	22-34-11
Fred Brathwaite	19	982	58	0	3.54	3-10-3

EDMONTON OILERS
1994-1995
STRIKE THREE

Just when Oiler fans thought there could be nothing worse than not winning the Stanley Cup, and certainly nothing worse than missing the playoffs two straight years, they found out differently.

There was something worse.

Some called it a strike. Others called it a lockout. And everybody called it a long, cold winter.

There had been little hint of a major labour tempest brewing with the National Hockey League during the early summer of 1994. The Oilers drafted Jason Bonsignore, another big centre in the Jason Arnott mould, and Ryan Smyth in the second round. They brought in former utility player Curt Brackenbury to run players through performance training, which he explained as "a mind-body-spirit kind of thing." Sort of a cross between Anthony Robbins and Richard Simmons.

And perhaps most enticing for hockey fans dulled by the 14-month soap opera between Oilers owner Peter Pocklington, the City of Edmonton and Edmonton Northlands, was that a restructuring of the Coliseum lease agreement finally seemed settled.

The new deal had Pocklington taking control of the Coliseum in exchange for a $2.8-million annual payment to Northlands. The city would contribute $15 million of federal infrastructure grants for Coliseum renovations and for Pocklington to build a new baseball park for his Triple A Edmonton Trappers. Pocklington would spend $4 million on Coliseum improvements and another $4 million on the ball park. And the city would forsake a seven-per-cent surcharge on Coliseum tickets, which would give Pocklington $1.5 million a year towards his lease payment.

Most comforting for Edmonton fans was that, under the first of three 10-year leases, the team could not be moved until at least 2004.

Pocklington held an information session at the Convention Centre, showing fans the revamped Coliseum seating structure. At the same time, general manager Glen Sather unveiled the club's new head coach, George Burnett, who after two years with the Oilers' Cape Breton farm club would become the youngest NHL head coach at age 32.

"If the bus is leaving at 10, we're leaving at 10," said Burnett, a former school teacher. "That's a priority for me, being well-organized and being prepared. That's the first step in gaining respect."

Then came signs of labour unrest in the NHL.

On Aug. 18, the first collective bargaining meeting in five months between the NHL and the NHL Players' Association ended with both sides saying "nothing of substance was accomplished."

NHL commissioner Gary Bettman said the average salary of $520,000 a year was out of whack and salaries should be tied to revenues. Bob Goodenow of the Players' Association viewed the proposal as a thinly disguised salary cap that would restrict the marketplace.

But teams went to training camp, where Sather marvelled at Bonsignore, who figured to be the last significant recommendation of chief scout Barry Fraser.

"When did we ever get a shot at a player like that?" said Sather.

"Fifteen years ago?"

Fraser, the man responsible for drafting successes like Kevin Lowe and Paul Coffey and Grant Fuhr, was winding down his role, having moved to Baja California to live life under the freshly anointed nickname Senor Fraser.

The Oilers' future would now be charted by Kevin Prendergast.

But the labour impasse caused the NHL season to be officially postponed on Oct. 1, with one of the few benefits being a throttle-back in the warp speed of renovations to the Coliseum.

NHL teams began laying off office staff, some 50 NHL players went to Europe to play, and Oiler assistant coach Kevin Primeau took a coaching job with Preussen Berlin in Germany.

And then there was Joey Moss.

Moss, born with Down syndrome, lived for his time spent as the Oilers' dressing room attendant. He'd been a fixture since the days of the World Hockey Association and had achieved celebrity status making commercials with his buddy Wayne Gretzky. Now he had nobody to vacuum up after.

Asked about the prospect of no NHL season, Joey said: "My feelings will be hurt."

"For all of us it's a job, but for Joey it's a way of life," said Oiler assistant trainer Lyle Kulchisky, who looked out for the immensely likable youngster.

The labour dispute lasted for 103 days, until on Jan. 11, 1995, a deal was struck. A schedule of 48 games per team in 101 days was issued, and teams were given a week for a mini-training camp.

And when the season was finally ready to face off, Doug Weight proclaimed Phase 1 of the Oilers' rebuilding project over.

"We've got everyone out who didn't want to be here," said Weight. "Nobody's looking to become a free agent and get the heck out of here."

Weight and Arnott figured to lead the scorers. Bryan Marchment and Luke Richardson would be the stalwarts on defence. And goalie Bill Ranford would keep victory within reach. A good start, but not a lot of depth.

Wearing the captain's 'C' would be Shayne Corson. "All I can do is lead by example, be the hardest worker in practice and the hardest worker in games and, hopefully, we'll

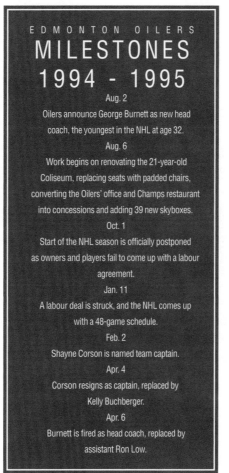

E D M O N T O N   O I L E R S
MILESTONES
1994 - 1995

Aug. 2
Oilers announce George Burnett as new head coach, the youngest in the NHL at age 32.

Aug. 6
Work begins on renovating the 21-year-old Coliseum, replacing seats with padded chairs, converting the Oilers' office and Champs restaurant into concessions and adding 39 new skyboxes.

Oct. 1
Start of the NHL season is officially postponed as owners and players fail to come up with a labour agreement.

Jan. 11
A labour deal is struck, and the NHL comes up with a 48-game schedule.

Feb. 2
Shayne Corson is named team captain.

Apr. 4
Corson resigns as captain, replaced by Kelly Buchberger.

Apr. 6
Burnett is fired as head coach, replaced by assistant Ron Low.

come out of this," said Corson.

But the team started with two wins, then five losses, and a pattern was set for the *Reader's Digest* version of the 1995 season.

"Pretty well every game this year we play 20 or 40 minutes, never a solid 60," said Arnott.

At that point, the club had a 2-42-10 record when trailing after two periods, dating back over two seasons.

With season ticket holders having fallen to 7,000 and fans still miffed by the labour dispute and increased ticket prices, Pocklington made a special television address asking the people for understanding and patience. "In order to keep one of the great hockey events in this city I need you back," he told the cameras. "Glen (Sather) needs you back. The players need you back. If we hope to be competitive (on the ice) we need our fans to come back."

Opposite: In a topsy-turvy strike-shortened season, Shayne Corson is first named captain and then stripped of the captaincy.

1994 - 1995
LOW GIVES
IT A GO

When the Edmonton Oilers were looking for a saviour after the team fell off the rails under head coach George Burnett in 1995, there was one in waiting.

During the stretch drive of the team's inaugural 1979-80 NHL season, the Oilers had traded Ron Chipperfield for goalie Ron Low, who posted an 8-2-1 record to squeeze the Oilers into the playoffs.

It was empathy for Low, who was with the New Jersey Devils during a 13-4 loss to the Oilers in 1983, that caused Wayne Gretzky to label the Devils "a Mickey Mouse operation."

But the Oilers in 1995 were almost an equal challenge. "I asked Ronnie if he was ready for the challenge and he said, 'Yeah, I'll wear an asbestos suit,' " said general manager Glen Sather.

"One thing I'd like to do is lighten up the dressing room," said Low. "Everything has been very tense for the last couple of weeks."

When his NHL head coaching debut ended in a 5-0 loss to the San Jose Sharks, Low joked: "If I'd expected this, I wouldn't have taken the job."

It was the Oilers' eighth straight defeat.

He had a 5-7-1 record that season, but would return the team to the playoffs for the first time in five years in 1997. He re-signed as head coach after the 1998-99 season, with a 139-162-40 regular season record.

During a nine-game losing streak, Burnett made a novel move to turn the season around. He relieved Corson of the captaincy, the first involuntary removal in Oiler history.

"Obviously, the relationship between Corson and myself is a little strained," said Burnett.

"If that's the way he wants to use his captain, I don't want to be that person," said Corson.

"I'm not that type of guy."

The clash between Burnett, a disciplinarian, and Corson, a free spirit, did not come as a shock.

Two days later, with the team 12-20-3, the club made a more traditional stab at salvaging the season.

Burnett was fired and the reins were turned over to assistant coach Ron Low. Kevin Primeau would return to his old

Oiler players get into it with the fans on the road, as security personnel wrestle with an offending fan.

Rugged defenceman Bryan Marchment (above) eyes St. Louis sniper Brett Hull, while even goalie Bill Ranford (above right) mixes it up with the Calgary Flames.

EDMONTON OILERS
1994-1995

assistant's job, after coaching in Germany.

"You have to find a way to motivate them and I'm not sure that it was there," said Sather.

"The way I look at it, it's costing me money every playoff game I miss," said Pocklington.

Six days later, a seven-game team losing streak finally ended, but it wasn't enough to prevent the team from missing the playoffs for the third straight year.

Yet there was at least a sense that the tension that had been suffocating the team had lifted.

"Youth, growing pains, a combination of events," said Sather, summing up the season. "Things that happened that never should have happened. That slump of 10 games killed us. We couldn't get out of it."

The Battle of Alberta was alive and well in 1994-95. Above left: Luke Richardson and Louie DeBrusk take out a Flame in Calgary, while back in Edmonton (right), Richardson tries to douse at least two Flames.

Edmonton Oilers
1994-95
Results & Statistics

COACH	REGULAR SEASON					
	GP	W	L T	PTS	GF	GA
George Burnett (12-20-3) &						
& Ron Low (5-7-1)						
	48	17	27 4	38	136	183

5th Pacific Division, 22nd Overall. Playoffs: Did not qualify.

PLAYER	REGULAR SEASON				
	GP	G	A	PTS	PIM
Doug Weight	48	7	33	40	69
Jason Arnott	42	15	22	37	128
Shayne Corson	48	12	24	36	86
David Oliver	44	16	14	30	20
Todd Marchant	45	13	14	27	32
Kelly Buchberger	48	7	17	24	82
Scott Thornton	47	10	12	22	89
Igor Kravchuk	36	7	11	18	29
Mike Stapleton	46	6	11	17	21
Roman Oksiuta	26	11	2	13	8
Luke Richardson	46	3	10	13	40
Jiri Slegr (VAN)	19	1	5	6	32
Jiri Slegr (EDM)	12	1	5	6	14
Jiri Slegr (TOT)	31	2	10	12	46
Kirk Maltby	47	8	3	11	49
Dean Kennedy	40	2	8	10	25
Fredrik Olausson	33	0	10	10	10
Boris Mironov	29	1	7	8	40
Ken Sutton (BUF)	12	1	2	3	30
Ken Sutton (EDM)	12	3	1	4	12
Ken Sutton (TOT)	24	4	3	7	42
Peter White	9	2	4	6	0
Bryan Marchment	40	1	5	6	184
Len Esau	14	0	6	6	15
Scott Pearson	28	1	4	5	54
Zdeno Ciger	5	2	2	4	0
Iain Fraser (DAL)	4	0	0	0	0
Iain Fraser (EDM)	9	3	0	3	0
Iain Fraser (TOT)	13	3	0	3	0
Louie DeBrusk	34	2	0	2	93
Gord Mark	18	0	2	2	35
Bill Ranford	40	0	2	2	2
Jason Bonsignore	1	1	0	1	0
Kent Nilsson	6	1	0	1	0
Tyler Wright	6	1	0	1	14
Ralph Intranuovo	1	0	1	1	0
Joaquin Gage	2	0	1	1	0
Micah Aivazoff	21	0	1	1	2
Dennis Bonvie	2	0	0	0	0
Ryan Smyth	3	0	0	0	0
Marko Tuomainen	4	0	0	0	0
Dean McAmmond	6	0	0	0	0
Fred Brathwaite	14	0	0	0	0
Ryan McGill (PHI)	12	0	0	0	13
Ryan McGill (EDM)	8	0	0	0	8
Ryan McGill (TOT)	20	0	0	0	21

GOALTENDER	REGULAR SEASON					
	GP	MINS	GA	SO	GAA.	W-L-T
Bill Ranford	40	2203	133	2	3.62	15-20-3
Fred Brathwaite	14	601	40	0	3.99	2-5-1
Joaquin Gage	2	99	7	0	4.24	0-2-0

PLAYOFF HUNTING

The 1995-96 season was pivotal in the resurrection of the Edmonton Oilers franchise. Facing a real threat of relocation due to an eroded fan base, there came hints of financial stability and long-term improvement on the ice.

The National Hockey League came up with the Canadian Assistance Plan, an offer of financial help for small market teams, which would prompt an annual battle among those teams to sell enough season tickets to earn a form of equalization money.

And on the ice, a different rite of spring would begin. During the 1980s, the Oiler season had reached a crescendo of excitement in May, as the team stretched its tentacles towards the Stanley Cup. Then, in recent times, playoff hopes usually faded by the end of February.

But in 1996, the fans would have a new movement to incite them to cheer, a feeling that in short time would consume the city late each March and early each April. Would they or would they not make the playoffs?

The annual race to the wire would whip the city into a frenzy, bringing tattooed faces to sold-out games and rekindling memories of the way we were.

Doug Weight would emerge as a leader, with a warmth that was precisely the tonic needed to melt the hearts of fans who had felt jilted during the 1994 labour dispute.

Another foreshadowing of stability came with the summer acquisition of goalie Curtis Joseph and gargantuan winger Mike Grier from the St. Louis Blues, in exchange for two first-round Oiler draft picks, acquired as compensation after St. Louis signed Oiler free agent Shayne Corson for $6.95 million over five years.

Grier had taken 28 stitches in the palm of his right hand when he skated over it at the USA Olympic festival while trying to pick up a dropped glove.

As the season started, there was hope that the Oilers might have their best line in years in Weight, Zdeno Ciger and Jason Arnott. Ciger was back after spending virtually all the previous season in Slovakia, and Arnott figured to be more focused without the influence of Corson and his penchant for the nightlife.

Gazing ahead at the season, coach Ron Low said: "If you do work every night, you can beat people who are better than you, because you can just grind them down. We're going to have to do that a lot of nights if we're going to be successful, because there are teams out there that have talent, not potential."

The team opened with four straight losses and was 7-15-5 by early December. That's when the NHL announced a plan offering Canadian small market teams a total of $7 million Cdn a year to help them keep some of their top talent. But it wasn't a handout, it had to be earned, by teams selling at least 13,000 season tickets by May 31, plus all rink board and arena advertising and luxury suites. The stickler for Edmonton would be finding season-ticket holders, at the time numbering only 6,487.

The new year started with a 5-0 loss to Tampa Bay that left the Oilers 13-21-6, causing general manager Glen Sather to lock the dressing room door and tell the players that if they didn't want to play for the club to let him know, or else quit

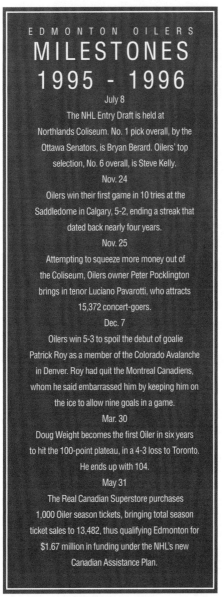

EDMONTON OILERS
MILESTONES
1995 - 1996

July 8
The NHL Entry Draft is held at Northlands Coliseum. No. 1 pick overall, by the Ottawa Senators, is Bryan Berard. Oilers' top selection, No. 6 overall, is Steve Kelly.

Nov. 24
Oilers win their first game in 10 tries at the Saddledome in Calgary, 5-2, ending a streak that dated back nearly four years.

Nov. 25
Attempting to squeeze more money out of the Coliseum, Oilers owner Peter Pocklington brings in tenor Luciano Pavarotti, who attracts 15,372 concert-goers.

Dec. 7
Oilers win 5-3 to spoil the debut of goalie Patrick Roy as a member of the Colorado Avalanche in Denver. Roy had quit the Montreal Canadiens, whom he said embarrassed him by keeping him on the ice to allow nine goals in a game.

Mar. 30
Doug Weight becomes the first Oiler in six years to hit the 100-point plateau, in a 4-3 loss to Toronto. He ends up with 104.

May 31
The Real Canadian Superstore purchases 1,000 Oiler season tickets, bringing total season ticket sales to 13,482, thus qualifying Edmonton for $1.67 million in funding under the NHL's new Canadian Assistance Plan.

embarrassing themselves.

"People had a right to boo us," said Weight. "We should have given their money back at the door."

Sather wondered if the fine mess the Oilers had got themselves into was due to the organization's inability to read the technical evolution in the way the game was being played. The so-called "trap" had arrived, a strategy of X's and O's that had players clog up the neutral zone like cholesterol plugging up arteries.

"In my opinion, we've screwed the game of hockey up over here," said Sather. "Flow doesn't exist. Defencemen can't carry the puck anymore. It's all dump-and-chase."

Weight was chosen to play in the NHL All-Star game, a well-deserved honour according to *Edmonton Journal* columnist Cam Cole: "Weight is the one who has taken the biggest step forward into another class entirely this season."

Public sentiment was that Curtis Joseph, who had been playing with the Las Vegas Thunder of the International League during the season, was being used by Sather as trade bait. But in mid-January, Sather signed Joseph, then traded fellow goaltender Bill Ranford to the Boston Bruins for Mariusz Czerkawski, Sean Brown and a first-round draft pick.

Said Ranford, as he left: "I hope the people realize that I wanted to be in this city and that'll never change. After eight years here, many guys have said it and I don't think I'll be any different. That Oil blood is always in you. That'll never change."

That left Kelly Buchberger as the last remaining member of an Oiler Stanley Cup-winning team.

The love affair with Joseph started with his first game as an Oiler. Fans appeared with painted faces spelling out his name, and serenaded him with "Cu-jo! Cu-jo!" from the upper blues. When the Oilers beat the Buffalo Sabres and Dominik Hasek 5-4 in overtime, Weight pointed at Joseph and the two of them skated toward each other and met in mid-leap at the Oiler blue-line.

Late in the season, NHL president Gary Bettman came to town trumpeting the Canadian Assistance Plan, and said if the Oilers couldn't increase their fan base by May 31, the team would be gone. With the Quebec Nordiques having become the Colorado Avalanche and the Winnipeg Jets headed for Phoenix in 1996-97, the warning was not taken lightly. Bettman's visit was a kick-off for the Friends of the Oilers, a group trying to rally support for the team within the business community.

A blast from the past came when Sather plucked 35-year-old Glenn Anderson off the waiver wire, although the former Oiler preferred to return to the NHL with the Vancouver Canucks. He played 17 games with Edmonton during the season, managing four goals and 10 points.

Meanwhile, Arnott's promise started to dim, and one of the reasons came to light — he had fathered a five-month-old son and confessed: "My contract's due this year and I'd love to stay here. But it's hard — if the fans are ashamed of you, it's

Opposite: Another in a long line of great Oiler netminders, Curtis Joseph, was acquired in the summer of '95.

It was dubbed D-Day — July 8, 1995, the only time the National Hockey League held its entry draft in Edmonton.

More than 15,000 fans joined hundreds of hopeful young players in the stands as the clubs waded through nine rounds of picks.

And there was little surprise when the Ottawa Senators made Bryan Berard of the junior Detroit Whalers the No. 1 draft overall.

The son of a mechanic from Woonsocket, R.I., Berard never did play for the Senators, spending four seasons with the New York Islanders and Toronto Maple Leafs from 1996 through 2000, retiring after a freak eye injury, but making a comeback a few years later.

The second overall pick in 1995 was Wade Redden by the Islanders, No. 3 was Aki-Petteri Berg of Finland by the Los Angeles Kings and No. 4 was Chad Kilger by the Anaheim Mighty Ducks.

The host Oilers chose Steve Kelly of the Prince Albert Raiders in the first round, sixth overall, and Georges Laraque of the St. Jean Lynx in the second round, 31st overall.

"He almost broke the power-measuring machine for grip," said Oilers general manager Glen Sather, of Laraque. "He's very strong, focused, kind of quiet-spoken. His attitude reminds me of Dave Semenko a little bit."

Kelly would score one goal as an Oiler, before moving on for cameo appearances with Tampa Bay, New Jersey and Los Angeles. Laraque became a fan favourite with the Oilers for his toughness, with 35 goals, 82 points, and 654 penalty minutes in his first three seasons — and counting.

Jarome Iginla of St. Albert, drafted No. 11 overall in the first round by the Dallas Stars, was later traded to the Calgary Flames and won the 2001-02 Art Ross Trophy with 96 points and Maurice Richard Trophy with 52 goals.

pretty hard to play in a city like that."

Conversely, fans couldn't have been happier with Joseph, who announced he was buying out of his own pocket "Cloud Nine," a luxury box for sick kids to watch games from. The program would be administered by the Children's Health Foundation of Northern Alberta.

With March came the first "Playoff Race At A Glance," with newspaper stories laying out all the permutations and combinations facing teams in the running.

And Anderson waded in with his words on what the Oilers needed to return to post-season play: "It's the chemistry that's lacking. You can't rely on Jason or Doug every night to come to the forefront.

"We need the third- and fourth-liners stepping up to the plate and taking control of some of the games."

The next day, Anderson was picked up on waivers by the St. Louis Blues.

In March, the Oilers started a 17-game stretch run by going 8-3-1 to excite the locals.

"It's nice to be racing for the playoffs instead of tee times,"

Mike Grier (top) joined the team in 1995-96, while Glenn Anderson (above) made a cameo re-appearance with the Oilers late in the season.

1995-1996

said Weight, who became the first Oiler since Mark Messier in 1989-90 — and only the seventh overall — to score 100 points in a season. Unfortunately, with six games left in the regular season, the wheels fell off. Joseph was felled with a second-degree sprain of his right knee and Edmonton lost its last five games of the season, missing the playoffs. A seasonal home record less than .500 did them in.

The playoff race gave way to a race to sell 13,000 season tickets, and qualify for $1.67 million US of the $5 million available through the Canadian Assistance Plan.

On May 31, the final day, The Real Canadian Superstore purchased 1,000 season tickets to reach 13,482, more than doubling the previous year's number.

"This is a huge day in this franchise," said Oilers owner Peter Pocklington. "We could have been announcing our arrival in St. Paul, Minn., or, God forbid, Nashville or some other American city. I think it's a bigger day for the city — the fact that it had the strength and commitment to step up and do something that I don't think has been done in any other city that I know of."

The arrival and stellar play of Curtis Joseph made Bill Ranford expendable (Ranford's mask shown at bottom right). Ranford was traded to Boston in January. Fred Brathwaite (top right) remained a capable backup netminder.

Edmonton Oilers 1995-96 Results & Statistics

REGULAR SEASON

COACH	GP	W	L	T	PTS	GF	G
Ron Low	82	30	44	8	68	240	30

5th Pacific Division, 21st Overall. Playoffs: Did not qualify.

REGULAR SEASON

PLAYER	GP	G	A	PTS	PIM
Doug Weight	82	25	79	104	9
Zdeno Ciger	78	31	39	70	4
Jason Arnott	64	28	31	59	8
Mariusz Czerkawski (BOS)	32	5	6	11	10
Mariusz Czerkawski (EDM)	37	12	17	29	8
Mariusz Czerkawski (TOT)	70	17	23	40	1
David Oliver	80	20	19	39	34
Todd Marchant	81	19	19	38	66
Miroslav Satan	62	18	17	35	22
Boris Mironov	78	8	24	32	10
Jeff Norton (STL)	36	4	7	11	2
Jeff Norton (EDM)	30	4	16	20	16
Jeff Norton (TOT)	66	8	23	31	4
Dean McAmmond	53	15	15	30	22
Kelly Buchberger	82	11	14	25	18
Scott Thornton	77	9	9	18	149
Bryan Marchment	78	3	15	18	20
Jiri Slegr	57	4	13	17	7
David Roberts (STL)	28	1	6	7	1
David Roberts (EDM)	6	2	4	6	
David Roberts (TOT)	34	3	10	13	1
Ryan Smyth	48	2	9	11	2
Luke Richardson	82	2	9	11	108
Glenn Anderson	17	4	6	10	2
Igor Kravchuk	26	4	4	8	1
Peter White	26	5	3	8	
Kent Manderville	37	3	5	8	3
Kirk Maltby	49	2	6	8	6
Donald Dufresne (STL)	3	0	0	0	
Donald Dufresne (EDM)	42	1	6	7	16
Donald Dufresne (TOT)	45	1	6	7	20
Brett Hauer	29	4	2	6	3
Fredrik Olausson	20	0	6	6	1
Louie DeBrusk	38	1	3	4	9
Ralph Intranuovo	13	1	2	3	
Greg de Vries	13	1	1	2	1
Jason Bonsignore	20	0	2	2	
Tyler Wright	23	1	0	1	3
Curtis Joseph	34	0	1	1	
Bill Ranford	37	0	1	1	2
Nick Stajduhar	2	0	0	0	
Bryan Muir	5	0	0	0	
Fred Brathwaite	7	0	0	0	
Dennis Bonvie	8	0	0	0	4
Joaquin Gage	16	0	0	0	

REGULAR SEASON

GOALTENDER	GP	MINS	GA	SO	GAA.	
Fred Brathwaite	7	293	12	0	2.46	
Curtis Joseph	34	1936	111	0	3.44	15
Joaquin Gage	16	717	45	0	3.77	
Bill Ranford	37	2015	128	1	3.81	13

EDMONTON OILERS
1996-1997
BACK WHERE THEY BELONG

The fortunes of the Edmonton Oilers diverged during the 1996-97 season. On the ice, the team made the National Hockey League playoffs for the first time in five years. In the boardroom, owner Peter Pocklington hung a For Sale sign on the franchise.

Before the season, the team unveiled new uniforms, which due to the team's Stanley Cup-winning history remained faithful to the original design, except orange gave way to copper and red trim. The blue was deeper than before, but not black; psychologists suggested teams with black or near-black uniforms get penalized more.

The Oilers traded centre Scott Thornton, who came over in the Grant Fuhr deal with Toronto, to the Montreal Canadiens for Russian Andrei Kovalenko. It was hoped he would pick up some of the scoring slack from the departed Zdeno Ciger, who headed back to Europe.

Former Oiler Dave Semenko was brought in to join Kevin Primeau and Bob McCammon as Ron Low's assistant coaches.

Part of the selling job that doubled the Oilers' season ticket base in spring had been that the new-found money would be used to sign stars Doug Weight and Jason Arnott. In September, Arnott was signed for $3.6 million US over two years. Weight joined on for $2 million US a year. They represented 29 per cent of the team's $13-million US payroll.

Kevin Lowe rejoined the team Sept. 19, 1996, at age 37, to nurture youngsters like Arnott and Jason Bonsignore. Lowe was also reported to have a handshake deal that would see him join the Oilers coaching staff or front office after his playing days.

For the first time, the NHL issued a crackdown on illegal goaltending equipment, as pads had grown wider, shoulder pads ballooned bigger, and catching gloves had become the size of lobster traps. Conversely, the NHL increased the maximum length of skaters' sticks from 60 to 63 inches, in deference to the growing boys now making it in the pros.

And speaking of equipment, Doug Risebrough, who as a Calgary Flame had used his skates to shred then-Oiler Marty McSorley's jersey in the Saddledome penalty box, signed on as Edmonton's new vice-president of hockey operations.

"It was a brain cramp," said Risebrough, of the sweater incident.

The Oilers got off to their best start in years, winning their first three games and engaging in one of their steadiest seasons in recent memory. They fell four games below .500 on Dec. 27, were five games above .500 on Feb. 12 and wound up 36-37-9.

In early December, Weight and Arnott mused aloud about not having enough ice time. But by the All-Star break, the most pleasant surprise on the team was Ryan Smyth. After a rookie season in which he had two goals and was minus-10 in 48 games, he was on his way to leading the team in goals with 39 and trail only Weight in points with 61. All at the tender age of 21.

In February, Pocklington called a news conference to announce he would be selling 45 per cent of all his sports and entertainment interests, including the Oilers, in a $50-million initial public offering. The money raised would go to pay down

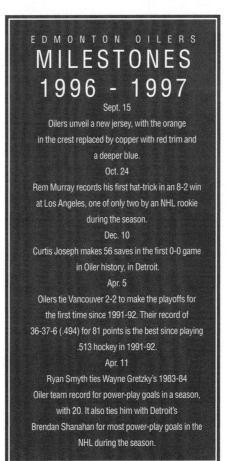

EDMONTON OILERS
MILESTONES
1996 - 1997

Sept. 15
Oilers unveil a new jersey, with the orange in the crest replaced by copper with red trim and a deeper blue.

Oct. 24
Rem Murray records his first hat-trick in an 8-2 win at Los Angeles, one of only two by an NHL rookie during the season.

Dec. 10
Curtis Joseph makes 56 saves in the first 0-0 game in Oiler history, in Detroit.

Apr. 5
Oilers tie Vancouver 2-2 to make the playoffs for the first time since 1991-92. Their record of 36-37-6 (.494) for 81 points is the best since playing .513 hockey in 1991-92.

Apr. 11
Ryan Smyth ties Wayne Gretzky's 1983-84 Oiler team record for power-play goals in a season, with 20. It also ties him with Detroit's Brendan Shanahan for most power-play goals in the NHL during the season.

loans to the Alberta Treasury Branches.

Back on the ice, Edmonton had won only one of their last nine games and dropped to .500 when March arrived.

"I really think our goal all year was just to make the playoffs," said Lowe. "Then we got onto a little bit of a roll and we thought: 'OK, now we've got that taken care of, let's think top half of the draw.'"

The February tailspin slapped them out of their daydream, but injuries would threaten their run at the playoffs. With 12 games left to play, Andrei Kovalenko, Boris Mironov and Todd Marchant were sidelined by injuries. Weight was fighting a bad ankle and sore shoulder. And Arnott had lost his scoring touch.

But the team went 5-2-2 in a nine-game stretch, and for the first time in five years, were back in the playoffs. It wasn't mere coincidence that the team had reduced its goals against from 304 the previous season to 247, with Joseph now firmly ensconced as the No. 1 netminder.

The stretch run produced sellouts of 17,099 fans in each of the last six home games, for an average of 15,993 on the year, compared to 12,335 the previous season.

"If we hadn't made the playoffs, I'm not sure this team would be here next year," said general manager Glen Sather.

The Oilers actually had a shot at fourth place in the Western Conference going into the final weekend of the regular season, but wound up seventh, earning them a playoff date against the second-place Dallas Stars, coached by local Edmonton product Ken Hitchcock. Thirteen Oilers had never played an NHL playoff game before.

Said Hitchcock, whose team hadn't lost to the Oilers in their last seven meetings: "Everybody has said this: the Oilers are the playoff wild card. They're the team with the highest upside going in."

Oiler coach Ron Low said the Oilers had lost those games to Dallas because of neutral-zone turnovers, with an inability to free-wheel like they like to do. And in the end, the series would hinge on three Oilers — Joseph, Kovalenko and Arnott.

"I think the room will have more electricity every time we come to the rink, knowing that we're in the playoffs," said Arnott, awaiting his first NHL post-season game. "It's going to be fantastic."

By contrast, Lowe was a veteran of 212 NHL playoff games. During his rookie days rooming with Wayne Gretzky, Lowe had captured how consuming playoffs become: "Dirty dishes keep piling up in the sink."

The first round was one for the ages. The Oilers scored three times in the last four minutes and then won Game 3 on captain Kelly Buchberger's goal at 9:15 of overtime, 4-3. Then it was Ryan Smyth scoring 22 seconds into the second overtime of Game 5, 1-0 Oilers. And finally Todd Marchant, at 12:26 of overtime in Game 7, sped past fallen Dallas defenceman Grant Ledyard and rifled the puck past the Stars' Andy Moog, making it 4-3 Oilers for the game and series.

The true series hero was Joseph, with two shutouts and a save on Joe Nieuwendyk 12 minutes into overtime of the final game that may be the most famous single save in Oiler history.

Down and out and beaten, Joseph never gave up, rolling and throwing the back

Opposite: Todd Marchant fires home the Game 7 overtime goal
that lifted the Oilers into the second round of the playoffs in the spring of 1997.

1996 - 1997
LOWE-DOWN
ON MR. OILER

On Jan. 20, 1997, Kevin Lowe became the first Edmonton Oiler to play 1,000 games for the NHL franchise during a game in his recent stomping grounds in New York.

"It's probably fitting that it's Kevin," said assistant coach Dave Semenko, who played 454 Oiler games with Lowe. "He was the (Oilers') first draft pick in the NHL; scored the first goal."

Lowe reflected on how he had needed the break from the public spotlight in Edmonton for his time on Broadway. "After 13 years in Edmonton, it kept growing and growing to the point where you didn't even go to the 7-Eleven without thinking, 'Should I comb my hair?' "

As for the 1,000 games, Lowe said: "Well I know I'm never going to score 1,000 points. So I need something to hang my hat on."

He talked about the evolution of the game during his time on the ice. "There is a different mentality and I'm glad I bridged that gap. I came in the late '70s and early '80s when the game on the ice had changed, led by the Oilers. The mentality was different then, not better, not worse, just different. I think that has to do with the international flavour of the game now. It used to be just a bunch of guys from Saskatchewan and handful of American guys."

Lowe wound up playing 1,037 regular season games with the Oilers, scoring 383 points. He was only the 27th NHL player to reach 1,000 games with the same team.

of an arm in front of a shot that was blasting into a seemingly open net.

"Best feeling I've ever had," said Joseph. "We've come so far, this team, from when I got here last season."

The dream came to an end in Round 2, as the defending Stanley Cup champion Colorado Avalanche could not be stopped. Colorado took the first two games, the Oilers won the third 4-3, then Colorado closed it out 3-2 on Claude Lemieux's overtime winner and 4-3 in the fifth and final game.

"We didn't lose this from lack of effort," said Joseph. "We can all look in the mirror and say we played our hearts out."

The Oilers returned home at 1:30 a.m., and were greeted by 400 fans at the airport. Barber Ben Gorodnitsky offered free hot towel and straight razor shaves to the players, who for the first

Defenceman Boris Mironov goes flying after an encounter with Dallas defenceman Derian Hatcher.

Curtis Joseph stops the Stars' Guy Carbonneau as Rem Murray tries to finish the check.

time in five years had playoff beards to shed. People wanted a public rally for the team.

Said Oilers director of public relations Bill Tuele: "Edmontonians have fallen in love again with this team."

But when Pocklington's plan for a public offering of his sports teams fell through, he announced on June 5, 1997, that the Oilers were for sale, for $85 million US.

"These money problems have taken a lot of the fun out of the business for me," said Pocklington. "Pro hockey is now a place for big corporations with very deep pockets or a group of very wealthy investors."

And with those words, another soap opera would start. Who would buy the Oilers? It was a matter that would not be solved quickly, without fear and some humour.

Kelly Buchberger crashes Avalanche goalie Patrick Roy's net.

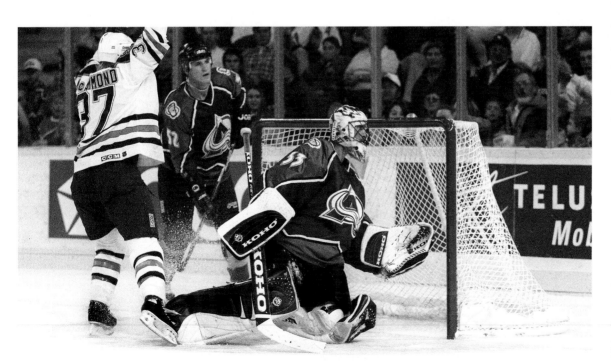

Dean McAmmond celebrates a goal on Roy as Colorado defenceman Adam Foote looks on.

Edmonton Oilers 1996-97 Results & Statistics

REGULAR SEASON

COACH	GP	W	L	T	PTS	GF	G
Ron Low	82	36	37	9	81	252	24

3rd Pacific Division, 13th Overall. Playoffs: Wor
Western Conference Quarter-Final
4-3 vs Dallas, Lost Western Conference Semifir
vs Colorado.

REGULAR SEASON

PLAYER	GP	G	A	PTS	PIM
Doug Weight	80	21	61	82	8
Ryan Smyth	82	39	22	61	7
Andrei Kovalenko	74	32	27	59	8
Jason Arnott	67	19	38	57	9
Mariusz Czerkawski	76	26	21	47	1
Kelly Buchberger	81	8	30	38	15
Todd Marchant	79	14	19	33	4
Mike Grier	79	15	17	32	4
Boris Mironov	55	6	26	32	8
Rem Murray	82	11	20	31	1
Dean McAmmond	57	12	17	29	2
Miroslav Satan	64	17	11	28	2
Mats Lindgren	69	11	14	25	1
Dan McGillis	73	6	16	22	5
Drew Bannister (TB)	64	4	13	17	4
Drew Bannister (EDM)	1	0	1	1	0
Drew Bannister (TOT)	65	4	14	18	4
Bryan Marchment	71	3	13	16	13
Petr Klima (LA)	8	0	4	4	
Petr Klima (PIT)	9	1	3	4	
Petr Klima (EDM)	16	1	5	6	
Petr Klima (TOT)	33	2	12	14	1
Kevin Lowe	64	1	13	14	5
Jeff Norton	62	2	11	13	4
Luke Richardson	82	1	11	12	9
Barrie Moore (BUF)	31	2	6	8	1
Barrie Moore (EDM)	4	0	0	0	
Barrie Moore (TOT)	35	2	6	8	1
Michel Petit	18	2	4	6	2
Greg de Vries	37	0	4	4	5
David Oliver	17	1	2	3	
Louie DeBrusk	32	2	0	2	9
Ralph Intranuovo (TOR)	3	0	1	1	
Ralph Intranuovo (EDM)	5	1	0	1	
Ralph Intranuovo (TOT)	8	1	1	2	
Curtis Joseph	72	0	2	2	2
Steve Kelly	8	1	0	1	
Donald Dufresne	22	0	1	1	1
Craig Millar	1	0	0	0	
Sean Brown	5	0	0	0	
Jesse Belanger	6	0	0	0	
Joe Hulbig	6	0	0	0	
Bob Essensa	19	0	0	0	
Bryan Muir	-	-	-	-	

REGULAR SEASON

GOALTENDER	GP	MINS	GA	SO	GAA.	W
Bob Essensa	19	869	41	1	2.83	4
Curtis Joseph	72	4100	200	6	2.93	32

REASON FOR OPTIMISM

The Edmonton Oilers took their fans on a rousing roller-coaster ride in 1997-98, reigniting their passions with another playoff run, yet worrying them sick that the franchise's impending sale would result in the team moving away.

The good news was that the Oilers would once again advance to the second round of the playoffs.

Even better news was that by season's end, the team seemed assured of staying in Edmonton under new local ownership.

The Oilers had been officially put up for sale by owner Peter Pocklington in June of 1997, prompting a parade of buyers to come forward.

Among those interested: a group of local businessmen; Edmonton developer Robert Proznik; Les Alexander of Houston; rivals Robert McNair and Chuck Watson, also of Houston; Michael Largue of New York; and, for a moment, Bernie Ebbers.

"I talked to Peter Pocklington about buying the Edmonton Oilers a couple of weeks ago," said Ebbers, a former University of Alberta basketball player, whose company WorldCom had just paid $37 billion US for MCI, the second-largest long-distance company in the United States.

As it turned out, WorldCom collapsed in 2002 with $41 billion US in debt, the largest corporate failure in U.S. history.

As the off-ice drama swirled in the background, the hockey team entered the season with a tremendous amount of optimism after the previous spring's playoff run.

The inevitable summer shuffle of personnel had seen Ted Green return and Kevin Primeau leave as assistant coach to Ron Low. The Oilers lost defenceman Luke Richardson to the Philadelphia Flyers and Louie DeBrusk to the Tampa Bay Lightning, both through free agency, and 26-goal scorer Mariusz Czerkawski was dealt to the New York Islanders for Dan Lacouture. Oilers general manager Glen Sather also rescued Drake Berehowsky and former club stickboy Ray Whitney from the minors as free agents.

Even with all the changes, the club's starting lineup was solid, featuring Ryan Smyth, Doug Weight and Todd Marchant up front, Bryan Marchment and Greg de Vries on defence and Curtis Joseph in goal.

Captain Kelly Buchberger stressed the importance of a strong start: "We have to carry the confidence we gained last year in the playoffs and which seems to have continued right through pre-season."

Said veteran defenceman Kevin Lowe: "The question now is: how much better can we get? What did we learn as a team last season?

"That, if we can take it another step, creates some pretty exciting possibilities."

The Oilers' home-opener attracted a sell-out crowd of 17,099 fans wearing painted faces and baggy hockey jerseys. As fan Shane Reykdal said: "The way last season ended, it's easy to be pumped. This place is very vibrant again."

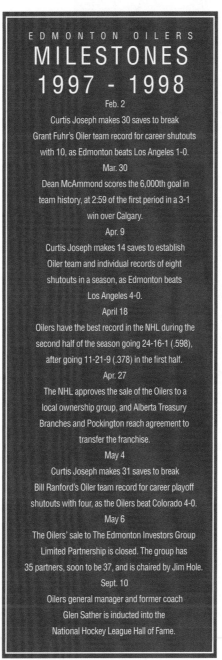

EDMONTON OILERS
MILESTONES
1997 - 1998

Feb. 2
Curtis Joseph makes 30 saves to break Grant Fuhr's Oiler team record for career shutouts with 10, as Edmonton beats Los Angeles 1-0.

Mar. 30
Dean McAmmond scores the 6,000th goal in team history, at 2:59 of the first period in a 3-1 win over Calgary.

Apr. 9
Curtis Joseph makes 14 saves to establish Oiler team and individual records of eight shutouts in a season, as Edmonton beats Los Angeles 4-0.

April 18
Oilers have the best record in the NHL during the second half of the season going 24-16-1 (.598), after going 11-21-9 (.378) in the first half.

Apr. 27
The NHL approves the sale of the Oilers to a local ownership group, and Alberta Treasury Branches and Pocklington reach agreement to transfer the franchise.

May 4
Curtis Joseph makes 31 saves to break Bill Ranford's Oiler team record for career playoff shutouts with four, as the Oilers beat Colorado 4-0.

May 6
The Oilers' sale to The Edmonton Investors Group Limited Partnership is closed. The group has 35 partners, soon to be 37, and is chaired by Jim Hole.

Sept. 10
Oilers general manager and former coach Glen Sather is inducted into the National Hockey League Hall of Fame.

Despite the fans' and the players' enthusiasm, the team got off to a shaky 5-12-5 start.

By the end of December, with the team still struggling, Sather traded Marchment, Steve Kelly and Jason Bonsignore to the Tampa Bay Lightning for Roman Hamrlik and Paul Comrie.

"It's a gamble, but to me it's a great gamble," said Sather, of losing Marchment.

Then came the big shakeup. With the Oilers sporting a 11-22-9 record at midseason, Jason Arnott and Bryan Muir were sent to the New Jersey Devils for Bill Guerin and Valeri Zelepukin.

Make it three Oiler first-rounders gone in four days — Arnott (1993), Bonsignore (1994) and Kelly (1995).

"He's always been the one who had the pressure on him to perform every night, and that's tough on a guy when you're that big and that young, and especially when you're also a sensitive guy," said Weight, of Arnott. "I think it did get the best of him at the end."

Coach Low now knew the tools he had to work with: "What we've got right now has got to be good enough. It if isn't, I'm not.

"And that's going to be the problem."

The shakeup worked, as the team added Tony Hrkac on waivers from St. Louis for good measure, and swapped defenceman Dan McGillis to Philadelphia for Finnish blue-liner Janne Niinimaa.

The Oilers went 19-15-1 the rest of the season, clinching a playoff spot just before its second-last game of the regular season.

The playoffs would be a carbon copy of the 1997 eliminations, with only the opponents reversed. Instead of beating Dallas in seven games before losing to Colorado in five, this time the Oilers would beat Colorado in seven before losing to Dallas in five.

The Oilers fell behind 3-1 in the first series but came back to take the seventh game 4-0, dominating a dispirited Avalanche team that only two years before had won a Stanley Cup.

"We deserved every bit of this," said Weight. "We dominated certain parts of this series. We didn't need Cujo to be this unbelievable god in seven straight games as he was last year in the Dallas series."

In the next round, Dallas won the opener 3-1, Edmonton responded with a 2-0 win and then Dallas took the third game 1-0 on Benoit Hogue's goal at 13:07 of overtime. It was that goal that seemed to break the Oilers' backs.

"We seemed to lose a lot of energy after that game," said Sather. "But this (series) was played with cautious optimism and smart hockey. We lost a lot of really close hockey games.

"The team certainly never quit."

While the hockey team took the fans on a wild playoff ride, the ownership question also heated up. In mid-December, Alberta Treasury Branches had basically taken control of the Oilers, as part payment of

EDMONTON OILERS
1997-1998

1997 - 1998
TALE OF THE SALE

The year-long sale of the Oilers unfolded sometimes as a tragedy, other times like a situation comedy and, in the end, a drama.

The tragedy was Les Alexander, a Texan who appeared destined to purchase the team, making its tenure in Edmonton insecure at best. Alexander, a failed bidder for an NHL expansion franchise, said Oct. 23 he had a handshake deal to buy the Edmonton Oilers from Peter Pocklington for $82.5 million US, and move them in three years.

When Pocklington showed up at a Nov. 4 news conference to announce the deal, Alexander didn't. In January, he amended his offer, with no provision for keeping the team in Edmonton past 1998 and no equity in the team for Pocklington.

The comedy was Michael Largue, 36, a New York investor who said he wanted to be part of the local group trying to buy the Oilers. Largue claimed he played for Northeastern University on a hockey scholarship, got a degree in political science, played for the Bern Bears in the Swiss Elite League and was a partner of Swiss banker Lester Mittendorf.

The *Edmonton Journal* then discovered Largue had neither played at Northeastern University nor received a degree there. He also hadn't played with Bern and there was no record that Mittendorf even existed. It turned out Largue was a con artist who once pleaded guilty to fraud on Long Island.

The drama in the Oilers' sale was the month-long spring countdown, as local investors tried to prod, cajole or otherwise entice friends and relatives to come up with $60 million Cdn — half the purchase price — by the April 30 deadline.

On April 29, the goal was reached, and on May 6, the sale to the Edmonton Investors Group Limited Partnership closed.

Rem Murray mixes it up with two Dallas Stars in the playoffs.

Defenceman Roman Hamrlik hammers this Star into the boards.

Mats Lindgren bats at the puck as Stars goalie Eddie Belfour defends the Dallas net.

Curtis Joseph bobbles this shot, but quickly covers up.

Pocklington's debts. ATB said it would work with the NHL to find a buyer, while Pocklington stayed on as co-director.

After a number of potential buyers dropped out one by one, the sole local group left pleaded for more investors to keep the team in Edmonton, needing to raise one-half of the $102 million Cdn. According to NHL rules, the other half could come from a lender.

The *Edmonton Journal* joined the ownership group, which on March 13 delivered an offer and deposit to purchase the team.

During the playoffs, the NHL approved the Oilers' sale to the local ownership group, the ATB and Pocklington reached an agreement to transfer the lease, and in May the deal was closed.

EDMONTON OILERS
1997-1998

Tony Hrkac (20) of the Oilers remains up, the Dallas Star is down, but it's the Star who gets the penalty.

Oilers' Todd Marchant and Boris Mironov congratulate a teammate after a goal.

Dallas gets one by Curtis Joseph.

Joseph was brilliant against Colorado in Round 1, but his heroics weren't enough against Dallas in Round 2.

The team was now owned by the Edmonton Investors Group Limited Partnership, chaired by Jim Hole, with 35 partners who would eventually become 38.

Amidst the ownership uncertainty and the team's spunky play-off performance, it was announced that general manager Sather would be inducted into the National Hockey League Hall of Fame as a builder. After just 80 goals in 658 NHL games as a player, he rolled off 464 wins and four Stanley Cups as a coach, adding a fifth Cup as general manager exclusively.

"I don't want to leave this organization," said Sather. "How many teams have the depth we have, the upside we have? It's incredible."

Edmonton Oilers
1997-98
Results & Statistics

REGULAR SEASON

COACH	GP	W	L	T	PTS	GF	G
Ron Low	82	35	37	10	80	215	22

3rd Pacific Division, 15th Overall. Playoffs: Won Western Conference Quarter-Final 4-3 vs Colorado, Lost Western Conference Sem 4-1 vs Dallas.

REGULAR SEASON

PLAYER	GP	G	A	PTS	PIM
Doug Weight	79	26	44	70	69
Dean McAmmond	77	19	31	50	4
Boris Mironov	81	16	30	46	100
Janne Niinimaa (PHI)	66	3	31	34	56
Janne Niinimaa (EDM)	11	1	8	9	
Janne Niinimaa (TOT)	77	4	39	43	6
Roman Hamrlik (TB)	37	3	12	15	22
Roman Hamrlik (EDM)	41	6	20	26	4
Roman Hamrlik (TOT)	78	9	32	41	7
Bill Guerin (NJ)	19	5	5	10	1
Bill Guerin (EDM)	40	13	16	29	80
Bill Guerin (TOT)	59	18	21	39	9
Todd Marchant	76	14	21	35	7
Ryan Smyth	65	20	13	33	4
Tony Hrkac (DAL)	13	5	3	8	0
Tony Hrkac (EDM)	36	8	11	19	10
Tony Hrkac (TOT)	49	13	14	27	10
Mats Lindgren	82	13	13	26	4
Dan McGillis	67	10	15	25	7
Scott Fraser	29	12	11	23	
Andrei Kovalenko	59	6	17	23	2
Kelly Buchberger	82	6	17	23	12
Valeri Zelepukin (NJ)	35	2	8	10	3
Valeri Zelepukin (EDM)	33	2	10	12	5
Valeri Zelepukin (TOT)	68	4	18	22	8
Rem Murray	61	9	9	18	3
Jason Arnott	35	5	13	18	7
Mike Grier	66	9	6	15	7
Greg de Vries	65	7	4	11	80
Bobby Dollas (ANA)	22	0	1	1	2
Bobby Dollas (EDM)	30	2	5	7	2
Bobby Dollas (TOT)	52	2	6	8	4
Drake Berehowsky	67	1	6	7	16
Boyd Devereaux	38	1	4	5	
Craig Millar	11	4	0	4	8
Joe Hulbig	17	2	2	4	
Ray Whitney	9	1	3	4	0
Bryan Marchment	27	0	4	4	5
Mike Watt	14	1	2	3	
Frank Musil	17	1	2	3	
Steve Kelly	19	0	2	2	8
Drew Bannister	34	0	2	2	4
Curtis Joseph	71	0	2	2	
Sean Brown	18	0	1	1	4
Bill Huard	30	0	1	1	7
Scott Ferguson	1	0	0	0	
Ladislav Benysek	2	0	0	0	0
Jason Bowen	4	0	0	0	1
Dennis Bonvie	4	0	0	0	2
Bryan Muir	7	0	0	0	1
Kevin Lowe	7	0	0	0	2
Terran Sandwith	8	0	0	0	6
Georges Laraque	11	0	0	0	59
Bob Essensa	16	0	0	0	0
Doug Friedman	16	0	0	0	2

REGULAR SEASON

GOALTENDER	GP	MINS	GA	SO	GAA.	W
Bob Essensa	16	825	45	0	2.55	6
Curtis Joseph	71	4132	181	8	2.63	29

NOT PRETTY, BUT GRITTY

A new era dawned on the Edmonton Oilers in the 1998-99 season, with a new local ownership group in place and no end of questions about the future.

But first, former owner Peter Pocklington took time out to say goodbye, saying he would sell off his remaining assets and move to "greener pastures."

"I don't have any bad words for the province or the city of Edmonton," said Pocklington. "It's a wonderful place. I'd do it all over again. It's just I need a change."

A sign of where the Oilers' franchise was headed came when defenceman Kevin Lowe retired and was appointed an assistant coach, causing Bob McCammon to be shuffled into a scouting position.

Lowe saw his role as "not trying to talk too much about the old years, but just the right amount to give the guys that type of enthusiasm."

A major blow came when the Oilers couldn't keep fan-favourite Curtis Joseph, as the free-agent goalie was signed by the Toronto Maple Leafs for $24 million over four years.

The Oilers did sign Pat Falloon, the second overall pick in the 1991 entry draft, who would be counted on for some offence, especially with Doug Weight holding out as training camp started. Edmonton also reacquired Marty McSorley, who had been part of the club's Cup-winning era, but shipped to L.A. in the 1988 Wayne Gretzky trade.

The regular season opened with two major questions — how would goalies Bob Essensa, Mikhail Shtalenkov and Steve Passmore pick up the slack for the departed Joseph, and how long would the scoring power of holdouts Weight and Ryan Smyth go missing?

Smyth came to terms after the regular season opener. And Weight followed suit on Oct. 19, four games into the season. "It was very difficult to sit out and watch the games on TV," said Weight, whose two-year deal was worth $7.75 million. Alas, two weeks later he hurt his right knee and needed surgery to repair a torn medial collateral ligament.

The Oilers managed to tread water without Weight, posting a 13-9-1 record by the beginning of December. Then the wheels fell off. A seven-game winless streak during early December laid the foundation for a 15-18-10 record during the next four months.

The Weight loss and inconsistent netminding were major factors. Captain Kelly Buchberger was sidelined for two months with a broken forearm, leaving Bill Guerin as interim captain, before Weight returned in mid-January and assumed the interim captaincy.

But one of the emerging highlights of the season was the play of rookie defenceman Tom Poti, the club's fourth choice in the 1996 entry draft.

At the end of January, the Oilers acquired Alexander Selivanov in a three-way deal that sent Andrei Kovalenko to the Philadelphia Flyers and Alexandre Daigle to the Tampa Bay Lightning. Then goalie Shtalenkov was traded to the Phoenix Coyotes.

"There's got to be an awful big change in the psyche of this hockey club about winning close hockey games," said Low, who on March 18 briefly considered

walking into Sather's office and resigning.

Then, the phoenix stirred.

Sather brought in motivational guru Don Smith to rekindle the fire in Weight's belly.

When the New York Islanders looked at trading their goalie Tommy Salo to the Oilers for Mats Lindgren, Low moved Lindgren onto a line with Weight and Guerin to showcase him at a game with Islanders pro scout Ken Morrow in attendance. Five days later, on March 20, Lindgren and an eighth-round draft pick went to the Islanders for Salo.

And Sather also bartered Boris Mironov and Dean McAmmond to the Chicago Blackhawks for Christian Laflamme, Dan Cleary, Chad Kilger and Ethan Moreau.

"It was obvious that we needed a goaltender," said Sather, who also acquired Jason Smith from the Toronto Maple Leafs for second- and fourth-round drafts.

"It makes a big difference when you have a GM and coaches who believe in you when you play," said Salo, who had led Sweden to the 1994 Olympic gold medal and 1998 World Championship.

He posted an 8-2-2 record and the Oilers went undefeated in their final six games of the season, clinching a playoff spot with two games remaining. It rekindled memories of the Oilers' very first season in the NHL, when they traded for then-goalie Ron Low at the end of the season and he went 8-2-1 to squeak Edmonton into the final playoff spot.

"Thank God that everybody has fit together as well as they have," said Low. "That says something about the people who we brought in, but it also says a lot about the people already here."

In the post-season, the Oilers were pitted against the Dallas Stars, who seemed to have vowed to haunt the Oilers every playoff season ever since the Oilers' crushing seventh-game overtime win in the 1997 Western Conference quarter-final.

This time, each game would be decided by one goal, but the winner would not waiver — 2-1, 3-2, 3-2 and finally 3-2 for Dallas, with Joe Nieuwendyk scoring at 17:34 of the third overtime, the longest game in the history of each franchise.

"We may not be pretty, and we may not be a first-place team, but everybody knows — especially the Dallas Stars — that we show up to play," said Bill Guerin. "Especially in the playoffs."

But showing up to play is one thing. Actually winning in the playoffs is another. Coach Low was not offered a raise in salary — a definite vote of non-confidence — and so he decided to resign on June 6. Low had spent 13 years in the organization spanning two decades, including four years as head coach — the second-longest span behind the bench in franchise history.

"When I walked out of Glen's place, I felt pretty brutal, actually," said Low. "I'll have an Oiler logo stamped on my butt for a long time."

His replacement, though, had been part of the Oilers' grand scheme of things for some time.

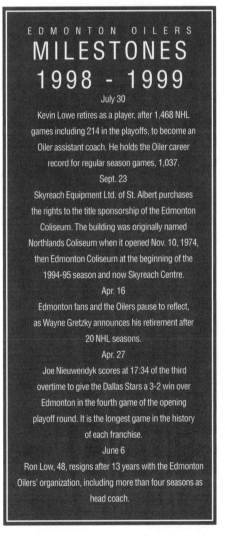

EDMONTON OILERS
MILESTONES
1998 - 1999

July 30
Kevin Lowe retires as a player, after 1,468 NHL games including 214 in the playoffs, to become an Oiler assistant coach. He holds the Oiler career record for regular season games, 1,037.

Sept. 23
Skyreach Equipment Ltd. of St. Albert purchases the rights to the title sponsorship of the Edmonton Coliseum. The building was originally named Northlands Coliseum when it opened Nov. 10, 1974, then Edmonton Coliseum at the beginning of the 1994-95 season and now Skyreach Centre.

Apr. 16
Edmonton fans and the Oilers pause to reflect, as Wayne Gretzky announces his retirement after 20 NHL seasons.

Apr. 27
Joe Nieuwendyk scores at 17:34 of the third overtime to give the Dallas Stars a 3-2 win over Edmonton in the fourth game of the opening playoff round. It is the longest game in the history of each franchise.

June 6
Ron Low, 48, resigns after 13 years with the Edmonton Oilers' organization, including more than four seasons as head coach.

Opposite: Tommy Salo arrived late in the 1998-99 season, but backstopped the struggling Oilers into the playoffs down the stretch.

1998 - 1999
STREET SIGN
FOR 99

In November of 1986, Don Lucas, the manager of a local oil-patch trucking operation, wrote the City of Edmonton about adding "Gretzky Way" to the city's signs along 99th Street.

"I'm excited about the idea," said Mayor Laurence Decore, who asked the city's names advisory committee to consider the matter.

Names such as Gretzky Street, Wayne Boulevard, and The Great One Way were also suggested.

The idea lay dormant until the spring of 1999, when Gretzky retired from hockey. Edmonton city council formed a Civic Recognition of Wayne Gretzky Selection Committee, chaired by Coun. Terry Cavanagh, a former hockey teammate of Gretzky's idol, Gordie Howe.

The committee received more than 5,000 submissions with 160 suggestions.

Just as Northlands Coliseum, where Gretzky did most of his scoring, would be renamed the Skyreach Centre, it was suggested that the Capilano freeway, which meanders past the Oilers' building, be renamed Wayne Gretzky Way.

But it was decreed that the word "Way" be reserved for a short stretch of city road.

So Cavanagh suggested Wayne Gretzky Drive and, on July 6, the name was approved by council.

Gretzky returned to Edmonton on Oct. 1, 1999, when his sweater was officially retired, and he officially unveiled Wayne Gretzky Drive.

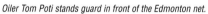
Oiler Tom Poti stands guard in front of the Edmonton net.

Doug Weight and company congratulate each other after another Oilers' score.

EDMONTON OILERS
1998-1999

Doug Weight, left, and Jason Smith converse with Ryan Smyth.

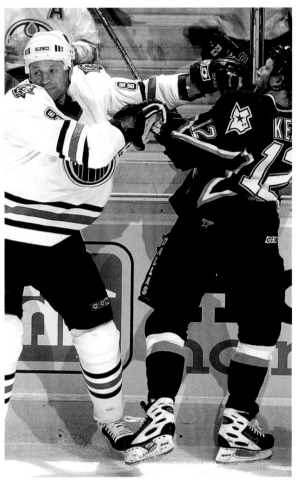

The Oilers' Frank Musil rubs out Dallas winger Mike Keane.

Todd Marchant, (right) battles for the puck with the Stars' Brian Skrudland.

Edmonton Oilers
1998-99
Results & Statistics

COACH	GP	W	L	T	PTS	GF	GA
			REGULAR SEASON				
Ron Low	82	33	37	12	78	230	226

2nd Northwest Division, 16th Overall, Playoffs: Lost Western Conference Quarter-Final 4-0 vs Dallas.

		REGULAR SEASON			
PLAYER	GP	G	A	PTS	PIM
Bill Guerin	80	30	34	64	133
Josef Beranek	66	19	30	49	23
Mike Grier	82	20	24	44	54
Pat Falloon	82	17	23	40	20
Boris Mironov	63	11	29	40	104
Rem Murray	78	21	18	39	20
Doug Weight	43	6	31	37	12
Todd Marchant	82	14	22	36	65
Alex Selivanov (TB)	43	6	13	19	18
Alex Selivanov (EDM)	29	8	6	14	24
Alex Selivanov (TOT)	72	14	19	33	42
Roman Hamrlik	75	8	24	32	70
Ryan Smyth	71	13	18	31	62
Janne Niinimaa	81	4	24	28	88
Chad Kilger (CHI)	64	14	11	25	30
Chad Kilger (EDM)	13	1	1	2	4
Chad Kilger (TOT)	77	15	12	27	34
Andrei Kovalenko	43	13	14	27	30
Dean McAmmond	65	9	16	25	36
Ethan Moreau (CHI)	66	9	6	15	84
Ethan Moreau (EDM)	14	1	5	6	8
Ethan Moreau (TOT)	80	10	11	21	92
Tom Poti	73	5	16	21	42
Mats Lindgren	48	5	12	17	22
Jason Smith (TOR)	60	2	11	13	40
Jason Smith (EDM)	12	1	1	2	11
Jason Smith (TOT)	72	3	12	15	51
Boyd Devereaux	61	6	8	14	23
Christian Laflamme (CHI)	62	2	11	13	70
Christian Laflamme (EDM)	11	0	1	1	0
Christian Laflamme (TOT)	73	2	12	14	70
Kelly Buchberger	52	4	4	8	68
Sean Brown	51	0	7	7	188
Kevin Brown	12	4	2	6	0
Georges Laraque	39	3	2	5	57
Todd Reirden	17	2	3	5	20
Marty McSorley	46	2	3	5	101
Frank Musil	39	0	3	3	34
Vladimir Vorobiev	2	2	0	2	2
Craig Millar	24	0	2	2	19
Chris Ferraro	2	1	0	1	0
Steve Passmore	6	0	1	1	2
Bob Essensa	39	0	1	1	0
Jim Dowd	1	0	0	0	0
Joe Hulbig	1	0	0	0	2
Bill Huard	3	0	0	0	0
Dan LaCouture	3	0	0	0	0
Daniel Lacroix	4	0	0	0	13
Fredrik Lindquist	8	0	0	0	2
Mikhail Shtalenkov	34	0	0	0	2
Tommy Salo (NYI)	51	0	0	0	12
Tommy Salo (EDM)	13	0	0	0	0
Tommy Salo (TOT)	64	0	0	0	12

			REGULAR SEASON			
GOALTENDER	GP	MINS	GA	SO	GAA.	W-L-T
Tommy Salo	13	700	27	0	2.31	8-2-2
M. Shtalenkov	34	1819	81	3	2.67	12-17-3
Bob Essensa	39	2091	96	0	2.75	12-14-6
Steve Passmore	6	362	17	0	2.82	1-4-1

SEEING STARS YET AGAIN

It took a mere 12 days for Kevin Lowe to be named the replacement for Ron Low as head coach of the Edmonton Oilers, a move that had seemed inevitable since Lowe's return to the Oilers as a player in 1996.

"It's not by coincidence," said general manager Glen Sather. "These things don't happen by osmosis."

Lowe was taking over a team that had made the playoffs the past three years, but seemed to have stalled, failing to make it past the first round in 1998-99.

In that context, Lowe listed his expectations shortly after being hired to his new job: "Work ethic. Accountability. Recognizing it's a privilege to play in the NHL and to understand, as Vince Lombardi said, 'Winning isn't everything, it's the only thing.'"

Lowe's philosophy seemed to have paid off. The Oilers played better than .500 during 1999-2000 for the first time in eight seasons. And one statistic was a telling sign of stability — during the entire season, only two players joined the Oilers from other NHL teams, German Titov from Pittsburgh and Igor Ulanov from Montreal.

Lowe also hired another former Oiler captain, Craig MacTavish, as an assistant coach after he spent two years as an assistant coach in New York.

"It's a situation that Kevin and I have talked about for a long time prior to the both of us retiring from the game," said MacTavish, 40. "Even if you leave, you never forget that. It's no coincidence players come back here."

And come back they did. Sather brought back goalie Bill Ranford, who led the Oilers to their last Stanley Cup in 1990. His former Oiler teammate Esa Tikkanen was also given a shot at making the lineup.

Leaving the front office was Doug Risebrough, who became general manager of the expansion Minnesota Wild. Kevin Prendergast became vice-president of hockey operations, and was instrumental in Edmonton's picks at the entry draft — Jani Rita in the first round, and a local youngster named Mike Comrie, their fifth overall pick, in the third round.

During training camp, MacTavish came up with the idea of having players divided into teams for scrimmages and competing for the Joey Moss Cup, acknowledging the longtime dressing-room attendant. Moss made the inaugural presentation to Doug Weight, as Team White beat Team Blue 4-0 in the final.

Weight was then named the Oilers' 10th captain.

Edmonton started the season much improved in goal compared to a year earlier, with Tommy Salo and Ranford replacing Bob Essensa and Mikhail Shtalenkov. Defensively, the question was just how good Roman Hamrlik would be. And on offence, things could only look up after a knee injury had limited Weight to 43 games the previous year.

The season marked the introduction of the "overtime loss," worth one point, which combined with four-on-four play in overtime would lead to more outright victories, or so the NHL hoped.

Ironically, the Oilers would instead set a team record for overtime appearances, 28, which was eight more than the last season and twice as many as five years previous.

On Oct. 1, the club started its season with — naturally — a 1-1 overtime tie with the New York Rangers, as Wayne Gretzky's No. 99 was officially retired during an emotional 55-minute pre-game ceremony, and raised to the Skyreach Centre rafters.

With the Oilers' record at 4-3-2-2, the latter digit for overtime losses, the club welcomed the previous year's top scorer, Bill Guerin, back to the fold after an 11-game holdout.

"Certainly, if we were going to have success this year, he was going to factor into it," said Lowe, in announcing the signing.

On Nov. 14, the Oilers won their first road game of the season in nine outings, 6-3 over the Chicago Blackhawks, as Alex Selivanov scored four times, the first Oiler to do so since Vincent Damphousse in 1991-92.

"I get lots of ice time and I play with great guys," said Selivanov. "This is it."

At the midway point in the season, with the team 13-12-11-5, Lowe expounded on his first year as a head coach: "The part that you struggle with is when to push and when to ease up," he said. "When are the guys overtired and when are the times they need to be pushed a little more?"

Salo emerged as the latest in a tradition of great Oiler goalies — Grant Fuhr, Andy Moog, Ranford and Curtis Joseph.

Largely due to Salo's stellar play, the Oilers were in first place in the Northwest Division by mid-February, in the midst of a 13-game stretch that would see them go 8-2-2-1, and aiming at third place overall in the Western Conference.

"They say that when you're winning you don't look back, you look ahead," said Lowe. "We've had a sense of that lately."

By March, the team had become a powerhouse at home, with a 15-4-9-3 record at Skyreach Centre. "Last year we played fine, or adequate, on the road, but we just weren't playing well at home, for whatever reason," said Lowe. "That became a bit of a focus this year."

But then, there was a reminder that the Oilers' fate might be beyond their control. The Colorado Avalanche acquired Ray Bourque and Dave Andreychuk for the stretch run, something that would have been well beyond the means of the small-budget Oilers.

"Obviously it's a major deal, but we can't let that affect us," said captain Weight.

The Oilers did make a minor deal of their own, acquiring Titov from Pittsburgh for Josef Beranek, who had been Edmonton's second-leading scorer the previous year with 49 points.

With Salo playing in 70 games and Ranford 16, the Oilers ended the season with just 212 goals against in 82

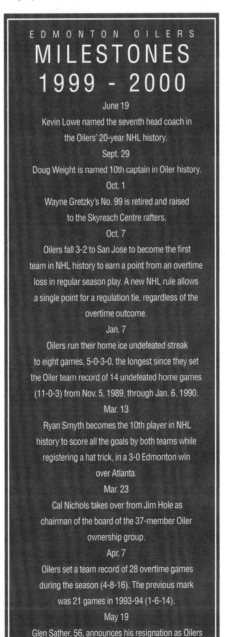

EDMONTON OILERS
MILESTONES
1999 - 2000

June 19
Kevin Lowe named the seventh head coach in the Oilers' 20-year NHL history.

Sept. 29
Doug Weight is named 10th captain in Oiler history.

Oct. 1
Wayne Gretzky's No. 99 is retired and raised to the Skyreach Centre rafters.

Oct. 7
Oilers fall 3-2 to San Jose to become the first team in NHL history to earn a point from an overtime loss in regular season play. A new NHL rule allows a single point for a regulation tie, regardless of the overtime outcome.

Jan. 7
Oilers run their home ice undefeated streak to eight games, 5-0-3-0, the longest since they set the Oiler team record of 14 undefeated home games (11-0-3) from Nov. 5, 1989, through Jan. 6, 1990.

Mar. 13
Ryan Smyth becomes the 10th player in NHL history to score all the goals by both teams while registering a hat trick, in a 3-0 Edmonton win over Atlanta.

Mar. 23
Cal Nichols takes over from Jim Hole as chairman of the board of the 37-member Oiler ownership group.

Apr. 7
Oilers set a team record of 28 overtime games during the season (4-8-16). The previous mark was 21 games in 1993-94 (1-6-14).

May 19
Glen Sather, 56, announces his resignation as Oilers general manager, having started 25 years earlier as team captain during the days of the World Hockey Association, before becoming coach and GM.

Opposite: It wouldn't be spring in Edmonton without a date with Dallas in the playoffs. Doug Weight tries to shake the Stars' Derian Hatcher during Dallas's opening round win.

1999 - 2000
REUNITING THE
BOYS ON THE BUS

A generation earlier they had been *The Boys on The Bus*, the subject of a candid video of greatness in the making.

Now, in August of 1999, they came together again for a reunion, celebrating 20 years of the franchise in the National Hockey League, with a banquet and golf tournament. "It's really great to put this Oilers' sweater back on," said Wayne Gretzky, wearing it for the first time since his trade to L. A. 11 years earlier.

Cam Connor recalled the early years, when Gretzky asked him to look after his new car, a Lincoln, during the summer. Neighbourhood kids found out about it and would ask to sit in Gretzky's car. "My wife would go out, roll the windows down in the car, and six to eight kids would just sit in there for two to three hours," said Connor.

Kevin Lowe remembered his first training camp.

"The climate was, well, a little different," said Lowe. "There were the WHA guys, and a lot of them had always had the feeling they were good enough to play in the NHL all along, but at the same time they didn't know for sure. Guys like Brett Callighen and Blair MacDonald had chosen to go the WHA route and they felt they had something to prove. Then there were some of the more senior guys, NHL guys who were holdovers, who had come from other teams. The rest of the guys were like me and Mess and Gretz. We just wanted to play hockey."

The players also took time during the reunion to acknowledge Bill Hunter, who had founded the Oilers, paving the way for Edmonton's entry in the NHL in 1979. Three months earlier, Hunter had been diagnosed with prostate and bone cancer.

Tommy Salo readies himself against the Dallas Stars. Salo played in a whopping 70 games for the Oilers in 1999-2000.

games, better than the club's previous low of 224 in 1997-98.

"Unless you have eight hall-of-famers on offence, you have to rely on being sound defensively," said Weight, in reference to an earlier era.

But the Oilers went through an eight-game stretch in early March with only two wins, and it took until the second-last game of the season, a 5-4 overtime victory in Vancouver, to clinch a playoff spot.

"The thing about this team is that we're so excited to get to the post-season," said Guerin. "It's a different feeling."

Once again, the Oilers faced the Dallas Stars in the playoffs, a team that hadn't lost to Edmonton in their last 15 regular season meetings.

The game plan posted in the Oilers' dressing room was courtesy of Normand and Tyler from Miss Panas's Grade 1 class at Kirkness elementary school: "Work hard. Beet Dallas."

Edmonton lost the first two games 2-1 and 3-0 in Dallas, before Weight scored three times for a 5-2 Edmonton win that revived the club's spirits.

But the revival was short.

Salo prepares for another NHL test at the Skyreach Centre.

Captain Doug Weight rights the Oilers' ship
with one of his 21 regular season goals

Edmonton Oilers 1999-2000 Results & Statistics

COACH	GP	W	L	T	OTL	PTS	GF	GA
Kevin Lowe	82	32	26	16	8	88	226	212

REGULAR SEASON

2nd Northwest Division, 14th Overall. Playoffs: Lost Western Conference Quarter-Final 4-1 vs Dallas.

REGULAR SEASON

PLAYER	GP	G	A	PTS	PIM
Doug Weight	77	21	51	72	54
Ryan Smyth	82	28	26	54	58
Alex Selivanov	67	20	27	47	46
Bill Guerin	70	24	22	46	123
German Titov (PIT)	63	17	25	42	34
German Titov (EDM)	7	0	4	4	4
German Titov (TOT)	70	17	29	46	38
Roman Hamrlik	80	8	37	45	68
Todd Marchant	82	17	23	40	70
Tom Poti	76	9	26	35	65
Janne Niinimaa	81	8	25	33	89
Mike Grier	65	9	22	31	68
Ethan Moreau	73	17	10	27	62
Boyd Devereaux	76	8	19	27	20
Jim Dowd	69	5	18	23	45
Pat Falloon	33	5	13	18	4
Josef Beranek	58	9	8	17	39
Georges Laraque	76	8	8	16	123
Rem Murray	44	9	5	14	8
Jason Smith	80	3	11	14	60
Sean Brown	72	4	8	12	192
Igor Ulanov (MTL)	43	1	5	6	76
Igor Ulanov (EDM)	14	0	3	3	10
Igor Ulanov (TOT)	57	1	8	9	86
Daniel Cleary	17	3	2	5	8
Chad Kilger	40	3	2	5	18
Christian Laflamme	50	0	5	5	32
Bert Robertsson	52	0	4	4	34
Paul Comrie	15	1	2	3	4
Brett Hauer	5	0	2	2	2
Tommy Salo	70	0	1	1	8
Mike Minard	1	0	0	0	0
Michel Picard	2	0	0	0	2
Dan LaCouture	5	0	0	0	10
Kevin Brown	7	0	0	0	0
Bill Ranford	16	0	0	0	2

REGULAR SEASON

GOALTENDER	GP	MINS	GA	SO	GAA.	W-L-T
Tommy Salo	70	4164	162	2	2.33	27-28-13
Mike Minard	1	60	3	0	3.00	1-0-0
Bill Ranford	16	785	47	0	3.59	4-6-3

Dallas came back with 4-3 and 3-2 wins.

"I haven't regretted a lot in my career," said Weight, "but I regret how we came in here and played the first two games. We didn't have the grit, played it a little too cautious. I really regret that."

Once the season was over, attention turned to the Oilers' front office. Tensions between general manager Sather and the new Oilers' ownership group had become increasingly evident. On May 19, Sather resigned, staying on as a consultant until the entry draft.

Sather and the Oilers had become synonymous over the previous 25 years. He progressed from team captain with the Oilers' World Hockey Association team to coach and GM after the team joined the NHL, playing a large part in the team's Stanley Cup success, eventually being inducted into the Hockey Hall of Fame in the builders category.

"I've had a wonderful 25 years in Edmonton, given 25 years of my life and tried to do things honourably," said Sather. "Today is the anniversary of the first Stanley Cup the Oilers won. Sort of ironic that I'm resigning today."

BACK TO 'OILERS HOCKEY'

The Edmonton Oilers strolled down memory lane during the 2000-01 season, as rookie general manager Kevin Lowe and rookie head coach Craig MacTavish brought out some old-fashioned results.

The Oilers put together the longest winning steak in club history — nine games — during the final half of the season. That propelled the team to finish 12th overall among National Hockey League teams, the club's highest finish since they were 12th overall in 1991-92.

Lowe, the first player drafted by the Oilers upon entry in the NHL in 1979, the first Oiler to score a goal in the NHL, and the record-holder for most games played by an Oiler, became GM in June.

"I have some good new ideas and I plan on being as innovative as any of the bright young people in this game," he said.

Less than a fortnight later, MacTavish followed Glen Sather and Lowe as former Oiler captains to become the team's head coach.

After Ted Green left the coaching group, MacTavish named Charlie Huddy and Mark Lamb, teammates during Edmonton's Cup-winning era, plus Billy Moores, a former junior Edmonton Oil King and University of Alberta Golden Bears coach, as assistants.

Lowe made his first player move at the entry draft, trading Roman Hamrlik to the New York Islanders for former first-round pick Eric Brewer, Josh Green and New York's second-round pick, which the Oilers turned into Brad Winchester.

On the business side, the Oilers' ownership board picked Patrick LaForge from 11 candidates to be the club's new president and chief executive officer. "I can't say that I woke up a long time ago and said I wanted to be in this position with an NHL franchise," said LaForge, who had served as CEO of Alpine Canada and vice-president of international marketing for Molson's Breweries. "But I must say this franchise and this opportunity and me is one of those marriages made in heaven."

In August, the club's last link to the World Hockey Association, Bruce MacGregor, announced he would be retiring as assistant general manager after 20 years. His replacement was Scott Howson.

The Oilers' goal for the season was to advance beyond the first round of the Stanley Cup playoffs.

"There's been a core group with this team that's been here for a number of years and has pretty much achieved similar things the past three or four years," said MacTavish. "Collectively, we all have to raise our expectations."

Gone from the previous season were Hamrlik, Boyd Devereaux, Alex Selivanov, German Titov, Jim Dowd, Pat Falloon, Josef Beranek, Christian Laflamme, Bert Robertsson and the retired Bill Ranford.

New to the lineup were Scott Ferguson, Brewer, Joaquin Gage, Domenic Pittis and Brian Swanson.

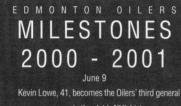

EDMONTON OILERS
MILESTONES
2000 - 2001

June 9
Kevin Lowe, 41, becomes the Oilers' third general manager in the club's NHL history.

June 22
Craig MacTavish, 41, becomes the eighth person to coach the Oilers in their NHL history.

July 6
Patrick LaForge, 47, is named Oilers' president and chief executive officer.

Oct. 6
Oilers honour Bruce MacGregor, 59, who resigns as assistant general manager after 20 years with the club. The Edmonton native spent 900 games in the NHL before returning to Edmonton in 1974, playing with the WHA Oilers before moving into the front office.

Nov. 13
Edmonton Journal hockey writer Jim Matheson is inducted into the Hockey Hall of Fame. Matheson started at *The Journal* in 1971 and has covered the Oilers since their inception in the World Hockey Association.

Nov. 15
Oilers acquire Anson Carter from Boston, becoming the first team in NHL history with five black players — Anson Carter, Mike Grier, Georges Laraque, Sean Brown and Joaquin Gage.

Mar. 13
Oilers beat Tampa Bay 5-4 in overtime to establish a club record of nine consecutive wins, dating back to Feb. 20.

Mar. 21
Tommy Salo makes 28 saves to tie Curtis Joseph's Oiler team record for shutouts in a season with eight, as Edmonton beats L.A. 7-0.

Apr. 4
Oilers finally raise Al Hamilton's No. 3 to the rafters, after the number worn by the team's first NHL captain had been retired following the 1979-80 season.

Apr. 7
Oilers finish with 93 points, their most since 99 points in 1987-88, good enough for 12th place overall, the best since finishing 12th in 1991-92.

"It's huge, having everybody together from the get-go," said MacTavish, of Lowe having signed all free agents before the season started. "Not only that, but Kevin signed all those guys with the exception of Dougie (Weight) to long-term deals. The core of the team is here."

The Oilers rolled off four straight wins in early October for a 5-1-1 record, their best start to a season since opening 11-2-1 in 1985.

In November, original general manager Bill Hunter, who founded the team and helped start the World Hockey Association, was brought in as chair of Operation Sell-Out, a campaign to increase ticket sales. "I'm supposed to be a sick man, but I've never felt better in my life," said Hunter, suffering from prostate and bone cancer.

The future of the franchise looked brighter on Nov. 2, when goalie Tommy Salo signed the richest contract in the history of the Oilers, $10.4 million US for three years, with an option of $4.15 million US for a fourth season.

"We figured, from the club's perspective, this season and three more allows us to breathe comfortably that, barring injury, our goaltending situation is solid," said Lowe.

In mid-November, the Oilers traded Bill Guerin, the club's top scorer two years earlier, to the Boston Bruins for Anson Carter plus draft choices.

"With the way things were going, I thought I'd found a home here," said Guerin.

From mid-November on, Edmonton would never lose more than two games in a row.

There was talk of an emerging style of play, "Edmonton Oilers hockey," a throwback to the Oilers of the 1980s and the Montreal Canadiens of the 1970s. In it, speed is used to create offensive opportunities and to press the opposition deep in its own end, rather than the defensive tactics used in the pervasive "neutral zone trap."

"They're not a team to sit back and wait for mistakes," said Vancouver Canucks goalie Bob Essensa, a former Oiler.

For Edmonton, staying aggressive and on the offensive would be a continuous challenge. But another step in that direction came with the signing of Mike Comrie, son of former Edmonton Oil King and The Brick owner Bill Comrie. Born in the year Lowe was an Oiler rookie, 1979, the five-foot-nine Comrie played his first game Dec. 30, 2000, against the Montreal Canadiens.

"When you break into the league, you do tend to hold the stick a little tighter," said Comrie, after scoring his first NHL goal Jan. 20. "It's nice to relieve the pressure."

Then came Edmonton's record winning streak, nine straight wins, from Feb. 20 through March 13.

A sign of the team's invincibility came in the sixth game of the streak, when they beat former Oiler goalie Curtis Joseph for the first time in nine tries since he defected to the Toronto Maple Leafs, 4-0.

"We were believing there was a curse," said MacTavish.

Opposite: Mike Comrie made the jump to the NHL on Dec. 30 vs. Montreal.

2000 - 2001
KEVIN AND CRAIG
— PART 2

A plot conceived in their days as New York Ranger teammates came to fruition during the summer of 2000 when Kevin Lowe emerged as general manager and Craig MacTavish as head coach of the Edmonton Oilers.

They had been teammates together with the Oilers and Rangers, both had been Oiler captains, and they had won four Stanley Cups together.

"We used to talk in New York when we roomed together," said MacTavish. "We started to discuss the possibility of the two of us getting involved in hockey in some capacity.

"It was just two guys, back then, discussing our aspirations. I don't think either one of us, in our wildest expectations or dreams, thought it would all transpire as quickly as it has."

Despite being the last helmetless player in the NHL, which made him a trivia question answer on the TV show *Who Wants To Be a Millionaire?*, MacTavish set the Oiler record of 518 consecutive games played, from Oct. 11, 1986, through Jan. 2, 1994. He recorded 213 goals and 267 assists in 1,093 career games.

In 1997, then general manager Glen Sather lured Lowe back to the Oilers with the promise that he would be given a job coaching or in the front office down the line. Lowe became an assistant coach in 1998, then head coach in 1999, and hired MacTavish as an assistant. MacTavish was announced as head coach on June 22, 2000.

"I've got the utmost confidence this is going to be a great ride for all of us," said MacTavish. "The style of play is going to be aggressive, Oiler-style hockey. I don't think any other style of play will be tolerated by anybody — certainly not the general manager or the fans who have grown accustomed to that exciting, fast-paced hockey."

MacTavish signed a new three-year deal in the summer of 2003.

Above: Mike Comrie and Anson Carter crash the Dallas net.
Below: Me and my shadow — super checker Todd Marchant lays the lumber on Dallas centre Mike Modano.

The ninth straight win, 5-4 over the Tampa Bay Lightning, came on a goal at 1:17 of overtime by Eric Brewer. He had been five years old when the Oilers set the previous mark of eight straight wins, Jan. 19 through Feb. 3 of 1985.

"We were hearing all the names of all the players who were on the team when they were involved in their streaks back in the old days and there's a lot of world-class players in there," said Brewer. "It's something special."

And young Comrie carried his own reminder of how historic the streak was — a dog-eared picture of himself and brother Paul posing with a young Wayne Gretzky and the Stanley Cup.

The streak ended March 14 in Fort Lauderdale, Fla, with a 2-2 tie against the Florida Panthers.

"We've been taking small, small steps over the last five years," said Weight. "This was a big step."

The next game pitted the Oilers, undefeated in 10 games, against the New Jersey Devils, who were on a nine-game winning streak of their own. The result: 5-4 New Jersey on a goal by Patrick Elias with 8.4 seconds left in overtime.

Tommy Salo sprawls to make a save against Dallas while Jason Smith keeps the Stars away from his goaltender.

Above: Stars behemoth Derian Hatcher puts the Oilers' Anson Carter in a headlock. Below right: Mike Comrie gets mugged by his teammates after scoring the overtime goal in Game 4 of the Western Conference quarter-final against, who else, but Dallas. Below left: Anson Carter and Ryan Smyth are a might happy after Comrie's goal got past Eddie Belfour.

Edmonton Oilers 2000-2001 Results & Statistics

COACH	GP	REGULAR SEASON						
		W	L	T	OTL	PTS	GF	GA
Craig MacTavish	82	39	28	12	3	93	243	222

2nd Northwest Division, 12th Overall. Playoffs: Lost Western Conference Quarter-Final 4-2 vs Dallas.

PLAYER	REGULAR SEASON				
	GP	G	A	PTS	PIM
Doug Weight	82	25	65	90	91
Ryan Smyth	82	31	39	70	58
Janne Niinimaa	82	12	34	46	90
Anson Carter	61	16	26	42	23
Todd Marchant	71	13	26	39	51
Mike Grier	74	20	16	36	20
Rem Murray	82	15	21	36	24
Daniel Cleary	81	14	21	35	37
Tom Poti	81	12	20	32	60
Sergei Zholtok (Mtl)	32	1	10	11	8
Sergei Zholtok (Edm)	37	4	16	20	22
Sergei Zholtok (TOT)	69	5	26	31	30
Georges Laraque	82	13	16	29	148
Igor Ulanov	67	3	20	23	90
Bill Guerin	21	12	10	22	18
Mike Comrie	41	8	14	22	14
Eric Brewer	77	7	14	21	53
Jason Smith	82	5	15	20	120
Ethan Moreau	68	9	10	19	90
Shawn Horcoff	49	9	7	16	10
Domenic Pittis	47	4	5	9	49
Chad Kilger	34	5	2	7	17
Dan LaCouture	37	2	4	6	29
Sean Brown	62	2	3	5	110
Sven Butenschon (Pit)	5	0	1	1	2
Sven Butenschon (Edm)	7	1	1	2	2
Sven Butenschon (TOT)	12	1	2	3	4
Brian Swanson	16	1	1	2	6
Frank Musil	13	0	2	2	4
Michel Riesen	12	0	1	1	4
Scott Ferguson	20	0	1	1	13
Tommy Salo	73	0	1	1	4
Chris Hajt	1	0	0	0	0
Jason Chimera	1	0	0	0	0
Joaquin Gage	5	0	0	0	0
Patrick Cote	6	0	0	0	18
Dominic Roussel (Ana)	13	0	0	0	0
Dominic Roussel (Edm)	8	0	0	0	2
Dominic Roussel (TOT)	21	0	0	0	2
Josh Green	-	-	-	-	-

GOALTENDER	REGULAR SEASON					
	GP	MINS	GA	SO	GAA.	W-L-T
Tommy Salo	73	4364	179	8	2.46	36-25-12
Joaquin Gage	5	260	15	0	3.46	2-2-0
Dominic Roussel	8	348	21	0	3.62	1-4-0

Despite the success, it wasn't until after the club's second-last game of the regular season that it locked up a playoff berth, finishing with 39 wins and 93 points, the most since the 1987-88 season.

And of course, where there's playoffs, there's Dallas. For the fifth straight year, the teams met in post-season play, Dallas finishing third overall in the Western Conference and the Oilers sixth. The series was a barnburner, with four of the six games decided in overtime. Dallas took the opener 2-1 on Jamie Langenbrunner's goal in overtime, Edmonton came back to take the second game 4-3, Dallas captured the third 3-2 on Benoit Hogue's overtime winner, Edmonton took the fourth 2-1 on Comrie's overtime marker, then Dallas scored a 4-3 overtime win on Kirk Muller's goal. The Stars finally closed it out with a 3-1 victory in Game 6.

"Craig, to me, is coaching the way this game has to be played in the year 2001," said Dallas coach Ken Hitchcock, of his counterpart, MacTavish. "His attention to detail is incredible. He coaches the way he played. Attention to detail, because of the closeness in this league, is vital."

TOUGH TEST IN THE WILD WEST

Normally, if you lose only one of your first six games of the season and have a nine-game undefeated streak in March, it's good enough to make the playoffs.

Usually, if you finish a season with six more wins than losses, you make the playoffs.

But the 2001-02 National Hockey League season was abnormal and unusual.

The Edmonton Oilers finished with 92 points, one less than the previous year when they finished sixth in the Western Conference, but this time around it wasn't good enough to be among the top-eight teams making the playoffs.

Perhaps it was an omen in July of 2001 when general manager Kevin Lowe looked at his budget and saw only one way to keep the purse strings from bursting. Doug Weight, who had made $205,000 US a season when he came from the New York Rangers for Esa Tikkanen in 1994, was now 30 years old and in line to make $6 million a year.

The only option to keep Lowe's promising youngsters in the fold was to free up some payroll cash, so he regretfully traded Weight, the team captain, along with Michel Riesen to the St. Louis Blues for Jochen Hecht, Marty Reasoner and Jan Horacek.

"It was necessary to move to solidify the organization until 2004 (when the collective bargaining agreement expires), which is our goal line," explained Lowe.

"It's hard to explain how close a team it is," said Weight of his old team after the trade was consummated. "That's what I told a lot of the guys — for a team like Edmonton, with a small budget, they need more camaraderie, more heart, to be competitive."

Weight called Mike Comrie his protege, and Comrie was just as effusive in his praise of Weight.

"I was 14 and he was stepping up his play," said Comrie, 20. "He started to become a superstar. Then to actually be able to play with him was remarkable."

Lowe added: "I don't want to put a lot on Mike Comrie's shoulders, but certainly his development will help expedite this."

The flip side of the coin in Comrie family fortunes was that in late August, Mike's brother Paul, who had a goal and two assists in 15 games with the Oilers in 2000, announced he was retiring after spending 18 months trying to recover from a concussion.

And there was even more sadness when it was confirmed that former Oiler player Garnet "Ace" Bailey, who spent 13 years as a scout for the team, had been on the plane hijacked by terrorists that crashed into the south tower of the World Trade Center on Sept. 11, 2001.

"Ace may not have been the greatest hockey player to play in the NHL, but he taught many players how to win championships and, more importantly, he was a winner as a person," said Wayne Gretzky, an Oiler teammate in 1979-80. "We will all miss him greatly."

Edmonton entered the season with Jason Smith, nicknamed Gator, as the 11th captain in team history, leading newcomers Hecht, Reasoner, free-agent signing Steve Staios and back-up goalie Jussi Markkanen.

"To get an opportunity on a team with such a great tradition of leaders like there is here is something special," said Smith.

Lowe, the current general manager, became a regular hospital visitor of Bill Hunter, the original Oiler general manager, who was battling cancer.

"Without trying to teach me anything, he talks about his values," said Lowe. "It kind of brings me back to the things that are important in hockey players, and life in general. All I know is we would sit down for two or three hours, and I'd much rather stay and talk to him for the rest of the afternoon than leave to go to work."

Defenceman Tom Poti joined the team after an eight-game holdout as the team was getting off to a 6-2-1 start.

In the boardroom, the 38-member Edmonton Investors Group came up with another $13.9 million to make sure the team survives until the current collective bargaining agreement expires in 2004.

Warned chairman Cal Nichols: "Our goal is just to get to 2004 because this thing just simply has to be fixed."

As the season progressed, the Oilers were gaining a reputation as The Come-From-Behind Kids, outscoring the opposition 21-10 in the third period.

Anson Carter chalked the comebacks up to resolve and confidence in goalie Tommy Salo.

The Oilers were 17-8-3-1 on Dec. 5, eight games above .500. "A lot of things we needed to have happen for us to have a successful start have happened," summarized coach Craig MacTavish. "Ryan Smyth, Anson Carter ... there was added responsibility for them and they've delivered. Our young guys have played very well, Tommy Salo has played brilliantly, the defence has played well.

"We just can't get too comfortable."

Midway through the season, Comrie had 13 goals and 28 points in 40 games, and was fulfilling all expectations to compensate for the departure of Weight. Comrie was small yet played big, like a junior version of Mark Messier. At times, he showed hints of Gretzky's natural hockey sense. And he was a home-town product. It all made him a fan favourite.

"He's so smart positionally and so good at hunting the puck," said MacTavish. "It's difficult for a guy that size to dominate somebody physically, so he makes up for it with smarts and positioning and a great stick."

Then the Oilers started to falter. Starting in mid-January, they won only twice in 14 games, scoring more than two goals only three times during the skid. "When you're having trouble scoring goals, you have to score ugly goals," said MacTavish. "You have to hack and whack and hope that something is going to get in."

After a loss against the Atlanta Thrashers, MacTavish playfully wrote on the dressing-room chalkboard: "Bus leaves for the airport at 10:50, be under it."

The season was interrupted in February for the Salt Lake City Winter Olympics, in which Canada (Ryan Smyth, Eric Brewer and GM Kevin Lowe were part of that team) captured hockey gold.

The break seemed to energize the Oilers. They made a good charge, going

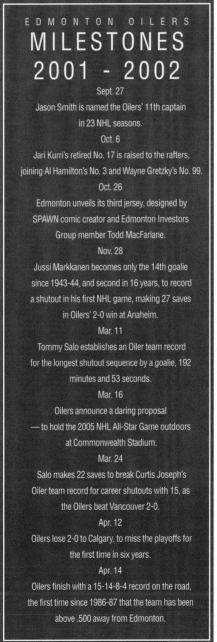

EDMONTON OILERS
MILESTONES
2001 - 2002

Sept. 27
Jason Smith is named the Oilers' 11th captain in 23 NHL seasons.

Oct. 6
Jari Kurri's retired No. 17 is raised to the rafters, joining Al Hamilton's No. 3 and Wayne Gretzky's No. 99.

Oct. 26
Edmonton unveils its third jersey, designed by SPAWN comic creator and Edmonton Investors Group member Todd MacFarlane.

Nov. 28
Jussi Markkanen becomes only the 14th goalie since 1943-44, and second in 16 years, to record a shutout in his first NHL game, making 27 saves in Oilers' 2-0 win at Anaheim.

Mar. 11
Tommy Salo establishes an Oiler team record for the longest shutout sequence by a goalie, 192 minutes and 53 seconds.

Mar. 16
Oilers announce a daring proposal — to hold the 2005 NHL All-Star Game outdoors at Commonwealth Stadium.

Mar. 24
Salo makes 22 saves to break Curtis Joseph's Oiler team record for career shutouts with 15, as the Oilers beat Vancouver 2-0.

Apr. 12
Oilers lose 2-0 to Calgary, to miss the playoffs for the first time in six years.

Apr. 14
Oilers finish with a 15-14-8-4 record on the road, the first time since 1986-87 that the team has been above .500 away from Edmonton.

2001-2002

2001 - 2002
THE LUCKY LOONIE

When Skyreach Centre supervisor of event operations Trent Evans was brought to Salt Lake City to make the ice for the 2002 Olympic Games, he dropped a dime onto the concrete floor to mark centre ice.

With flooding partly done, Evans placed a loonie on the same spot as a good luck charm for Canada's teams. When an American icemaker complained, Evans craftily scraped away some ice, applied a splotch of gold paint, and reflooded, with the loonie still in place.

The Games began with seven members of the Edmonton Oilers in various lineups — Eric Brewer and Ryan Smyth (Team Canada), Janne Niinimaa and Jussi Markkanen (Finland), Tom Poti (United States), Tommy Salo (Sweden) and Jochen Hecht (Germany). The Team Canada entourage also included former Oiler Wayne Gretzky as executive director, Oiler general manager Kevin Lowe as assistant executive director, plus medical trainer Ken Lowe, equipment manager Barrie Stafford and massage therapist Stewart Poirier.

Canada finished 1-1-1 in the round robin, then swept Finland 2-1 in the quarter-final, Belarus 7-1 in the semifinal, and the U.S. 5-2 in the final, to become the first Canadian team to win Olympic men's gold since the 1952 Edmonton Waterloo Mercurys.

"I know one thing: the medal is very heavy," said Smyth. "I had to take it off a couple of times."

"The quality of play was so high," said Brewer. "You played 30- or 40-second shifts and got off. With the big ice, making plays wasn't easy. You had to skate more to do less."

As for the lucky 1987 loonie, it wound up in the Hockey Hall of Fame. "It's pretty special to have my name mentioned here with the loonie," said Evans.

11-5-2-2 down the stretch in a drive to make the playoffs.

Before the trade deadline, Lowe sent Rem Murray and Tom Poti to the New York Rangers for Mike York and a draft pick, while trading Sean Brown to Boston for Bobby Allen.

The Oilers sat in the eighth and final playoff playoff position with a three-point margin and five games remaining as the season drew to a close.

During the five previous years, the Oilers had clinched a playoff spot in the last three games of the season — game 79 in 1997, game 81 in 1998, game 80 in 1999, game 81 in 2000 and

Left: Todd Marchant looks up at the clock. The Oilers season ended sooner than anyone had hoped after the team failed to make the playoffs for the first time since 1995-96.
Below: Tommy Salo, with the capable assistance of defenceman Janne Niinimaa, couldn't coax the Oilers into the post-season this time around.

2001-2002

after game 81 in 2001, when San Jose eliminated Phoenix.

But this time, Edmonton lost three of their next four games, and a 2-0 defeat to Calgary in game 81, the second-last game of the season, eliminated Edmonton from the playoffs.

"That just shows the competitiveness and how equal teams are throughout the league," said Oiler captain Smith.

"Losing at home is tough. Being shut out is tough. Losing to Calgary is tough. Go down the list," said Carter.

Comrie led the team with 33 goals and York had a combined 61 points with two teams.

Right: Mike Grier had a tough season, managing only eight goals after a 20-goal season previously.
Below: Salo was again the work horse in the Oilers net, appearing in 69 regular season games.

Edmonton Oilers
2001-2002
Results & Statistics

	REGULAR SEASON							
COACH	GP	W	L	T	OTL	PTS	GF	GA
Craig MacTavish	82	38	28	12	4	92	205	182

3rd Northwest Division, 15th Overall. Playoffs: Did Not Qualify.

	REGULAR SEASON				
PLAYER	GP	G	A	PTS	PIM
Mike York (NYR)	69	18	39	57	16
Mike York (Edm)	12	2	2	4	0
Mike York (TOT)	81	20	41	61	16
Mike Comrie	82	33	27	60	45
Anson Carter	82	28	32	60	25
Ryan Smyth	61	15	35	50	48
Janne Niinimaa	81	5	39	44	80
Jochen Hecht	82	16	24	40	60
Todd Marchant	82	12	22	34	41
Daniel Cleary	65	10	19	29	51
Mike Grier	82	8	17	25	32
Eric Brewer	81	7	18	25	45
Rem Murray	69	7	17	24	14
Shawn Horcoff	61	8	14	22	18
Georges Laraque	80	5	14	19	157
Jason Smith	74	5	13	18	103
Tom Poti	55	1	16	17	42
Ethan Moreau	80	11	5	16	81
Josh Green	61	10	5	15	52
Marty Reasoner	52	6	5	11	41
Sean Brown	61	6	4	10	127
Steve Staios	73	5	5	10	108
Domenic Pittis	22	0	6	6	8
Scott Ferguson	50	3	2	5	75
Brian Swanson	8	1	1	2	0
Jason Chimera	3	1	0	1	0
Tommy Salo	69	0	1	1	0
Jani Rita	1	0	0	0	0
Ales Pisa	2	0	0	0	2
Ty Conklin	4	0	0	0	0
Jussi Markkanen	14	0	0	0	0
Sven Butenschon	14	0	0	0	4

	REGULAR SEASON					
GOALTENDER	GP	MINS	GA	SO	GAA.	W-L-T
Ty Conklin	4	148	4	0	1.62	2-0-0
Jussi Markkanen	14	784	24	2	1.84	6-4-2
Tommy Salo	69	4035	149	6	2.22	30-28-10

2002-2003
EYES BACK ON THE PRIZE

After missing the playoffs for the first time in six years, the Edmonton Oilers faced having to refocus for the 2002-03 season.

There would be no more thinking beyond the first round of post-season play, or even beyond the regular season. While they had the second-fewest goals allowed the previous year, 182, they had tied for 21st in goals scored with only 205. The offence had to come alive.

Having missed the playoffs the previous year became an albatross. "I hate talking about last year," said Ryan Smyth. "It's over and done with. We didn't make it. We're frustrated. We're upset because we're a team that thrives on the playoffs."

During the summer, the team acquired Jiri Dopita from the Philadelphia Flyers for draft picks, and dealt Jochen Hecht to the Buffalo Sabres for draft picks, one of which turned out to be Jarret Stoll, captain of the Memorial Cup champion Kootenay Ice, formerly the Edmonton Ice.

Then two days before the regular schedule opened, Edmonton sent rugged Mike Grier — whose goal production had fallen from 20 to eight the previous year — to the Washington Capitals for two draft picks.

"Kevin (general manager Lowe) said I did everything they had asked of me," said Grier. "I think when you leave a hockey team feeling that you did as much as you could, it is a good feeling."

So the team started the season with newcomers Dopita, Ales Hemsky from the Quebec junior league and local product Jason Chimera from the Hamilton farm club in the lineup.

"We made a determination that we had to fill out our top-six forwards so we could get more scoring," said Oilers assistant general manager Scott Howson.

But from the word go, this was a season of inconsistency, boiled down to six distinct segments:

◗ *Oct. 10 - Nov. 8 (3-6-3-1)* — The worst start since 1993-94 had coach Craig MacTavish oozing with anguish. "You're left guessing who's ready to play," he said. "But you learn more about your team when you go through stretches like this. You learn who's capable of handling it, who can elevate their game and maybe you sort out some of your problems early on in the year." Sure enough, things turned around.

◗ *Nov. 9 - Dec. 13 (13-3-1-1)* — This period included a 12-game stretch with only one loss. "All of a sudden you gain your confidence. And everybody feels great out there," said defenceman Steve Staios. But coach MacTavish looked like a prophet when he said: "We all realize and recognize what a fine line it is between a 10-game unbeaten streak and winning a game or two in 10 games. We're getting bailed out by Tommy (goalie Salo) or a post or a lucky bounce."

◗ *Dec. 14 - Jan. 2 (1-4-0-4)* — The good fortune ended with a splat, as Markus Naslund scored four goals in a 6-2 Vancouver win, starting a slide that brought Edmonton below .500 at the midway mark in the season.

◗ *Jan. 4 - Feb. 11 (9-5-2-1)* — Despite Mike Comrie being out with a broken

thumb, the Oilers soldiered on. And the buzz in the city was the new line of rookies Chimera, Brian Swanson and Fernando Pisani, who had played together on the American Hockey League farm team in Hamilton the previous year. They brought back memories of the Oilers' Kid Line in the 1990 Stanley Cup finals — Martin Gelinas, Joe Murphy and Adam Graves. "You almost forget they're rookies because of the way they've played," said MacTavish. At the team skills competition, Chimera was the fastest Oiler around the ice in 13.332 seconds, faster than Mike Gartner's 1996 official NHL record of 13.386 seconds, and Alexei Semenov won the hardest shot event at 104.6 miles per hour.

◗ *Feb. 12 - Mar. 1 (0-5-2-2)* — During this stretch, the Oilers had a closed door meeting instead of a practice. "When you're a young team and you're winning, you want to order the rings," said Anson Carter. "When you're losing, it feels like you're going to be out playing golf the first week of the off-season. The guys who have been around have to relay the message that we're going to go through these spells. It's just a matter of not getting down, of not pointing fingers, and really pumping up the guy beside you to get out of this predicament."

◗ *Mar. 4 - Apr. 5 (10-3-3-1)* — The Oilers' nine-game winless streak ended when Smyth returned after missing nine games due to a separated shoulder. It's one of those connections that players mention at contract renegotiation time, and that fans mention when selecting a team most valuable player. Smyth returned with a goal and assist in a 2-1 win over San Jose Sharks that kick-started a stretch run that got them into the playoffs. "It just goes to show the type of player he is and how much he's missed," said Todd Marchant.

At the March 11 trade deadline, the Oilers sent Carter and defenceman Ales Pisa to the New York Rangers for Radek Dvorak and Cory Cross, then Edmonton bartered Janne Niinimaa and a draft pick to the New York Islanders for Brad Isbister and Raffi Torres.

It was tough letting go of Carter, who had tied Mike Comrie for the scoring lead among full-year Oilers the previous season, and Niinimaa, who had been picked the team's best defenceman that year.

"As players, we can't let it affect us," said Comrie, of the trades. "As professionals, we have to go out and play. That's our job."

The team's sprint down the stretch allowed it to clinch a playoff spot with a whopping five games left in the regular season.

"It was very prominent in everybody's memory banks what a feeling of devastation it was when the season wrapped up," said MacTavish, of missing the playoffs the previous year.

Lowe pointed out how much more important the regular season had become and how much more difficult mak-

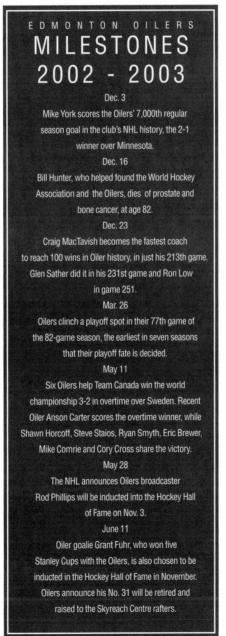

E D M O N T O N   O I L E R S

MILESTONES
2002 - 2003

Dec. 3

Mike York scores the Oilers' 7,000th regular season goal in the club's NHL history, the 2-1 winner over Minnesota.

Dec. 16

Bill Hunter, who helped found the World Hockey Association and the Oilers, dies of prostate and bone cancer, at age 82.

Dec. 23

Craig MacTavish becomes the fastest coach to reach 100 wins in Oiler history, in just his 213th game. Glen Sather did it in his 231st game and Ron Low in game 251.

Mar. 26

Oilers clinch a playoff spot in their 77th game of the 82-game season, the earliest in seven seasons that their playoff fate is decided.

May 11

Six Oilers help Team Canada win the world championship 3-2 in overtime over Sweden. Recent Oiler Anson Carter scores the overtime winner, while Shawn Horcoff, Steve Staios, Ryan Smyth, Eric Brewer, Mike Comrie and Cory Cross share the victory.

May 28

The NHL announces Oilers broadcaster Rod Phillips will be inducted into the Hockey Hall of Fame on Nov. 3.

June 11

Oiler goalie Grant Fuhr, who won five Stanley Cups with the Oilers, is also chosen to be inducted into the Hockey Hall of Fame in November. Oilers announce his No. 31 will be retired and raised to the Skyreach Centre rafters.

ing the playoffs is. He noted that the regular season had been viewed as a giant round of exhibition games back in 1979 when 16 of 21 teams reached the playoffs, compared to 16 out of 30 teams advancing now.

Opposite: With his enthusiasm and toughness, Georges Laraque is a fan favourite in Edmonton.

2002-2003
GOODBYE, BILL

He may be the only person who had mourners at his funeral receive hockey pucks as a memento of his life. But then, "Wild Bill" Hunter had always done things with flair.

For 14 years, starting as general manager of the junior Edmonton Oil Kings in 1965, Hunter had been the pulse of hockey in Edmonton. Without him, there would have been no Edmonton Oilers, no Wayne Gretzky in Edmonton, no five Stanley Cups.

"In the hockey circle, especially in Edmonton, he should be immortalized," said Oilers general manager Kevin Lowe. "The greatness of Gretzky and Messier and the championship teams, maybe one of the greatest teams of all time, is linked to him because if it wasn't for his efforts, the team wouldn't have been here."

Hunter helped form the World Hockey Association in 1971 and brought what would later become the Edmonton Oilers into the league in 1972. Then Hunter and one of his partners, Zane Feldman, announced plans to buy land for a new arena. A week later, Edmonton Northlands announced it would build the Coliseum.

The building was one reason Gretzky wound up in Edmonton, and Gretzky was a big reason the Oilers were accepted into the National Hockey League and became Cup winners.

Jasper Place Arena was renamed Bill Hunter Arena, Hunter was made a companion of the Order of Canada and was inducted into the Canadian Sports Hall of Fame.

"If to be passionate and emotional looks wild to some people, so be it," wrote Hunter, in his autobiography *Wild Bill*. "Other people call me an eternal optimist. To them I say, 'Thank you.'"

After years of battling prostate and bone cancer, Hunter died on Dec. 16, 2002, at age 82. Feldman, his former partner with the Oilers, died four months later at age 80.

And if it's April, that means Dallas. The clubs would meet in the playoffs for the sixth time in the last seven years; in fact, every year during that period that Edmonton made the playoffs. But only 10 Oilers and nine Stars were back from the last series two years earlier. Back to the future.

"It's not going to be the same old matchups and same old strategies," said MacTavish.

However, it was the same old results. The Stars took the

Big Georges Laraque charges in front of the Dallas net while Derian Hatcher, left, and Kirk Muller try to contain him.

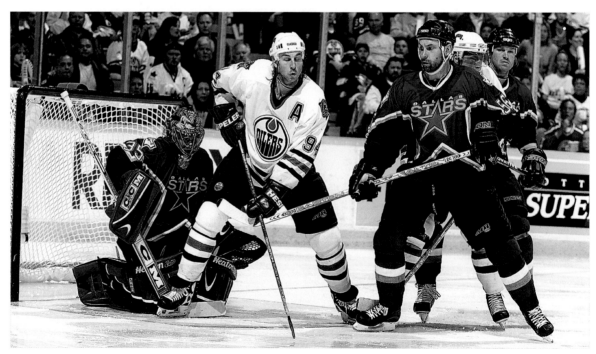

Ryan Smyth parks himself in a familiar spot in front of the Dallas net, looking for a deflection, as the Stars' Sergei Zubov defends.

2002-2003

series for the fifth straight time, in six games.

Edmonton won the first game 2-1 and the third 3-2, then Dallas took three straight — 3-1, 5-2 and 3-2. Mike Modano, Sergei Zubov and Scott Young scored 12 of the Stars' 20 goals, including three of four game winners. "The most frustrating thing was that it was them again," said Smyth.

"I think everybody had grown tired of the same scenario," added MacTavish.

Edmonton Oilers
2002-2003
Results & Statistics

COACH	GP	W	L	T	OTL	PTS	GF	GA
REGULAR SEASON								
Craig MacTavish	82	36	26	11	9	92	232	230

4th Northwest Division, 14th Overall. Playoffs: Lost Western Conference Quarter-Final 4-2 vs Dallas.

REGULAR SEASON

PLAYER	GP	G	A	PTS	PIM
Ryan Smyth	66	27	34	61	67
Todd Marchant	77	20	40	60	48
Anson Carter	68	25	30	55	20
Mike York	71	22	29	51	10
Mike Comrie	69	20	31	51	90
Radek Dvorak (NYR)	63	6	21	27	16
Radek Dvorak (Edm)	12	4	4	8	14
Radek Dvorak (TOT)	75	10	25	35	30
Shawn Horcoff	78	12	21	33	55
Ethan Moreau	78	14	17	31	112
Marty Reasoner	70	11	20	31	28
Ales Hemsky	59	6	24	30	14
Eric Brewer	80	8	21	29	45
Janne Niinimaa	63	4	24	28	66
Brad Isbister (NYI)	53	10	13	23	34
Brad Isbister (Edm)	13	3	2	5	9
Brad Isbister (TOT)	66	13	15	28	43
Steve Staios	76	5	21	26	96
Jason Chimera	66	14	9	23	36
Daniel Cleary	57	4	13	17	31
Fernando Pisani	35	8	5	13	10
Georges Laraque	64	6	7	13	110
Jason Smith	68	4	8	12	64
Brian Swanson	44	2	10	12	10
Cory Cross (NYR)	26	0	4	4	16
Cory Cross (Edm)	11	2	3	5	8
Cory Cross (TOT)	37	2	7	9	24
Scott Ferguson	78	3	5	8	120
Alexei Semenov	46	1	6	7	58
Jiri Dopita	21	1	5	6	11
Jani Rita	12	3	1	4	0
Ales Pisa	48	1	3	4	24
Marc-Andre Bergeron	5	1	1	2	9
Josh Green	20	0	2	2	12
Jussi Markkanen	22	0	1	1	2
Bobby Allen	1	0	0	0	0
Alex Henry	3	0	0	0	0
Kari Haakana	13	0	0	0	4
Tommy Salo	65	0	0	0	4

REGULAR SEASON

GOALTENDER	GP	MINS	GA	SO	GAA	W-L-T
Jussi Markkanen	22	1180	51	3	2.59	7-8-3
Tommy Salo	65	3814	172	4	2.71	29-27-8

Ales Hemsky showed flashes of brilliance in his rookie season with the Oilers, but here he is hooked by the Stars' Derian Hatcher and has his stick hooked by Jere Lehtinen.

Ryan Smyth, Todd Marchant, their teammates and the Skyreach Centre crowd go nuts after this goal.

CHAPTER 3

The Stanley Cups

For those who saw the Edmonton Oilers win their first Stanley Cup, a picture of balloons may pop into their heads.

As the final minutes counted down at Northlands Coliseum, with Dave Lumley's empty-net goal giving the Oilers a 5-2 margin and a five-game series win over the New York Islanders, the ice became an ocean of balloons — orange and blue ones.

Then there was that other picture, the one snapped by *Edmonton Journal* photographer Mike Pinder, that would be the paper's front page poster the next day. In it, Wayne Gretzky was circling the ice, hoisting the Cup above his head, like a weightlifter who had taken the weight of the world off a bunch of youthful shoulders.

"I've been in the NHL for five years, and all the time you pick up the paper and read, 'Well, they haven't won the Stanley Cup yet, so they're not that good,' " said Gretzky. "Well, we'll never have to hear that again. There's no feeling like this. Nothing compares. When I was carrying the Cup, I thought of Jean Beliveau. I remembered when he picked it up and how good he looked with it. I was worried a lot about dropping it, though."

Before the final game, Gretzky, who had previously won five cars, the Art Ross Trophy for scoring and the Hart Trophy as most valuable player, delivered an impassioned speech, telling his teammates that all his individual baubles meant nothing unless he got the Stanley Cup. "I told him none of mine did either," said teammate Dave Semenko, keeping a straight face.

So it was that the Islanders' Drive For Five fell short, although New York captain Denis Potvin wasn't bitter about his role as carrier of the Cup. "I felt no shame turning the Cup over to them," said Potvin. "I'm damn proud. Several Oilers talked about idolizing us as we shook hands. One great team turning it over to a team that was great all year. They deserved it."

After the final game, more than a dozen people were injured as rowdiness swept over Jasper Avenue, and things were even worse after a parade for the team three days later, when an unruly mob caused a massive riot in which 65 people were arrested. Fifty were released after being held at police headquarters until they had calmed down, while another 15 were charged with offences that included mischief, possession of weapons (rocks and beer bottles) and committing indecent acts.

To get to the Cup finals, Edmonton romped through its first series three straight over the Winnipeg Jets, and were up 3-1 in games on the Calgary Flames when trouble arose. Consecutive 5-4 wins by Calgary — the latter on Lanny McDon-

ald's goal at 1:04 of overtime — forced Game 7. In that one, Al MacInnis put Calgary ahead 4-3 at 10:15 of the second period, but Edmonton retaliated with four straight goals for a 7-4 victory. Breathing easier, the Oilers swept the Minnesota North Stars four straight to set up a Cup final rematch with the Islanders.

Whereas the Isles had won 2-0 in the 1983 opener, this time Edmonton prevailed 1-0 in Uniondale.

"This takes the monkey off our back," said Kevin McClelland, whose goal early in the third period ended an Oiler streak of 10 consecutive losses to the Islanders.

"This may be the best game we've ever played," added defenceman Paul Coffey.

Goalie Grant Fuhr, who outduelled Islanders netminder Billy Smith, was asked by a philosophical New York reporter: "When there were seven seconds left, you looked at the clock. What was on your mind?"

Said Fuhr: "I wanted to know how much time was left."

The Islanders rebounded to even the series with a 6-1 victory in Game 2 on Long Island, with Clark Gillies scoring three goals for New York.

"The difference between tonight's game and the first one was we were more involved," said Islanders coach Al Arbour. "There was more intensity. We won the little battles in the pits."

During the game, Smith performed an acting job worthy of James Cagney, lifting his body skyward and falling with a thud when brushed by a passing Oiler.

But in Game 3 in Edmonton, the Coliseum erupted into delirious song — "Goodbye Bill-y" — when he was banished to the Islander bench after six pucks eluded him during the first 46 minutes of a 7-2 Edmonton victory. "It's nice to have that feeling we can finally score goals on Smith," said Oiler Kevin Lowe. "Psychologically, it was so important for us to stay close, not let them get a big jump. If they had, they could have gone into their defensive shell."

Game 4 was a variation on a theme. The Oilers scored early — six times in the first 30 minutes — and once again routed the Islanders 7-2. Smith let in two goals each by Gretzky and Willy Lindstrom, as Andy Moog played goal for Edmonton while Fuhr nursed a sore shoulder.

When Edmonton won Game 5 and the Stanley Cup, it was the fulfilment of a lot of dreams. They had captured the Cup in their fifth National Hockey League season. Only the 1940 New York Rangers, in their third NHL season, had won a Cup quicker. "I was pretty naive when I said it on a show with Dick Beddoes," said Oilers owner Peter Pocklington, of having predicted the time frame.

"But the players believed it."

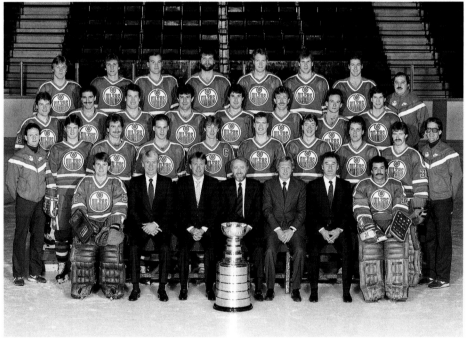

Back Row – Raimo Summanen, Kevin McClelland, Rick Chartraw, Dave Semenko, Randy Gregg, Don Jackson, Kevin Lowe, Lyle Kulchisky
3rd Row – Pat Conacher, Charlie Huddy, Dave Hunter, Jaroslav Pouzar, Paul Coffey, Willy Lindstrom, Ken Linseman, Larry Melnyk
2nd Row – Barrie Stafford, Pat Hughes, Glenn Anderson, Lee Fogolin, Wayne Gretzky, Mark Messier, Jari Kurri, Dave Lumley, Mike Zanier, Peter Millar
Front Row – Andy Moog, John Muckler, Glen Sather, Peter Pocklington, Bruce MacGregor, Ted Green, Grant Fuhr

Opposite: Bedlam! Wayne Gretzky and Paul Coffey hoist Edmonton's first-ever Stanley Cup.

Above: No one, it appears, celebrates with more enthusiasm than the Moose, Mark Messier.

Left: Coach and general manager Glen Sather experiences the sweet taste of success.

Bottom left: Wayne Gretzky struggles with the mother of all bottles of bubbly.

Below: The dynamic duo in the nets, Grant Fuhr (left) and Andy Moog (right) hold on tight to hockey's holy grail, the Stanley Cup.

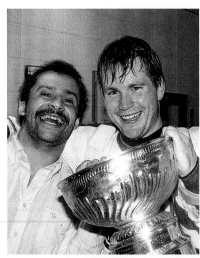

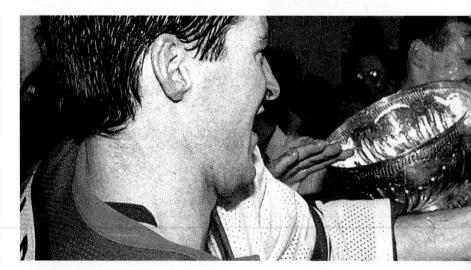

Top centre: *With the Stanley Cup comes a Stanley Cup parade.*

Left: *What seems like half the city comes downtown to fete the Oilers' victory.*

Bottom centre: *Oiler defenceman Kevin Lowe has a little fun with the bubbly.*

Top right: *The Great One has great fun hugging winning goalie Andy Moog.*

Right: *Smooch cam catches Dave Lumley about to plant one on Lord Stanley's mug.*

Bottom right: *Coach Glen Sather joins in the dressing room celebration with Barrie Stafford and Peter Millar.*

Below: *Dave Hunter hoists the Cup.*

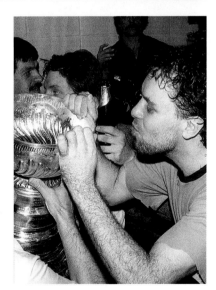

EDMONTON OILERS
Stanley Cup
1983 - 1984
PLAYOFFS RESULTS AND STATISTICS

		PLAYOFFS			
COACH	GP	W	L	GF	GA
Glen Sather	19	15	4	94	56

STANLEY CUP CHAMPIONS, 1st Smythe Division, 1st Overall. Playoffs: Won Smythe Division Semifinal 3-0 vs Winnipeg, Won Smythe Division Final 4-3 vs Calgary, Won Campbell Conference Final 4-0 vs Minnesota, Won Stanley Cup Final 4-1 vs NY Islanders.

		PLAYOFFS			
PLAYER	GP	G	A	PTS	PIM
Wayne Gretzky	19	13	22	35	12
Paul Coffey	19	8	14	22	21
Jari Kurri	19	14	14	28	13
Mark Messier	19	8	18	26	19
Glenn Anderson	19	6	11	17	33
Ken Linseman	19	10	4	14	65
Pat Hughes	19	2	11	13	12
Dave Hunter	17	5	5	10	14
Kevin Lowe	19	3	7	10	16
Charlie Huddy	12	1	9	10	8
Randy Gregg	19	3	7	10	21
Willy Lindstrom	19	5	5	10	10
Kevin McClelland	18	4	6	10	42
Jaroslav Pouzar	14	1	2	3	12
Dave Lumley	19	2	5	7	44
Lee Fogolin	19	1	4	5	23
Don Jackson	19	1	2	3	32
Dave Semenko	19	5	5	10	44
Grant Fuhr	16	0	3	3	4
Pat Conacher	3	1	0	1	2
Rick Chartraw	1	0	0	0	2
Raimo Summanen	5	1	4	5	0
Andy Moog	7	0	0	0	2
Larry Melnyk	6	0	1	1	2

			PLAYOFFS			
GOALTENDER	GP	MIN	GA	GAA.	W-L	
Andy Moog	7	263	12	2.74	4-0	
Grant Fuhr	16	883	44	2.99	11-4	

1984 PLAYOFFS

DATE	CITY	RESULTS
April 4	Edm	Edm 9, Win 2
Apr 5	Edm	Edm 5, Win 4*
Apr 7	Win	Edm 4, Win 1

* Randy Gregg scored at 0:21 overtime
(EDM WON SERIES 3-0)

Apr 12	Edm	Edm 5, Cgy 2
Apr 13	Edm	Cgy 6, Edm 5*
Apr 15	Cgy	Edm 3, Cgy 2
Apr 16	Cgy	Edm 5, Cgy 3
Apr 18	Edm	Cgy 5, Edm 4
Apr 20	Cgy	Cgy 5, Edm 4**
Apr 22	Edm	Edm 7, Cgy 4

* Carey Wilson scored at 3:42 overtime
** Lanny McDonald scored at 1:04 overtime
(EDM WON SERIES 4-3)

Apr 24	Edm	Edm 7, Min 1
Apr 26	Edm	Edm 4, Min 3
Apr 28	Min	Edm 8, Min 5
May 1	Min	Edm 3, Min 1

(EDM WON SERIES 4-0)

May 10	Unidle	Edm 1, NY Isld 0
May 12	Unidle	NY Isld 6, Edm 1
May 15	Edm	Edm 7, NY Isld 2
May 17	Edm	Edm 7, NY Isld 2
May 19	Edm	Edm 5, NY Isld 2

(EDM WON SERIES 4-1)

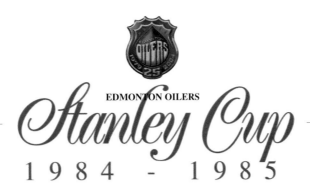

EDMONTON OILERS
Stanley Cup
1984 - 1985

A huge white sheet hung behind goaltender Grant Fuhr's shoulder during the fifth game of the 1985 Stanley Cup finals. The message read simply: "2Nite."

And so it came to pass. The Edmonton Oilers captured their second straight Cup at Northlands Coliseum by thumping the Philadelphia Flyers 8-3 to win the finals four games to one.

"This Cup victory may not have been tougher, but it was more interesting," said coach Glen Sather. "We had our ups and downs this year. But that sort of thing creates an attitude that gets things going. Like we hadn't beaten Philadelphia in eight games coming into the playoffs. But I guess we like a challenge. The players should be proud of themselves."

So dominant was the team's performance in the '85 playoffs that the Oilers virtually started their own section of the Stanley Cup record book, breaking 24 milestones.

Wayne Gretzky had won the Conn Smythe Trophy with records of 30 assists and 47 points. Jari Kurri's 19 goals tied the playoff high set in 1976 by Philadelphia's Reggie Leach. Fuhr's 15 playoff wins were also an NHL best.

The Oilers entered the playoffs facing the Los Angeles Kings, and memories of the

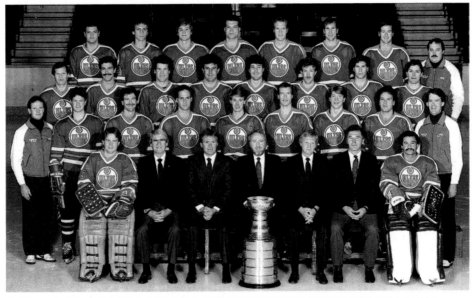

Back Row – Esa Tikkanen, Kevin McClelland, Mike Krushelnyski, Dave Semenko, Randy Gregg, Don Jackson, Kevin Lowe, Lyle Kulchisky
3rd Row – Mark Napier, Charlie Huddy, Dave Hunter, Jaroslav Pouzar, Paul Coffey, Willy Lindstrom, Larry Melnyk, Billy Carroll
2nd Row – Barrie Stafford, Pat Hughes, Glenn Anderson, Lee Fogolin, Wayne Gretzky, Mark Messier, Jari Kurri, Dave Lumley, Peter Millar
Front Row – Andy Moog, John Muckler, Glen Sather, Peter Pocklington, Bruce MacGregor, Ted Green, Grant Fuhr

Kings' five-game opening round upset of Edmonton in 1982 were everywhere.

"There's always the fear of failure," said Sather. "It's scared me all year long. Every time you start the playoffs you have a degree of uncertainty. But it's the challenge that motivates you." Lee Fogolin scored in overtime in the first game and Glenn Anderson in the third game, as the Oilers swept the Kings three straight.

"Maybe now they'll forget what happened in '82," said Gretzky.

With Dale Hawerchuk, the league's third-leading point-getter, out with an injury, the Winnipeg Jets fell four straight to the Oilers in Round 2. Paul Coffey scored the winner in the first game and tied an NHL playoff record with five points in the second. Then Gretzky took over, notching the winner in the third game and tallying seven points in the fourth meeting.

The Oilers captured the first two games of Round 3, 11-2 and 7-3 over the Chicago Blackhawks. But in Chicago, the 'Hawks posted 5-2 and 8-6 wins to even the series. Coffey's ankle was injured by a Pat Hughes' slapshot during the Game 5 warmup, but the defender returned to record an NHL record six points during a 10-5 Oiler win. In Game 6, Kurri potted three goals to join Doug Bentley in 1944 as the only players with back-to-back playoff hat tricks, helping Edmonton to an 8-2 decision.

The Oilers went into the final series against Philadelphia, whom they hadn't beaten in their last 10 meetings, and the Flyers had lost only five times in their last 49 games. In Game 1, Edmonton's offence vanished — Flyers netminder Pelle Lindbergh had to handle only three shots in the last 14 minutes of the first period

and two in the final 16 minutes of the second. In fact, only Willy Lindstrom's goal with three minutes remaining kept them from being blanked for the first time in 134 games, as Philly won 4-1. "I started thinking of all the good things that come from winning," said Oiler defenceman Kevin Lowe. "I didn't want to see it end. I didn't want to see them carrying the Cup instead of us."

Gretzky, who didn't muster a single shot on goal in the opener, scored early in Game 2, as a rookie from Finland named Esa Tikkanen was inserted into the lineup. Lindstrom netted the winner late in the second period as Edmonton won 3-1. Game 3 was a celebration of kids day, as Heather and Kirsten Ostrom, ages 7 and 9, came in from Tacoma, Wash., to sing the national anthems. Gretzky scored twice in the first 75 seconds and again during the 13th minute, then added an assist as the Oilers hung on for a 4-3 win.

The Oilers were spurred by the antics of Flyers defenceman Ed Hospodar, who knocked Kevin McClelland out cold in one game and three of Mark Napier's teeth out in another, which caused Sather to say: "If the league doesn't do something about this guy, we're going to get two boxes for him — one for his head and one for his body." Yet Game 4 was Philly's turn to bolt out of the blocks, with a 3-1 margin only 11 1/2 minutes into the action. But then Fuhr robbed Ron Sutter on a penalty shot, a save that Sather said "ignited us." The Oilers roared back with four power-play goals out of six tries — after going 1-for-16 in the first three games — and won the game 5-3. Philadelphia coach Mike Keenan yanked Lindbergh due to dehydration, saying: "I think this is a good case for having water bottles on top of the net, especially if you go this long in the playoffs. I can't see why a guy playing 60 minutes can't get a drink." Sather's response: "Maybe we'll order a bucket of chicken and a bottle of wine and have a picnic on the nets."

Lindbergh missed Game 5 due to a sore knee, but nobody could stop the Oilers that night, as Coffey and Mark Messier each scored twice. With five minutes to play in the season, Oiler Don Jackson fought Dave Brown and then Brad Marsh, then threw a water bottle at Keenan, who had been jawing profusely with Sather about the fisticuffs. When it was all over, Flyers captain Dave Poulin reflected: "The first game was our style of hockey, the last game was theirs. And there were three in the middle that were a mixture and they came out ahead in all three."

In the Oilers' dressing room, there was talk of a dynasty. "Right now I'm just happy I won this one to give us two," said Coffey. "That's enough for me. I don't want to look into the future. But if I have to, I'm sure we can be a dynasty. We've got good players, good management, good coaching. I'd say we haven't started peaking yet." He was right.

Opposite: This, hoisting the Cup, is a habit Wayne Gretzky would prefer not to break.

Above: For the second straight year, a Stanley Cup parade winds its way through the downtown of Edmonton.

Left: Esa Tikkanen, who made his Oilers' debut in the playoffs, has a Stanley Cup to show for it.

Bottom left: Mark Napier flashes the teeth he has left as he holds the Cup.

Below: Jari Kurri, Gretzky's high-scoring sidekick, savours his second Cup victory.

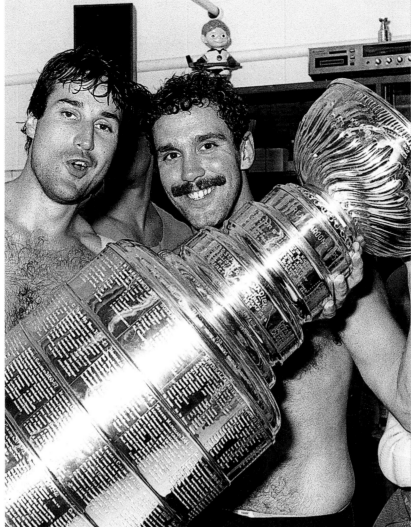

PLAYOFFS

COACH	GP	W	L	GF	GA
Glen Sather	18	15	3	98	57

STANLEY CUP CHAMPIONS, 1st Smythe Division, 2nd Overall. Playoffs: Won Smythe Division Semifinal 3-0 vs Los Angeles, Won Smythe Division Final 4-0 vs Winnipeg, Won Campbell Conference Final 4-2 vs Chicago, Won Stanley Cup Final 4-1 vs Philadelphia.

PLAYOFFS

PLAYER	GP	G	A	PTS	PIM
Wayne Gretzky	18	17	30	47	4
Jari Kurri	18	19	12	31	6
Paul Coffey	18	12	25	37	44
Mike Krushelnyski	18	5	8	13	22
Glenn Anderson	18	10	16	26	38
Mark Napier	18	5	5	10	7
Mark Messier	18	12	13	25	12
Charlie Huddy	18	3	17	20	17
Dave Hunter	18	2	5	7	33
Willy Lindstrom	18	5	1	6	8
Dave Lumley	8	0	0	0	29
Pat Hughes	10	1	1	2	4
Kevin Lowe	16	0	5	5	8
Kevin McClelland	18	1	3	4	75
Randy Gregg	17	0	6	6	12
Don Jackson	9	0	0	0	64
Dave Semenko	14	0	0	0	39
Bill Carroll	9	0	0	0	4
Lee Fogolin	18	3	1	4	16
Jaroslav Pouzar	9	2	1	3	2
Larry Melnyk	12	1	3	4	26
Grant Fuhr	18	0	3	3	2
Andy Moog	2	0	0	0	0
Esa Tikkanen	3	0	0	0	2

PLAYOFFS

GOALTENDER	GP	MIN	GA	GAA.	W-L
Andy Moog	2	20	0	0.00	0-0
Grant Fuhr	18	1064	55	3.10	15-3

1985 PLAYOFFS

DATE	CITY	RESULTS
Apr 10	Edm	Edm 3, LA 2*
Apr 11	Edm	Edm 4, LA 2
Apr 13	LA	Edm 4, LA 3**

* Lee Fogolin scored at 3:01 overtime
** Glenn Anderson scored at 0:46 overtime
(EDM WON SERIES 3-0)

Apr 18	Edm	Edm 4, Win 2
Apr 20	Edm	Edm 5, Win 2
Apr 23	Win	Edm 5, Win 4
Apr 25	Win	Edm 8, Win 3

(EDM WON SERIES 4-0)

May 4	Edm	Edm 11, Chi 2
May 7	Edm	Edm 7, Chi 3
May 9	Chi	Chi 5, Edm 2
May 12	Chi	Chi 8, Edm 6
May 14	Edm	Edm 10, Chi 5
May 16	Chi	Edm 8, Chi 2

(EDM WON SERIES 4-2)

May 21	Phil	Phil 4, Edm 1
May 23	Phil	Edm 3, Phil 1
May 25	Edm	Edm 4, Phil 3
May 28	Edm	Edm 5, Phil 3
May 30	Edm	Edm 8, Phil 3

(EDM WON SERIES 4-1)

Top centre: *That's two and counting, indicates Kevin Lowe (left) with Glen Sather and Lee Fogolin in complete agreement.*

Left: *Fans spill out onto the street in the aftermath of the Oilers' win over the Flyers.*

Bottom centre: *Wayne Gretzky and Bill Carroll seem pretty satisfied with themselves — and well they should be.*

Top right: *Paul Coffey (left) and Charlie Huddy anchored the Oilers' defence.*

Right: *Oiler players show off their new Stanley Cup rings.*

Bottom right: *Willy Lindstrom gets set for a taste of champagne.*

Below: *Muscleman Dave Semenko deserves a swig, too.*

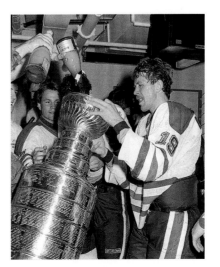

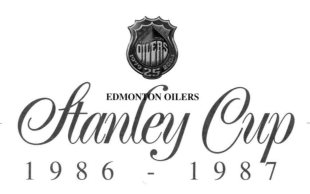

EDMONTON OILERS
Stanley Cup
1986 - 1987

There had been little foreshadowing of the emotion that would pour out when the Edmonton Oilers won the 1987 Stanley Cup, given that it was their third such victory in four years.

Perhaps it was because the Oilers had been slapped in the face by the Calgary Flames the previous year, Edmonton's sense of omnipotence suddenly shaken if not shattered. Perhaps it was because one tends to forget the drama that builds up when the Cup is decided in the seventh game of the final series, something that had not happened in 16 years. Whatever, there was no denying the feeling that flowed when Jari Kurri's goal at 14:59 of the second proved to be the winner, as the Oilers came from behind to beat the Philadelphia Flyers 3-1 in the winner-take-all finale.

For Wayne Gretzky, hoisting the Cup over his head was anything but blase. "A lot of people say they'd like to fly, or skydive," said Gretzky, as champagne dripped from his hair and stung his eyes in the post-game celebrations. "Well, all I can say is the greatest high in my life is when I have that Stanley Cup in my hand and I raise it over my head."

Marty McSorley, a ruffian who would rather chew his arm off than be seen crying in public, had carted the Cup over his head for the first time with remarkable decorum. But then, when he finally saw his father Bill amid the sea of fans in the stands, both bawled like babies. On the ice they hugged, head to head, and they cried. "I wanted to thank him for the support and everything," said the younger McSorley. "I'd said to him earlier, 'We're going to get our name on the Cup.' It was because of the support, whether I was playing ball hockey or in Pittsburgh or in the minors. The first time I ever dreamed of winning a Stanley Cup was when my dad gave me my older brother's skates and said: 'Go to the pond.' Every time you won a game, whether it was in rubber boots or street hockey ... it was the seventh game of the Stanley Cup. And this is it. We just won the seventh game."

It was a scene that touched even referee Dave Newell. "I've been in hockey a long time," said Newell. "But when McSorley found his dad and started hugging him, and the old man's tears were just running down his cheeks ... that's one of the nicest things I've ever seen in the game. He's a helluva kid, that McSorley."

The path to the finals had been fairly easy for the Oilers. They lost the opener of the first round 5-2 to the Los Angeles Kings, but Edmonton won the second game 13-3 and took the best-of-seven series in five games.

The Winnipeg Jets were more burdensome in Round 2, but Glenn Anderson's goal on Daniel Berthiaume just 36 seconds into overtime of the first game for a 3-2 Oilers win may have been the turning point. Edmonton then skated to 5-3, 5-2 and 4-2 wins for a series sweep. "I really think the further we would have gone, the better we would have played," said losing coach Dan Maloney.

"That's the best I've seen the Oilers play in six years," said Winnipeg's Paul MacLean. "I've never seen them play with so much discipline," added Jets captain Dale Hawerchuk.

In Round 3, the Oilers similarly dropped the opener 3-1 to the Detroit Red Wings, but then won four straight, including two by one goal. In the clincher, Mark Messier's two goals stole the show. "It was just too much Messier, as far as I'm concerned," said Detroit coach Jacques Demers. "He's a great, great player."

Oilers coach Glen Sather agreed. "He's got a look of that unbeatable spirit. He's like a galloping thoroughbred, running in the wind. When he gets them in the dressing room, and decides enough is enough ... well, I played against the Rocket (Maurice Richard) once, and he had that look." (When it was pointed out that Richard retired in 1960 and Sather turned pro six years later, Sather harrumphed: "It must have been in my imagination. I did play against the Pocket (Henri Richard) though.")

So the stage was set for a Cup final rematch of the series two years earlier, Oilers against Philadelphia.

"I think it was a big help for them (Flyers), going through it the first time," said Sather. "They can recall what happened and what you need."

Indeed, the Flyers were gritty opponents, with stars like Murray Craven, Ron Sutter, Mark Howe, Peter Zezel and Dave Poulin playing with severe injuries, the latter wearing a flak jacket to protect broken ribs. As usual, the Flyers presented a lightning rod to draw out the fire within the Oilers. In 1985, it had been Ed Hospodar, knocking out three of Mark Napier's teeth with his stick. This time around, it was goalie Ron Hextall, with a Paul Bunyonesque slash that felled Kent Nilsson.

When it was noted that Hextall's off-ice personality wasn't the same as on the ice, he said: "If it were, I think I'd probably be in jail."

The Oilers took a 3-1 lead in the series, including a 3-2 victory in the second game on Jari Kurri's winner at 6:50 of overtime. But Rick Tocchet had the 4-3 winner in Game 5 and J.J. Daigneault the 3-2 winner in Game 6, forcing the drama in Game 7. Craven and Messier scored in the first period for a 1-1 tie, and Kurri put Edmonton ahead in the second. But it wasn't until 17:42 of the final period that Oiler fans exhaled, when Glenn Anderson slipped a 30-foot insurance marker through the legs of Hextall, who would become only the fourth player from the losing team to win the Conn Smythe Trophy as top playoff performer.

"This one's the sweetest because we had to be gutsy," said defenceman Kevin Lowe. "I was thinking this afternoon, if we don't win the Stanley Cup, it'll be devastating. You go through the whole summer banging your head ... 'Why? Why? Why?' Well, we don't have to do that now."

Back Row – Kelly Buchberger, Randy Gregg, Jeff Beukeboom, Steve Smith, Mike Krushelnyski, Craig Muni, Kevin McClelland
3rd Row – Reijo Ruotsalainen, Moe Lemay, Paul Coffey, Glenn Anderson, Marty McSorley, Jaroslav Pouzar, Kent Nilsson, Craig MacTavish, Esa Tikkanen
2nd Row – Lyle Kulchisky, Juergen Merz, Jari Kurri, Charlie Huddy, Mark Messier, Wayne Gretzky, Kevin Lowe, Dave Hunter, Peter Millar, Barrie Stafford
Front Row – Andy Moog, John Muckler, Glen Sather, Peter Pocklington, Bruce MacGregor, Ted Green, Grant Fuhr

Opposite: After a year hiatus, Wayne Gretzky has the privilege of hoisting the Cup for a third time.

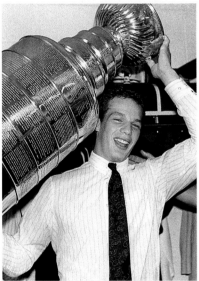

Above: Marty McSorley and his dad Bill share in an emotional moment on the Coliseum ice after the final game.

Left: Future captain Kelly Buchberger played in three playoff games, earning him a chance to hoist Lord Stanley's mug.

Bottom left: Coach/G.M. Glen Sather and his boss, team owner Peter Pocklington, share a swig from the Cup.

Below: Wayne Gretzky and Stanley — a perfect match?

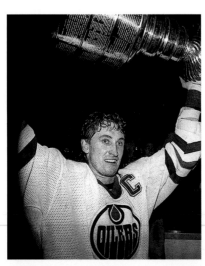

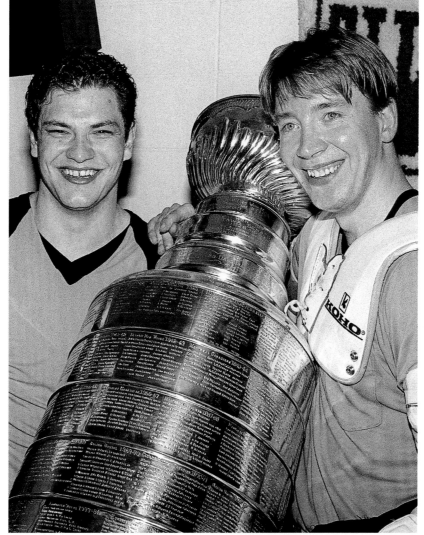

EDMONTON OILERS

Stanley Cup

1986 - 1987

PLAYOFFS RESULTS AND STATISTICS

	PLAYOFFS				
COACH	GP	W	L	GF	GA
Glen Sather	21	16	5	87	57

STANLEY CUP CHAMPIONS, 1st Smythe Division, 1st Overall. Playoffs: Won Smythe Division Semifinal 4-1 vs Los Angeles, Won Smythe Division Final 4-0 vs Winnipeg, Won Campbell Conference Final 4-1 vs Detroit, Won Stanley Cup Final 4-3 vs Philadelphia.

	PLAYOFFS				
PLAYER	GP	G	A	PTS	PIM
Wayne Gretzky	21	5	29	34	6
Jari Kurri	21	15	10	25	20
Mark Messier	21	12	16	28	16
Esa Tikkanen	21	7	2	9	20
Glenn Anderson	21	14	13	27	59
Paul Coffey	17	3	8	11	30
Kent Nilsson	21	6	13	19	6
Mike Krushelnyski	21	3	4	7	18
Craig MacTavish	21	1	9	10	16
Kevin Lowe	21	2	4	6	22
Moe Lemay	9	2	1	3	11
Craig Muni	14	0	2	2	17
Kevin McClelland	21	2	3	5	43
Randy Gregg	18	3	6	9	17
Steve Smith	15	1	3	4	45
Charlie Huddy	21	1	7	8	21
Dave Hunter	21	3	3	6	20
Reijo Ruotsalainen	21	2	5	7	10
Marty McSorley	21	4	3	7	65
Jaroslav Pouzar	5	1	1	2	2
Grant Fuhr	19	0	1	1	0
Andy Moog	2	0	0	0	0
Wayne Van Dorp	3	0	0	0	2
Kelly Buchberger	3	0	1	1	5

	PLAYOFFS					
GOALTENDER	GP	MIN	GA	GAA	W-L	
Grant Fuhr	19	1148	47	2.46	14-5	
Andy Moog	2	120	8	4.00	2-0	

1987 PLAYOFFS

DATE	CITY	RESULTS
Apr 8	Edm	LA 5, Edm 2
Apr 9	Edm	Edm 13, LA 3
Apr 11	LA	Edm 6, LA 5
Apr 12	LA	Edm 6, LA 3
Apr 14	Edm	Edm 5, LA 4

(EDM WON SERIES 4-1)

Apr 21	Edm	Edm 3, Win 2*
Apr 23	Edm	Edm 5, Win 3
Apr 25	Win	Edm 5, Win 2
Apr 27	Win	Edm 4, Win 2

* Glenn Anderson scored at 0:36 overtime
(EDM WON SERIES 4-0)

May 5	Edm	Det 3, Edm 1
May 7	Edm	Edm 4, Det 1
May 9	Det	Edm 2, Det 1
May 11	Det	Edm 3, Det 2
May 13	Edm	Edm 6, Det 3

(EDM WON SERIES 4-1)

May 17	Edm	Edm 4, Phi 2
May 20	Edm	Edm 3, Phi 2*
May 22	Phi	Phi 5, Edm 3
May 24	Phi	Edm 4, Phi 1
May 26	Edm	Phi 4, Edm 3
May 28	Phi	Phi 3, Edm 2
May 31	Edm	Edm 3, Phi 1

* Jari Kurri scored at 6:50 overtime
(EDM WON SERIES 4-3)

Top centre: Sipping champagne from the Stanley Cup for the third time with the Oilers is coach and GM Glen Sather.

Left: Capturing the Cup is especially sweet for newcomer Marty McSorley, who gets a hug from Mark Messier.

Bottom centre: Coaches John Muckler and Sather savour the moment.

Top right: Fantastic Finns — Esa Tikkanen and Jari Kurri had a big hand in the Oilers' third Cup victory.

Right: Defencemen Paul Coffey and Charlie Huddy have done this before.

Bottom right: No one deserves a swig more than Steve Smith, who cost the Oilers a shot at the Cup the year before with a gaffe against the Flames.

Below: Tikkanen quenches his thirst.

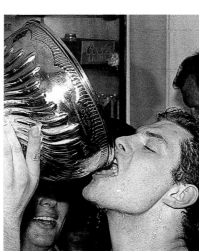

When the year was done and the Edmonton Oilers had scratched their names on the Stanley Cup for the fourth time in five years, coach Glen Sather admitted a distaste for the word dynasty. "It seems like bragging," said Sather, in a rare moment of humility. "When I think of dynasty, I think of the Ming dynasty. Hey, I'm only 39. It makes me feel old. Okay... I'm really 41."

It was the way the Oilers won the Cup that was so convincing, with a 16-2 playoff run. That included a five-game sweep of the Boston Bruins in the final — Game 4 having been declared a draw when the lights went out in the Boston Garden. "I'm not sure what makes a dynasty and what doesn't," said Wayne Gretzky. "A dynasty — that's a matter of individual opinion, really. But let's not kid ourselves ... ."

Kevin Lowe wasn't shy, however, outright trumpeting the team as one of the best ever. "I think we're one Cup away from being recognized as the greatest hockey team of all time," said defenceman Lowe, who spent the last three series of the playoffs with broken ribs.

As they entered the 1987-88 playoffs, finishing third overall in the NHL standings, the Oilers appeared to be on the eve of self-destruction. All season they had been shaken by labour disputes and cabin fever, players like Paul Coffey wanting a change of scenery, even if that meant the Canadian Olympic team.

"Our talent is still there but throughout the season we didn't play to our capability," said Sather. "Talent doesn't disappear, though. How can you say guys who've been talented for eight years suddenly don't have it? It doesn't work that way. It comes down to motivation.

"I feel with the people we have — once things get flowing and we have a real reason to play — we'll do a lot better than we did in the last month and a half."

In the first round, it was Craig Simpson, new to all this hoopla, who scored the first two game-winning goals as the Oilers beat the Winnipeg Jets in five games. "I don't think there was a flaw in the whole team," said Oilers co-coach John Muckler, after the 6-2 series finale. "That's the most complete game we've played in a long time. I'd say we're 30-per-cent stronger now than we were to start the series."

Edmonton eliminated the Calgary Flames four straight in an abbreviated version of The Battle of Alberta during Round 2, but no game was won by more than two goals. The most memorable event was Oiler Marty McSorley spearing the mid-section of Calgary's Mike Bullard during Edmonton's 4-2 win in Game 3, only to plead amnesia afterwards. "I remember the boys coming in and saying I was a bad kid," said McSorley, the day after his spearing major and game misconduct.

The series gave Simpson his first taste of the Oilers' ability to kick their game into overdrive. "It's hard to believe such great players can be that much greater in the playoffs," said Simpson. "Their ability to move it up, step it up so many notches ... I mean, it gives everyone the inspiration to work so much harder."

The Oilers won Round 3 in five games over the Detroit Red Wings, in a great demonstration of a team being able to beat others into submission. Said Sather: "When you're facing guys like Simpson and (Mark) Messier and (Glenn) Anderson and Gretzky and (Jari) Kurri continually — I mean night after night — and you know you've got one chance to stay alive in the playoffs, and if you make one mistake, these guys are going to score. Well, I think it must get intimidating."

In the finals against Boston, the Oilers took the opener 2-1 in a battle of longtime goaltending-mates, Edmonton's Grant Fuhr and former Oiler, now Bruin, Andy Moog. The winning goal was notched by Keith Acton, who had made an impression on Sather seven years earlier, as a Montreal Canadien being shocked by the upstart Oilers in a three-game precursor of Edmonton's future success.

"When I went to shake his hand, he was heartbroken," said Sather. "It showed me how much he cared. He's a tremendous competitor. He's a great character person."

Back Row – Craig Muni, Craig Simpson, Steve Smith, Jeff Beukeboom, Randy Gregg, Mike Krushelnyski, Daryl Reaugh
3rd Row – Dave Hannan, Geoff Courtnall, Craig MacTavish, Marty McSorley, Kevin McClelland, Normand Lacombe, Esa Tikkanen
2nd Row – Lyle Kulchisky, Juergen Merz, Charlie Huddy, Glenn Anderson, Mark Messier, Wayne Gretzky, Kevin Lowe, Jari Kurri, Keith Acton, Peter Millar, Barrie Stafford
Front Row – Bill Ranford, John Muckler, Glen Sather, Peter Pocklington, Bruce MacGregor, Ted Green, Grant Fuhr

Gretzky sported a new spiked hairdo for Game 2, but he was the same magician on the ice, with a goal and two assists in a 4-2 Edmonton win.

"I think we should thank the big fella in Philadelphia (Kjell Samuelsson) who hurt him (Dec. 30)," said Sather. "With the 16 games he missed, he's like a young kid now. He's got lots of energy. He can't be on the ice often enough."

Edmonton took the third game 6-3 and appeared ready to celebrate with a Garden party in Game 4. But with the score tied 3-3 and 3:23 left in the second period, the lights went out in the 60-year-old building, the result of an overload of a 4,000-volt transformer switch. NHL president John Zeigler then invoked NHL by-law No. 27.12, namely that the game would be replayed in its entirety at the end of the series if necessary. Thus the teams returned to Edmonton for Game 4A. That one was close for a while, then Eka Tikkanen's two goals and Gretzky's goal and two assists powered the Oilers to a 6-3 win and a series sweep. A 16-2 playoff record, a fourth Cup win in five years, a Conn Smythe for Gretzky; all by a team that had meandered without inspiration through a season of labour unrest and defections. "You can't predict it, but look at all the adversity we had this year and all the good that came of it," said Muckler. "We probably would not have been where we are if it had never happened."

"That's an important part of bringing young guys into the team and keeping it strong," said Gretzky. "It's what we can pass on to them, that feeling."

Unknown to anyone, Gretzky would never play another game as an Oiler.

Opposite: Wayne Gretzky hands off the Stanley Cup — the Oilers' fourth — to Mark Messier for his victory lap around the Coliseum ice.

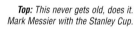

Top: This never gets old, does it. Mark Messier with the Stanley Cup.

Left: Defenceman Steve Smith samples the bubbly.

Bottom left: Wayne Gretzky is awarded the Conn Smythe trophy for the top playoff performer.

Below: Longtime dressing room attendant Joey Moss poses with the Cup.

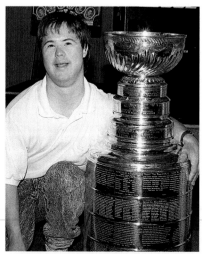

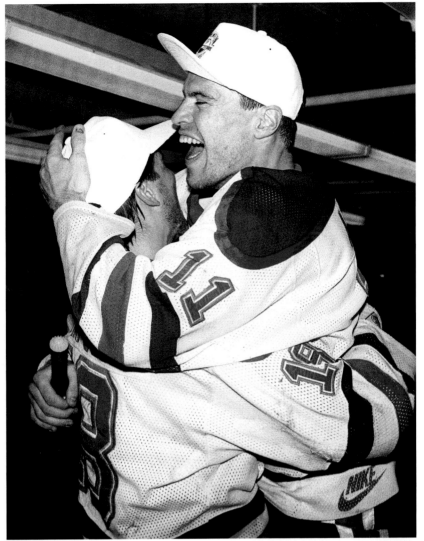

Stanley Cup
1987 - 1988
PLAYOFFS RESULTS AND STATISTICS

PLAYOFFS

COACH	GP	W	L	GF	GA
Glen Sather	18	16	2	84	53

STANLEY CUP CHAMPIONS, 2nd Smyth Division, 3rd Overall. Playoffs: Won Smythe Division Semi-final 4-1 vs Winnipeg, Won Smythe Division Final 4-0 vs Calgary, Won Campbell Conference Final 4-1 vs Detroit, Won Stanley Cup Final 4-0 vs Boston.

PLAYOFFS

PLAYER	GP	G	A	PTS	PIM
Wayne Gretzky	19	12	31	43	16
Mark Messier	19	11	23	34	29
Jari Kurri	19	14	17	31	12
Craig Simpson	19	13	6	19	26
Glenn Anderson	19	9	16	25	49
Esa Tikkanen	19	10	17	27	72
Geoff Courtnall	19	0	3	3	23
Steve Smith	19	1	11	12	55
Mike Krushelnyski	19	4	6	10	12
Charlie Huddy	13	4	5	9	10
Craig MacTavish	19	0	1	1	31
Keith Acton	7	2	0	2	16
Dave Hannan	12	1	1	2	8
Marty McSorley	16	0	3	3	67
Jeff Beukeboom	7	0	0	0	16
Kevin Lowe	19	0	2	2	26
Craig Muni	19	0	4	4	31
Normand Lacombe	19	3	0	3	28
Kevin McClelland	719	2	3	5	68
Grant Fuhr	19	0	1	1	6
Jim Wiemer	2	0	0	0	2
Randy Gregg	19	1	8	9	24

PLAYOFFS

GOALTENDER	GP	MIN	GA	GAA	W-L
Grant Fuhr	19	1136	55	2.90	16-2

1988 PLAYOFFS

DATE	CITY	RESULTS
Apr 6	Edm	Edm 7, Win 4
Apr 7	Edm	Edm 3, Win 2
Apr 9	Win	Win 6, Edm 4
Apr 10	Win	Edm 5, Win 3
Apr 12	Edm	Edm 6, Win 2

(EDM WON SERIES 4-1)

Apr 19	Clgy	Edm 3, Clgy 1
Apr 21	Clgy	Edm 5, Clgy 4*
Apr 23	Edm	Edm 4, Clgy 2
Apr 25	Edm	Edm 6, Clgy 4

* Wayne Gretzky scored at 7:54 of overtime.
(EDM WON SERIES 4-0)

May 3	Edm	Edm 4, Det 1
May 5	Edm	Edm 5, Det 3
May 7	Det	Det 5, Edm 2
May 9	Det	Edm 4, Det 3*
May 11	Edm	Edm 8, Det 4

* Jari Kurri scored at 11:02 of overtime.
(EDM WON SERIES 4-1)

May 18	Edm	Edm 2, Bos 1
May 20	Edm	Edm 4, Bos 2
May 22	Bos	Edm 6, Bos 3
May 24	Bos	Edm 3, Bos 3*
May 26	Edm	Edm 6, Bos 3

* Game cancelled due to power failure.
(EDM WON SERIES 4-0)

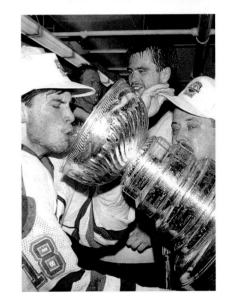

Top Centre: *Wayne Gretzky gathers his teammates for the Stanley Cup presentation.*

Left: *All decked out in black leather, Mark Messier addresses his adoring masses.*

Bottom Centre: *Mark Messier, Wayne Gretzky and Kevin Lowe, who reminds anyone who's watching that this is Cup No. 4 for the Oilers.*

Top Right: *The always sedate Messier gives Craig Simpson a hug. This was Simpson's first Stanley Cup.*

Right: *Simpson tastes the champagne from the Stanley Cup.*

Bottom right: *Messier and Charlie Huddy practise their champagne spraying technique.*
Below: *A relaxed Jari Kurri basks in the glory of Cup No. 4.*

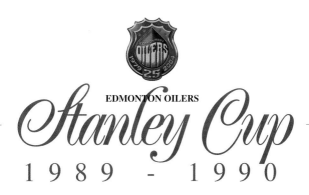

The 1990 format for what had become a tradition, the informal team photo of players and entourage sprawled around the Stanley Cup after the final game, would be five-by-seven. Five Cups in seven years. Five Cups for seven players — Mark Messier, Glenn Anderson, Jari Kurri, Charlie Huddy, Kevin Lowe, Randy Gregg and the injured Grant Fuhr.

When the Edmonton Oilers plucked off their last — and least expected — Stanley Cup with a five-game win over the Boston Bruins, there were two trains of thought as to how it had all come about. There was a Win-It-For-Gretzky faction of players on the team. "Although we won it without Wayne, there's always going to be a large part of him here, as long as I'm here and Mark's here," said Lowe. "He was the leader for all those years and I think he helped us develop into solid NHLers. Hopefully we can lend that leadership to the young players like he did to us."

Then there was a Win-It-For-The-New-Guys faction.

Billy Ranford seized the moment with Fuhr injured, and won the Conn Smythe Trophy as best playoff performer. Petr Klima scored the Game 1 winner at 15:13 of the third overtime period. And The Kid Line of Martin Gelinas, Joe Murphy and Adam Graves were the team's lifeblood, inspiring a lot of much older legs to keep pumping when they ached to rest. "This feels great, it's possibly the nicest of the five," said John Muckler, in his first year as head coach after four years helping Glen Sather. "Coming out of training camp we never expected to be in this position ... but we won again with a great *team* concept. I just can't say enough about Billy in goal, or the kids Gelinas, Murphy and Graves, or the leadership from the guys who've been here so many times."

There had been absolutely no hint of the final outcome when the season started, the second year the team played without Gretzky — traded to Los Angeles before the 1988-89 season. "I don't think anybody thought we had a Stanley Cup team," said Sather, now exclusively a general manager. "I think we had a team that was going to be competitive, but we knew we had to make some changes before we got to that stage."

His search was not just for players with speed, but for players "who can play with the puck at high speed and make plays at high speed and carry the puck in traffic." So the Oilers obtained Graves, Murphy, Klima and Jeff Sharples, who was later exchanged for Reijo Ruotsalainen. "It was a tough trade to make," said Sather. "The guys we got were really looked on as chances by everybody."

By the time the team entered the playoffs, Muckler's concept of "system" had been absorbed by the team. "We still have the big guns in here," said Klima. "But the team was built around Gretzky before. Now it's built around Mess, with everybody having their job to do."

"We do things in fives out on the ice," said Murphy. "We rely on each other. It's a group of guys willing to commit to it."

The Oilers got the playoffs off to an inauspicious start, falling behind the Winnipeg Jets three games to one, but became only the seventh team in NHL history to rebound with three straight wins. They took the seventh game 4-1 at home.

The Oilers then swept the Los Angeles Kings in four straight, including a 7-0 shutout by Ranford in the opener, and a 6-5 overtime winner by Murphy in the fourth game. Then came the Chicago Blackhawks, and Edmonton buckled, falling behind two games to one. But Messier spearheaded a 4-2 win in Chicago during the pivotal fourth game, and the Oilers added two more wins to end the series in six games.

That set up the second Oilers-Bruins Stanley Cup final in three years and, once again, the teams were de-lighted, as it were, playing in Boston Garden. Two years earlier, the lights went out with Game 4 tied 3-3, and the game was wiped out. This time it was during Game 1, in overtime, when the rink darkened at 12:33 a.m. EDT. Almost an hour later, the SOS went out to Klima, whose legs were fresh after spending most of the game on the bench, and he ended the ninth-longest game in NHL history 3-2, after 115 minutes and 13 seconds of overtime. The irony was that Klima had complained about his lack of ice time, issuing a quote that would live for ages: "You need an awful long stick to score from the bench."

Game 2 was all Kurri, who had three goals and two assists in a 7-2 Oilers win, causing Messier to say: "It's probably the best single performance I've ever seen. I mean he was absolutely unbelievable. He forechecked. He backchecked. He set up the goals. He scored the goals." The Bruins came back in Game 3 with rookie John Byce scoring 10 seconds after the opening faceoff, Greg Johnston adding another before the period ended, and then Andy Moog preserving a 2-1 win as the Bruins were outshot 29-22. Anderson and Simpson each had four points in Game 4, but it was Messier's physical determination that won the day during a 5-1 Edmonton victory. Then came Game 5 in Boston. Anderson scored on an end-to-end rush early in the second period and then made a behind-the-back pass to set up Simpson with another goal, as the Oilers skated the Bruins into the ice 4-1.

It was a sweet comeback for Ranford, winning the Conn Smythe Trophy after being a target of great criticism following the 7-5 loss to Winnipeg in the very first playoff game. "I took a lot of flak, but a lot of my teammates came to me and said it was one way for me to get back at everybody who jumped on me," said Ranford. "It was a thrill to get the opportunity to rebound."

The Kid Line combined for 30 points in 22 playoff games. Graves' father, paraded through the victorious dressing room by his son, was asked if he had ever thought Adam would get the family name engraved on the Stanley Cup.

"When he was six years old, no. But when he went to the Edmonton Oilers, yes."

Opposite: There is life after Gretzky after all. Mark Messier lifts the most unlikely one of them all, Edmonton's fifth Stanley Cup.

125

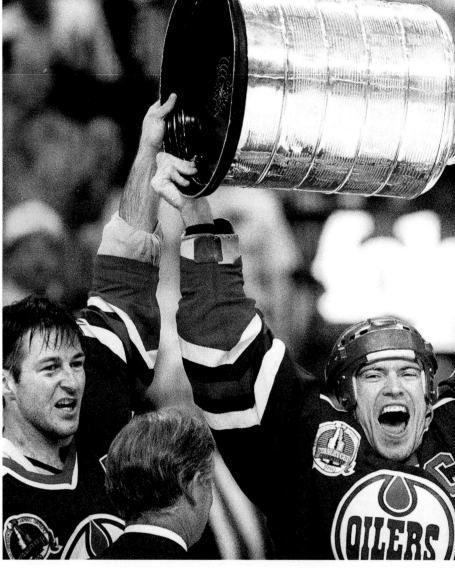

Above: Esa Tikkanen gives captain Mark Messier a champagne shower during a television interview, but Messier doesn't seem to mind one bit.

Left: Messier cavorts with Oiler fans.

Below left: Charlie Huddy and Tikkanen have been through this a few times before, as have many of the Oilers.

Below: Craig Simpson hoists the Cup for the second time in his career. Simpson led the Oilers in playoff goals in 1990 with 16.

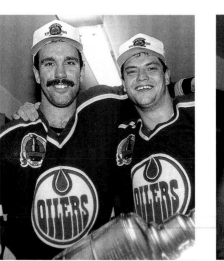

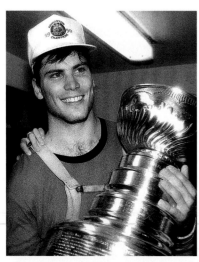

EDMONTON OILERS

Stanley Cup

1989 - 1990

PLAYOFFS RESULTS AND STATISTICS

		PLAYOFFS			
COACH	GP	W	L	GF	GA
John Muckler	22	16	6	93	60

STANLEY CUP CHAMPIONS, 2nd Smyth Division, 5th Overall. Playoffs: Won Smythe Division Semifinal 4-3 vs Winnipeg, Won Smythe Division Final 4-0 vs Los Angeles, Won Campbell Conference Final 4-2 vs Chicago, Won Stanley Cup Final 4-1 vs Boston.

		PLAYOFFS			
PLAYER	GP	G	A	PTS	PIM
Mark Messier	22	9	22	31	20
Jari Kurri	22	10	15	25	18
Glenn Anderson	22	10	12	22	20
Petr Klima (EDM)	21	5	0	5	8
Esa Tikkanen	22	13	11	24	26
Craig Simpson	22	16	15	31	8
Craig MacTavish	22	2	6	8	29
Steve Smith	22	5	10	15	37
Kevin Lowe	20	0	2	2	10
Joe Murphy (EDM)	22	6	8	14	16
Mark Lamb	22	6	11	17	2
Martin Gelinas	20	2	3	5	6
Randy Gregg	20	2	6	8	16
Charlie Huddy	22	0	6	6	10
Adam Graves (EDM)	22	5	6	11	17
Craig Muni	22	0	3	3	16
Geoff Smith	3	0	0	0	0
Reijo Ruotsalainen (EDM)	22	2	11	13	12
Jeff Beukeboom	2	0	0	0	0
Kelly Buchberger	19	0	5	5	13
Dave Brown	3	0	0	0	0
Bill Ranford	22	0	2	2	4
Eldon Reddick	1	0	0	0	0
Anatoli Semenov	2	0	0	0	0

		PLAYOFFS			
GOALTENDER	GP	MIN	GA	GAA.	W-L
Eldon Reddick	1	2	0	0.00	0-0
Bill Ranford	22	1401	59	2.53	16-6

1990 PLAYOFFS

DATE	CITY	RESULTS
Apr 4	Edm	Win 7, Edm 5
Apr 6	Edm	Edm 3, Win 2*
Apr 8	Win	Win 2, Edm 1
Apr 10	Win	Win 4, Edm 3**
Apr 12	Edm	Edm 4, Win 3
Apr 14	Win	Edm 4, Win 3
Apr 16	Edm	Edm 4, Win 1

* Mark Lamb scored at 4:21 of overtime.
** Dave Ellett scored at 21:08 of overtime.
(EDM WON SERIES 4-3)

Apr 18	Edm	Edm 7, LA 0
Apr 20	Edm	Edm 6, LA 1
Apr 22	LA	Edm 5, LA 4
Apr 24	LA	Edm 6, LA 5*

* Joe Murphy scored at 4:42 of overtime.
(EDM WON SERIES 4-0)

May 2	Edm	Edm 5, Chi 2
May 4	Edm	Chi 4, Edm 3
May 6	Chi	Chi 5, Edm 1
May 8	Chi	Edm 4, Chi 2
May 10	Edm	Edm 4, Chi 3
May 12	Chi	Edm 8, Chi 4

(EDM WON SERIES 4-2)

May 15	Bos	Edm 3, Bos 2*
May 18	Bos	Edm 7, Bos 2
May 20	Edm	Bos 2, Edm 1
May 22	Edm	Edm 5, Bos 1
May 24	Bos	Edm 4, Bos 1

* Petr Klima scored at 55:13 of overtime.
(EDM WON SERIES 4-1)

Top Centre: *Mark Messier gives credit to the contributions of the so-called Kid Line — from left, Adam Graves, Joe Murphy and Martin Gelinas.*

Left: *Alternate captains Kevin Lowe and Jari Kurri, along with captain Messier get the first shot at hoisting the Cup.*

Bottom Centre: *Mark Messier lets the fans touch the Stanley Cup.*

Top Right: *The Kid Line — Graves, Murphy and Gelinas, exalt in the Cup victory.*

Right: *Steve Smith, now a leader on the Oilers' defence, couldn't be happier.*

Bottom right: *Lowe, Messier and Kurri wave to fans at Commonwealth Stadium with the Stanley Cup.*

Below: *Goalie Bill Ranford was outstanding in the playoffs, earning him the nod for the Conn Smythe trophy.*

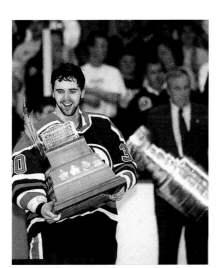

CHAPTER 4

THE LEGEND OF

Wayne Gretzky

Wayne Gretzky

THE MAN

On a January night in 1985, with the Edmonton Oilers on the road in Minneapolis, a reporter knocked on the hotel room door where Wayne Gretzky and Kevin Lowe were fast asleep at about 11 p.m.

The *Edmonton Journal* scribe had been asked to get Gretzky's reaction to a story in which disabled runner Steve Fonyo had called him a wimp.

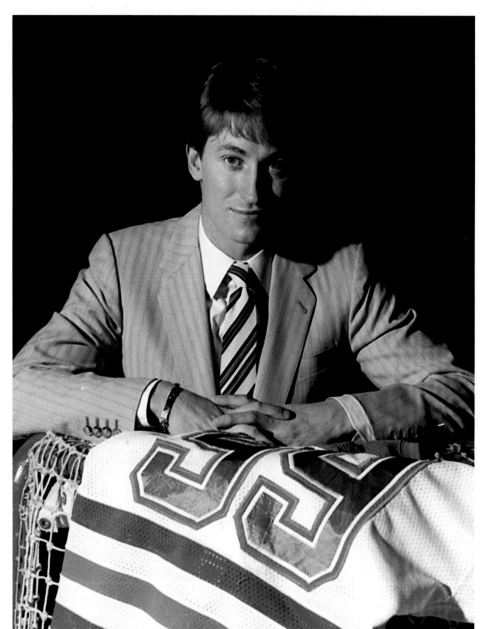

Lowe answered, aroused from a deep sleep in a darkened room. The reporter explained his request and Lowe woke up Gretzky.

Lying on his stomach in his bed, Gretzky propped himself up on his elbows and, despite the cobwebs in his head, he started: "I'm disappointed that it was said, if it was said. But it doesn't affect how I feel about charities, or how I feel about disabled people... ."

After a few more words, the reporter thanked him profusely, and Gretzky fell back onto his stomach, dead asleep.

The anecdote perfectly defines the makeup of Wayne Gretzky. There was this amazing ability to concentrate, an uncanny instinct to say and do the right thing, and a rare sense of being able to handle all the demands on his private life with class.

Some of it was the result of all the attention and expectations that engulfed him from a very tender age.

The first story about Gretzky in a major publication came in the now-defunct *Toronto Telegram*, on Oct. 28, 1971: "There's a little No. 9 in this town who has ambitions of replacing the recently retired Big No. 9 of the Detroit Red Wings, Gordie Howe."

The *Edmonton Journal*'s first story on Gretzky ran in 1972, when he was only 52 inches tall but had scored some 370 goals as a peewee.

It was the beginning of decades of people baiting and badgering him, trying to get him to let down his guard and explode, to expose his human fallibility.

But cracking that Gretzky exterior of propriety would not be easy.

One of the first to try was Dick Beddoes, who wore many hats — one of a journalist, one of a broadcaster, and many of the loud, checkered variety.

In a TV interview between periods of an early Edmonton Oilers game, Beddoes told a pimple-faced Gretzky he never would have been a star in the six-team NHL like Gordie Howe or Bobby Hull.

"You're probably right, Mr. Beddoes," said Gretzky. But he promptly noted that the four-minute mile was now being run in 3:50 and weightlifters were pressing a hundred pounds more than decades earlier. "I guess hockey is the only sport where athletes aren't improving."

In 1982, New York author Stan Fischler wrote: "It is a travesty of hockey history to discuss Gretzky in the same breath as Maurice (The Rocket) Richard, Howie Morenz, Gordie Howe or Jean Beliveau.

"I roar with laughter when I read a Michael Farber in the *Montreal Gazette* eulogize Gretzky at the expense of The Rocket or Howe. Farber and his ilk write in ignorance."

In 1985, Montreal writer Mordecai Richler came to interview Gretzky as he received the Edmonton Sports Reporters' Association award as Athlete of the Year.

In a *New York Times* article, Richler described Gretzky as "a curiously bland 24-year-old in a grey flannel suit."

Gretzky usually chose not to defend himself, knowing it was a no-win situation.

But on occasion he did respond, and brilliantly so.

The night after the Fonyo story came out, the Oilers won a game in the Met Centre at Minneapolis, 5-3 over the North Stars. As Gretzky was coming off the ice, a leather-lunged fan stood over the exit, yelling obscenities at him.

As Gretzky skated towards the exit, he asked the child standing beside the man: "Is he your father?"

The kid nodded.

"Aren't you embarrassed?" asked Gretzky.

The kid nodded again.

The father didn't say another word.

Gretzky absorbed his time in the spotlight without faltering. No drug charges, no drunk driving tickets, no illegitimate children. His most mortal sin was calling the New Jersey Devils a Mickey Mouse operation, after a 13-4 loss to Edmonton, and that came out of feeling for his former teammate Ron Low, who was a goalie with Jersey's sad-sack franchise.

"The only person I have to answer to is myself," said Gretzky, years later. "If I make a comment, as I did about New Jersey, some people thought I was wrong and I thought I was right."

Gretzky's parents, Walter and Phyllis, laid the foundation for his personality, but his role model in hockey was Gordie Howe.

During one of Gretzky's first trips to New York, he ended a morning practice by doing endless interviews, until yet another sportscaster — from a small station — asked for 10 minutes more. Gretzky finally said he didn't have any more time. An Edmonton sportswriter went over to Gretzky and said: "Gordie Howe would have found the time." Gretzky tracked down the sportscaster and talked to him for 30 minutes.

His willingness to accommodate hockey people amazed others.

After a Saturday night game in Detroit, the Oilers were up at 5 a.m. for plane rides to Toronto and then Edmonton. At 8:30 a.m. in the Toronto airport, a gaggle of 50 screaming 12-year-old girls destroyed the morning peace and made drinking a cup of coffee almost impossible for Gretzky.

"I'll sign everything, but no pictures," he pleaded, trying to save his weary eyes from flashing lights.

Mike Krushelnyski, then an Oiler newcomer on a scoring tear, couldn't believe his linemate's patience.

"See, you better slow down or that will happen to you," said Dave Semenko, of the perils of being a scoring sensation. "That's why I stopped."

At a baggage carousel on another trip, Gretzky was besieged by pen-wielding fans. When they departed with their autographs, he looked at his tan raincoat, which was covered in ink marks. "I go through two or three a year," he said of the ruined garment.

He once said he had different types of signatures: one type on items for special people; one on things like lithographs, items going for auctions or charity; one on things handed to him at rinks; and one when he was walking through a throng to the team bus. "Those ones aren't very good. I sometimes can't read them," he said.

On the ice, the wonderment of Gretzky included his innate attention to detail, his ability to accomplish so much while actually touching the puck so little, and his ability to lift others to approach his level.

If the scoreclock started a couple of seconds late while his team was trying to preserve a lead, Gretzky would point it out. And if the opposition had too many men on the ice during a line change, Gretzky's peripheral vision would spot it.

"We didn't need videotape because we had Wayne," said his former coach Glen Sather. "If you asked him who was on the ice, he always knew who they were and where they were."

Attention to detail, it's called.

And unlike other hockey superstars like Bobby Hull and Bobby Orr and Mario Lemieux, who drew your attention by lugging the puck the length of the ice, Gretzky was a give-and-go artist who accomplished magic through sleight of hand. He seldom held the puck more than a few seconds.

In the early years it was the "give" that got him points — 16 seasons he led the National Hockey League in assists. But soon after, there was also the "go" — five times he led the league in goals.

Then there was his effect on others.

As a 19-year-old, he would skate onto the ice at an Oilers practice, move over the opposing blue-line, then drop the puck from his stick back onto his skates and kick it back up to his stick again, freezing the defenceman just long enough to get by. After practice, there would be a half-dozen players staying out on the ice, dropping the puck onto their skates in imitation.

He made a commercial with his brother, tapping the side of the puck to put it on its edge, then flipping it into the air and smacking it like a baseball, all in one smooth motion. Great hand-eye co-ordination.

Guess what players were trying at practice the next day?

The result of those skills and intuition was that while other stars scored their goals from the coveted "slot" area in front of the net, Gretzky orchestrated most of his damage from behind the net, an area that became known as his office. Seeing the flow of play in front allowed him to set up others to score, or to emerge himself from nowhere to pounce on rebounds.

In 1985, David Hemery, who won the 1968 Olympic 400-metre hurdles gold medal, interviewed Gretzky as one of 65 athletes he was talking to in search of the fountain of greatness.

He agreed with former Montreal Canadiens' goalie Ken Dryden that what made Gretzky unique was that his "panic point" was so much later than that of other players.

"While everybody else is running around like they're leaving a burning building, Gretzky is calmly gathering up his possessions," said Dryden.

And when others enjoyed success, Gretzky let them savour it. If he were the story of the game, he would make himself readily available to the media, understanding their deadlines.

But if he had been a bit player in the night's drama and someone else had played the lead, eventually you would realize that Gretzky's delay in surfacing in the post-game dressing room was deliberate. He wanted that day's hero to savour the moment and attention.

He was the consummate professional.

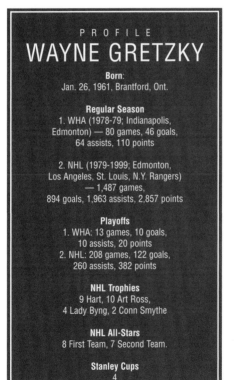

PROFILE
WAYNE GRETZKY

Born:
Jan. 26, 1961, Brantford, Ont.

Regular Season
1. WHA (1978-79; Indianapolis, Edmonton) — 80 games, 46 goals, 64 assists, 110 points

2. NHL (1979-1999; Edmonton, Los Angeles, St. Louis, N.Y. Rangers) — 1,487 games, 894 goals, 1,963 assists, 2,857 points

Playoffs
1. WHA: 13 games, 10 goals, 10 assists, 20 points
2. NHL: 208 games, 122 goals, 260 assists, 382 points

NHL Trophies
9 Hart, 10 Art Ross, 4 Lady Byng, 2 Conn Smythe

NHL All-Stars
8 First Team, 7 Second Team.

Stanley Cups
4

THE RECORDS

▶ *Dec. 30, 1981 — 50 Goals in 39 Games.*

Wayne Gretzky didn't fly his parents to Edmonton for this Oilers game. He planned to bring them in for the next one. After all, he needed five goals to set the record for the fastest 50 goals in NHL history. To do it in 39 games would shatter the 50-in-50 mark set by Rocket Richard in 1944-45 and equalled by the New York Islanders' Mike Bossy in 1980-81.

After a four-game scoring drought, Gretzky had scored in eight straight games, 14 goals in all, including four the game before against Los Angeles. And on this night, 17,490 fans showed up at Northlands Coliseum, unwilling to risk missing him get five more.

Philadelphia Flyers netminder Pete Peeters, an Edmonton resident, was on the bench for an extra player when, with just four seconds remaining in the game, Gretzky slid the puck 20 feet into the empty net for his fifth goal of the night.

Edmonton Journal columnist Terry Jones called it "the greatest hockey game ever played by the greatest player in the history of the game — to break the greatest record ever set in the game."

"Last year, I would have passed on three of the goals I scored on," said Gretzky. But nobody had thoughts of selfishness, just of awe.

"This is absolutely crazy," said Flyers playing coach Bobby Clarke. "At least with (Bobby) Orr, you'd see him wind up in his own end and you could try to set up some kind of defence to stop him. Gretzky just comes out of nowhere ... it's scary."

"I wouldn't have done anything differently on his other goals," said Peeters. "What he did was absolutely amazing."

Thirty minutes after the game, Flyers coach Pat Quinn went into the Oilers' dressing room to personally congratulate Gretzky. "Any superlatives I might offer would be inadequate," said Quinn.

Oilers coach Glen Sather, who mused correctly that Gretzky might score more goals in one season than the 80 Sather had in his career, said: "People are now going to have to re-evaluate their stars of the century. I don't think we've seen the best of Wayne yet."

▶ *Feb. 24, 1982 — Most Goals in a Season.*

One night in 1975, Phil Esposito received a phone call from his father in Sault Ste. Marie, Ont.

"Phil, there's a boy who will break all of your records one day," said the elder Esposito. "He's 14 years old and he's from the Soo. His name is Gretzky ... Wayne Gretzky."

Espo the younger told his father: "Well, that's great, Dad, but he's only 14. Let's wait and see."

Seven years later, on Feb. 24, 1982, Gretzky scored three goals in six minutes late in the game on Buffalo Sabres goalie Don Edwards for 79 on the year, smashing Esposito's NHL single-season record of 76 set in 1970-71.

"I wanted him to get it here, I was tired of following him around," said Esposito, who presented Gretzky with the historic puck in a brief on-ice ceremony at Memorial Auditorium.

"His total intensity and desire for the game outweighs everybody else. On top of that, God gave him an awful lot of talent."

Esposito had scored 76 goals in 78 games, while Gretzky got No. 77 in game 64.

The NHL had told referee Andy Van Hellemond to waive the league rule calling for a delay of game penalty to any team coming over the boards to celebrate a goal.

"I don't think I was nervous before the game," said Gretzky. "I went about my

regular routine. The only thing I felt anxious about was that Phil was here and I wanted to do it so he could get back to work."

After the game, Oilers owner Peter Pocklington said he was running out of things to say about Gretzky. "I'd never have thought I could fall in love with a hockey player," said Pocklington.

▶ *Oct. 5, 1983 - Jan. 27, 1984 — Longest Consecutive Point Scoring Streak.*

It was a streak so strange to hockey, that comparisons were made to Joe DiMaggio's 56-game hitting streak in baseball.

In 1982-83, Gretzky had extended Guy Lafleur's 28-game NHL point-scoring streak, set in 1976-77, by two games.

But what happened in 1983-84 was a saga. For 51 games from the start of the season, Gretzky earned at least one point an outing, running up 61 goals and 153 points.

Finally, on Jan. 28, 1984, his streak was snapped during a 4-2 loss to goalie Markus Mattsson and the Los Angeles Kings at Northlands Coliseum.

"I never dreamed I'd go 51 games," said Gretzky, who had faced 500-1 odds by Las Vegas bookmakers against scoring at least a point each game all season. "I went from 30 to 51 and bettered it by 21. Maybe next year, I'll go from 51 to 72. The thing I'm most glad about is the streak ended at home."

"He has enough pressure being a captain and a leader every game and being expected to score 200 points a year as though it's an ordinary thing," said teammate Mark Messier.

During the 3½-month streak, Gretzky went into the third period without a point eight times, waiting until the last three minutes to get on the board in Long Island on Dec. 13, and scoring into an empty net with two seconds left in

The night was Dec. 30, 1981 — Wayne Gretzky's 39th game of the season. He needed five goals to shatter the record of 50 goals in 50 games set by Maurice Richard and Mike Bossy. Gretzky methodically went to work (opposite page), scoring four goals to get to 49. Then, with just four seconds left in the game, Gretzky put his 50th into an empty net. 50 in 39 — amazing.

Chicago on Jan. 11.

"I feel bad, I was cheering for him too," said Kings interim coach Rogie Vachon after Los Angeles snapped the streak. "Fifty-one games? That's unbelievable."

Instead of using a centre to shadow Gretzky, the Kings used a defensive pairing — Jay Wells and Mark Hardy — to stymie The Great One.

"It's very tough to change lines against him, so I put two defencemen on against him all night and they did a tremendous job," said Vachon.

Gretzky refused to use an injured shoulder — he had been belted Jan. 21 by the Kings' Dave Taylor — as an excuse. "I can still slap the puck because I don't have to move my shoulder, but when I have to pass, it bothers me," said Gretzky. "But I can't make excuses, I'm a pro athlete. They did a great job."

▶ *Mar. 1, 1988 — Most Career Assists.*

Setting records had become so blase for Gretzky that when he set the NHL career mark with 1,050 assists on March 1, 1988, hardly any of the usual suspects were on hand.

NHL president John Ziegler was in meetings and missed the game. Previous record holder Gordie Howe was attending a charity function in Eastern Canada, but sent a taped message. Oilers owner Peter Pocklington was late flying home from Toronto and heard the play on the radio at 40,000 feet. Gretzky's fiance, Janet Jones, had flown to Los Angeles early in the day for a movie audition. Wayne's parents, Walter and Phyllis, were in Brantford, Ont., and phoned to get the satellite co-ordinates to watch the game on TV, but it wasn't televised.

The play was even missed by local broadcaster CFRN radio, which cut away

THE LEGEND OF
Wayne Gretzky

for a commercial after Gretzky had scored 18 seconds earlier and missed the milestone assist.

The play came when he slipped a pass to Jari Kurri, who blasted the puck past Los Angeles Kings' netminder Roland Melanson at 12:44 of the first period. It was Gretzky's 1,050th assist in 681 games over eight seasons, compared to the 1,049 assists in 1,767 games over 26 NHL seasons for Howe.

"When I came into the league, people questioned my consistency," said Gretzky. "I think I showed you can be 170 pounds and under six feet and play in this league. Brains are an important part in the game."

The NHL gave Gretzky a Tiffany-crafted mantle clock and the Oilers gave him a gold hockey stick plus a $50,000 bond payable upon his first child's 21st birthday.

▶ *Oct. 18, 1989 — Most Career Points.*

Howe admitted Gretzky, now with the Los Angeles Kings, had him worried at Northlands Coliseum on this night.

Howe had been following Gretzky around, waiting for the youngster to break his NHL career record of 1,850 points, which Gretzky tied with an assist five minutes into the game. But as public address announcer Mark Lewis announced the "last minute of play in the period" to 17,503 fans, the record hadn't been surpassed.

"He scared the daylights out of me," said Howe. "I told him I only had one suit to wear on record nights. I don't know what I'd have done if we'd had to go back to Los Angeles (tied)."

Then, with 53 seconds left in the game, Gretzky lifted a short backhander over Edmonton goalie Bill Ranford, giving Gretzky 1,851 points in 780 NHL games, eclipsing the mark Howe set in 26 seasons.

Gretzky then added the 5-4 winner for Los Angeles in overtime.

The game stopped when Gretzky broke the record, as a flood of dignitaries poured onto the ice.

NHL president John Ziegler presented him with a silver tea tray with the logos of the 21 NHL teams engraved, plus the following inscription: "Presented to Wayne Gretzky, whose greatness transcends goals and assists and is evidenced by the qualities of character and leadership he has come to symbolize while achieving this memorable record."

Gretzky was in tears as he hugged longtime teammate and friend Mark Messier, who presented him with a hand-crafted, 10-karat-gold bracelet containing diamonds weighing 1.851 carats, representing his point total.

"It was only fitting it happened here," said Gretzky. "I played a lot of years here and won four championships in this building. The fans were a great part of it."

He had been only five years old when he got his first autograph, from Howe. They played together at the 1980 NHL All-Star Game. And now Howe, at age 61, was more than ready to pass the torch to the youngster who idolized him.

"I'd like to say with all honesty, I've been waiting for this for a long time," said Howe. "I thought I knew him, but I've been with him for 10 days and he's grown an inch taller in my eyes.

"I don't know how he does these things so dramatically. I was cheering like hell when the puck went in. There's no sense of loss, I feel more gain than anything.

"I feel proud that Wayne calls me a friend. I said the other day the only tears I'd have would be tears of joy."

▶ *Mar. 23, 1994 — Most Career Goals.*

At 15:32 of the third period at Northlands Coliseum, New York Ranger centre Mark Messier moved in to take a faceoff when the voice of public address

announcer Mark Lewis filled the air.

"Ladies and gentlemen, the Edmonton Oilers would like to congratulate Wayne Gretzky on scoring the 802nd goal of his career."

Messier straightened up and backed away from the linesman. The Coliseum fans stood, issuing a standing ovation for a minute. "Everybody in the building, I know, was feeling a little something right then," said Messier.

Some 2,189 kilometres away, in Inglewood, Calif., Gretzky had just scored for Los Angeles at 14:47 of the second period against the Vancouver Canucks to break Howe's NHL record of 801 career regular season goals.

Gretzky, the trailer on a three-on-two rush against Canucks netminder Kirk McLean, took a pass from longtime Oiler and King teammate Marty McSorley and directed it past an out-of-position McLean.

The game was stopped and league commissioner Gary Bettman presented Gretzky with a book

containing scoresheets from each game Gretzky scored in. "You've always been the Great One," said Bettman. "Tonight you became the greatest."

"It's the greatest game in the world," said Gretzky. Later, he admitted: "There has been a lot of pressure for the last couple of weeks. Everyone was pulling for me. I wanted to make it an important goal, and it tied the game. And Marty got the assist, so it made it better."

Howe, who retired in 1980, scored 801 goals in 1,767 NHL games over 26 seasons. Gretzky set the record in his 1,117th career game over 15 NHL seasons.

It was the 60th record of Gretzky's career and gave him every major offensive record in the NHL, including total points.

Gretzky would retire in 1999, with 894 goals in 20 NHL seasons and 940 goals in 21 seasons in both leagues.

Howe had 801 goals in 26 NHL seasons and 875 during 32 seasons in both leagues.

"I think I showed you can be 170 pounds and under six feet and play in this league. Brains are an important part in this game."

Wayne Gretzky

Gretzky, now a King, comes back home to break Gordie Howe's record for 1,850 career points. Always with a flair for the dramatic, 99 scored the tying goal with 53 seconds left in the game for point 1,851 (opposite page). Then, for good measure, Gretzky scored in overtime to give Los Angeles the win over the Oilers. Howe was on hand, and ex-teammate Mark Messier congratulated him during a ceremony at centre ice.

"I thought I knew him, but I've been with him for 10 days and he's grown an inch taller in my eyes. I don't know how he does these things so dramatically."

Gordie Howe

THE WEDDING

Gretzky's essay on how he spent his 1983 summer vacation included launching a cereal called Pro Stars, playing an underworld thug named Wayne in the soap opera *The Young and The Restless*, and performing a dance number as a guest judge on the syndicated TV show *Dance Fever*.

"It was the most embarrassing 10 seconds of my life," said Gretzky, of his Fred Astaire impression.

But not everything about that show was forgettable. One of the dancers was Janet Jones, from Bridgeton, Mo., near St. Louis.

She would go on to appear in a chorus at Radio City Music Hall, plus act in the movies *Flamingo Kid*, *A Chorus Line*, *American Anthem* and *A League of Their Own*.

The attention led to a semi-nude photo spread in the March 1987 edition of *Playboy* magazine.

Jones was engaged to tennis star Vitas Gerulaitis for two years. And Gretzky had been going steady with Edmonton singer Vicki Moss for some time.

But in the spring of 1987, Gretzky and Jones met again.

"He already had a steady girlfriend, but he liked her (Jones) so much he

wanted to set her up with me," said Kevin Lowe, Gretzky's roommate during their first few years in the NHL.

During the summer of 1987, Gretzky and Jones started dating. On Jan. 11, 1988, he proposed marriage and she accepted. They both turned 27 that month.

On Saturday, July 16, 1988, they were united at St. Joseph's Basilica in Edmonton during a 33-minute ceremony by Rev. Mike McCaffrey, the pastor of St. Joseph's, and Rev. John Munro, a retired minister from an Anglican church in Gretzky's home town of Brantford, Ont.

It was billed as Edmonton's Royal Wedding, the city's very own version of Charles and Diana, and it lived up to the fanfare.

While the Basilica was packed with family, politicians and sports and entertainment celebrities, 5,000 fans and well-wishers sat on lawn chairs and curbs outside.

Members of the Edmonton Symphony Orchestra performed during the ceremony and singer Tim Feehan, an Edmonton native now performing out of Los Angeles, sang *Ode to Joy*.

Wrote the *Edmonton*

Edmonton's 'Royal Wedding' on Saturday, July 16, 1988. Gretzky's bride Janet Jones is led up the aisle at St. Joseph's Basilica on Jasper Avenue in Edmonton.

Journal: "Thousands of rhinestones, pearls and crystals adorned the 10-metre train of her fairy-tale $40,000 gown. The gown, cut almost to the navel in the front, featured leg o' mutton sleeves that came to points on the wrist, a beaded choker-style collar and silk organdie across the bust."

Wayne wore a black tuxedo.

Janet walked down the aisle with her brother, John.

"It's taken two clergy, Wayne and Janet, to bring you close together and God help you if anything tears you apart," said Rev. Munro, during the ceremony.

After the ceremony, the couple's white Rolls-Royce, followed by white Bentleys bearing the wedding party, rolled into Sandy Mactaggart's walled Riverbend residence, where formal wedding photos were taken.

The Westin Hotel was the scene of the reception, as 12 bars awaited the 610 guests.

There were 22 people at the two-tiered head table. Alberta Premier Don Getty sat with Soviet goaltending great Vladislav Tretiak, while Gordie

Howe sat with composer David Foster.

Telegrams were read from Prime Minister Brian Mulroney, rock star Bryan Adams, actor Lee Majors and basketball great Larry Bird.

The 200 wedding gifts filled an entire suite. Tretiak gave a wooden swan covered in gold, noting that swans "stay paired with the same partner for life. If one dies, or is killed, the other will die from despair."

Barry Tomalty, owner of Barry T's nightclub in Edmonton, commissioned Edmonton artist Joan Healey's painting of a young baseball player wearing an Oilers' cap. Oilers owner Peter Pocklington presented the couple with a pair of scooters.

Wayne's gift to Janet was a cream Corniche Rolls-Royce convertible.

Because of their late appearance after the photo shoot, dinner at the Westin was delayed an hour, before skinned capon stuffed with peaches in Madeira cream sauce was served with "Polish overtones" of potato pyrogies and cabbage rolls.

Wayne and Janet Jones Gretzky went on to have four children — Paulina, Trevor, Ty and Tristan.

Introducing, Mr. and Mrs. Wayne Gretzky.

THE TRADE

The rumours had swirled since the summer of 1982, that the New York Rangers had offered $20 million for Wayne Gretzky.

The rumours surfaced so often that an unofficial part of *Edmonton Journal* hockey writer Jim Matheson's job became that of Denials Editor, having to put to rest whatever far-flung tip would be phoned in from whatever bar was still open at the paper's deadline.

On Aug. 4, 1988, the rumour surfaced that Gretzky would be traded to the Los Angeles Kings for Jimmy Carson and Luc Robitaille and $15 million. It was

Then came Aug. 9.

Black Tuesday in Edmonton. Black and silver in Los Angeles. It was all made official by a teary-eyed Gretzky at a Molson House news conference.

"GRETZKY GONE," read *The Journal* the next day, using the largest type size for a headline since the Second World War had ended.

Gretzky, Marty McSorley and Mike Krushelnyski to the Los Angeles Kings for Jimmy Carson, Martin Gelinas and three first-round draft picks. Oh yes, and Pocklington got $15 million US from Kings owner Bruce McNall.

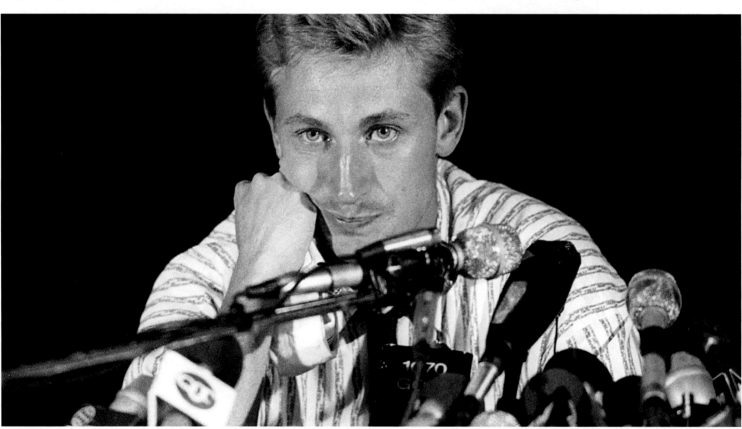

Wayne Gretzky tried to keep his composure during the news conference to announce his trade to Los Angeles, but he broke down. 'I promised Mess I wouldn't do this,' he said, fighting back tears.

also rumoured that Gretzky's wife, Janet Jones, was pregnant and might want to stay in L.A.

Oilers coach Glen Sather told Matheson: "Peter (owner Pocklington) says Wayne still belongs to the Oilers. He says the stories are all BS."

Wrote *Journal* columnist Cam Cole that day: "He (Gretzky) will not just walk away a free agent when his contract expires (in 1992). Pocklington will get something for him before that happens. This is a man who took the ring off his wife's finger to help buy the Oilers in the first place. Believe this: for the right price, anything Peter owns is for sale. Anything. And anybody."

On Aug. 8, a Montreal newspaper reported that Gretzky was being dealt to Los Angeles for $20 million plus Carson and three first-round draft picks. And Charlie Henry, the general manager of the junior team Gretzky owned in Hull, Que., said L.A.'s top draft pick that June, Martin Gelinas, was coming to Edmonton as part of a Gretzky trade. Pocklington told Matheson the stories were "pure speculation."

But before the deal was announced, a subplot took place among the parties involved, concerning the spin to be imparted saying just who wanted this trade. Whomever was perceived as the instigator would face a public relations disaster in Edmonton and likely all of Canada.

"I don't believe in misleading the public," said Pocklington during the news conference, insisting the trade was Gretzky's idea all along.

"I believe he has earned the right to determine his own destiny," said Pocklington. He started another sentence: "When Wayne approached me and asked to be traded to Los Angeles ... ."

Said Gretzky: "I decided that for the benefit of myself, my new wife and our expected child in the new year, it would be beneficial for everyone involved to let me play for the Los Angeles Kings."

But as he continually broke into tears, his words rang hollow.

Reaction to the trade was fast and furious. *The Journal* put out an entire supplement comprised of fans' sentiments and wishes.

Former teammate Paul Coffey said Gretzky had become "just a piece of meat," traded for hard cash. "There's no bloody way he wanted to go there (Los Angeles)."

In Ottawa, New Democrat Member of Parliament Nelson Riis urged the federal government to stop the sale, saying: "Wayne Gretzky is a national symbol, like the beaver."

The media and fans extrapolated Gretzky's explanation, fingering wife Janet as the cause of the trade, likening her role to that of Yoko Ono's in breaking up

In his book *Fun While it Lasted*, released in 2003, McNall explained that it was Gretzky's agent Michael Barnett who encouraged him to pursue Gretzky and in 1988 became a central figure in the deal.

McNall quotes Pocklington as saying of Gretzky: "His ego is out of control. He thinks that he's bigger than the game itself." McNall then had Wayne listen on a speaker phone as Pocklington denounced Janet for inflating Gretzky's ego and Walter Gretzky for being a pain. At that point, Wayne decided he did want to go to another team.

Gretzky sits in the background while his coach, Glen Sather, addresses the media. Oilers owner Peter Pocklington (left) and Kings owner Bruce McNall (back right) listen intently on the grave occasion.

the Beatles. The next day, Jones said the whole trade had been Pocklington's idea.

Pocklington got in more hot water, telling Matheson: "Wayne has an ego the size of Manhattan. He's a great actor. I thought he pulled it off beautifully when he showed how upset he was."

The following day, Pocklington tried to defuse a ticking bomb, saying his comments had been misconstrued, that his saying a person has an ego the size of Manhattan "is a complimentary thing." He added that the story "has caused more grief and heartache than you can imagine."

For his part, Gretzky went on Jay Leno's TV show and said that anyone who had seen his appearance in the TV soap opera *The Young And The Restless* knew he couldn't act.

Pocklington's final demands were that Gretzky call him and ask to be formally traded, and that the announcement be delayed for two weeks while Pocklington continued selling Oiler season tickets.

Then the deal was done.

Gretzky saw it as an opportunity and challenge to sell hockey to Los Angeles, the West Coast, and even all of the United States.

Ten years after the trade, having since gone from Los Angeles to the St. Louis Blues and then the New York Rangers, Gretzky looked back on that fateful Aug. 9.

"Hockey in 1988 was still hockey, but when I got traded it became big business," he said. "My going changed the way we look at hockey forever."

"I decided that for the benefit of myself, my new wife and our expected child in the new year,

it would be beneficial for everyone involved to let me play for the Los Angeles Kings."

THE END

The signs had been there, namely the extra equipment that had been lugged around. He had hauled bundles of sticks to various NHL rinks, giving them to former teammates and even members of the media. And he began wearing different jerseys each period.

Then, during the final week of the 1998-99 NHL season, Gretzky made it official, the final regular season game on Sunday would be the 1,487th and last of his 20-year NHL career.

"It's over. I'm officially retiring," he told a news conference. "Of course I'm sad. I haven't just played pro for the last 21 years (including one in the World Hockey Association). I've played this game for 35 years, since I was only three. But I'm done. I've known absolutely for the last five days that I was making the right decision."

After the final game, his skates would go to the Hockey Hall of Fame in Toronto. Gretzky would catch up with them on Nov. 22, when he would be inducted into the Hall, the minimum five-year retirement period being waived.

"It's funny, when I was a kid, 12 or 13 years old, I used to sneak down to the Hall. There was a fellow who would let me in and I used to just stand there for hours and stare."

Now, he has his own wing at the Hall, holding the NHL records for career goals (894), assists (1,963) and points (2,857), plus the single-season records for goals (92), assists (163) and points (215).

"No person in sports has done as much for their game as Wayne has," said NHL commissioner Gary Bettman. "He's the consummate ambassador."

"No longer will arenas be energized by his presence and electrified by his performance," said Prime Minister Jean Chretien. "No longer will we be able to thrill in anticipation of his next wondrous play."

"I don't think there was an awful lot that you could teach somebody like Wayne,"

Wayne Gretzky's famous No. 99 is raised to the Skyreach Centre rafters in October of 1999.

said former Oilers coach and general manager Glen Sather. "He has ability, he has a tremendous mind and sees the ice differently than the rest of us."

"Let's get this in perspective, it's a hockey player who is retiring, we're not curing cancer here," said former Oiler owner Peter Pocklington.

His former roommate and teammate Kevin Lowe attributed Gretzky's greatness to "his consummate love of the game."

"He was so consistent," said Lowe. "Some guys they get seven points one game and disappear the next. He'd be out there trying to get eight."

Gretzky returned to Edmonton in October of 1999 for a civic ceremony, to watch his No. 99 retired to the rafters at Skyreach Centre, and to unveil the renaming of Capilano Freeway as Wayne Gretzky Drive.

At the City Hall gathering, fans chanted: "One more year. One more year. One more year."

"This is one of the highlights of my life," said fan Rita Kelly, 67, who kept her winter parka open despite the freezing cold, to show off her Oilers jersey.

Fans then chanted: "Wayne for Mayor, Wayne for Mayor."

"Hey, he's got my vote," said Edmonton Mayor Bill Smith.

And later, when Gretzky's number was retired at Skyreach, he said: "It's fitting that the banner is parked behind the net where I spent so much time." He became misty-eyed as his buddy Joey Moss, the Oilers' long-time dressing room attendant, came out to give him a replica banner.

"I couldn't help smiling throughout the ceremony," said Gretzky. "I had nothing but good things to think about. The only time I got emotional was when the banner went up. I felt the saddest then. And yes, the most proud.

"I knew for sure it was over."

CHAPTER 5

The Supporting Cast

Kevin Lowe

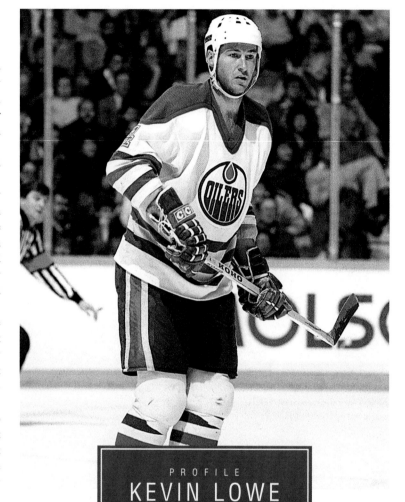

Clifford Lowe would take his three-year-old son Kevin to the hockey rink beside the Lowe Dairy in Lachute, Que., where Kevin would skate for hours before being given an ice cream cone and a colouring book.

Then, when Kevin was 13, Clifford died.

"I remember finding Kevin the day we buried our dad," said brother Ken Lowe, now a trainer with the Edmonton Oilers. "I remember him throwing his gloves against the wall and saying he didn't want to play hockey anymore. It was the first time he'd shown any emotion."

But in 1979, when the Oilers made their first-ever selection and the 21st pick overall in the National Hockey League entry draft, they chose the first English-speaking captain of the Quebec Remparts, Kevin Lowe.

"I had him rated anywhere from 10 to 13 overall," said Oilers chief scout Barry Fraser, expressing surprise that Lowe was still available so late. "He was the best player available, a steady defenceman who's good offensively, with a penchant for being tough."

"I think I got a signing bonus of $25,000 and I think my first year I was playing for $50,000 or $70,000," said Lowe.

"That seemed like a ton of money to me."

Thus began a relationship between Lowe and the Oilers that would span more than three decades.

He was the first Oiler NHL draft pick, scored the team's first NHL goal and eventually became the team's captain. After his playing days, Lowe began a rapid ascent up the ladder, spending a year as an assistant coach, a year as head coach, and then became general manager when Glen Sather left, who had been the Oilers' general manager for almost all of the team's NHL existence.

As a player, Lowe was a stalwart on defence, the stay-at-home guy who took care of business in his own end with great efficiency.

"The way I played my whole career was on heart and instinct," Lowe said.

Off the ice, he was perceived as the team's unofficial spokesman — analytical and articulate. Nobody was

surprised when he once said that he would likely go into politics after hockey.

But when it came time to retire, after stints with the Oilers from 1979-92 and 1996-98, he turned to coaching.

His favourite memory as a player was an easy choice.

"No doubt, May 19, 1984," he said, citing the date of the Oilers' first Stanley Cup win. "When Lummer (Dave Lumley) scored, it was pretty unbelievable. I guess I've always been one of those it's-never-over-'til-it's-over players. Even though we were up 4-2 with a minute left and about to win the Stanley Cup, I didn't feel like we actually had it. When the puck went in, that moment is forever in my mind."

Longtime Oilers coach and general manager Glen Sather summed up Lowe in one sentence: "He was the consummate team guy who helped keep everything together when things got a little bit scratchy."

Indeed, when Steve Smith banked the puck off Grant Fuhr into the Oilers net to end the team's drive for a third straight Stanley Cup in 1986, it was Lowe who stormed into the dressing room, trying to keep the media from conducting a Smithsonian inquisition.

In 1999, Lowe became the Oilers' seventh head coach in franchise history.

"You not only come to the rink to work for three hours a day," he said. "Hockey has got to be on their minds 24 hours a day. Having said that, you have to have the right feel for it. You can't be overly consumed by it — we all have a life and families — and I'm conscious of that. But you have to be thinking and preparing for that next game."

When he was offered the job of general manager, he carefully analyzed the free-agent situation and the team budget.

The day he accepted, a throng of people descended upon the Lowe house, causing his three-year-old daughter Darby to ask if the excitement meant they were all going to a movie.

"I told her, 'No dear, but where we're going will be just as exciting.' "

PROFILE

KEVIN LOWE

Born
April 15, 1959, Lachute, Que.

Player
Regular Season
NHL (1979-1998, Edmonton, N.Y. Rangers):
1,254 games, 84 goals,
347 assists, 431 points
Playoffs
NHL: 214 games, 10 goals,
48 assists, 58 points
Stanley Cups
6
Coach
Regular Season
NHL (1999-2000, Edmonton):
82 games, 32 wins,
34 losses, 16 ties
General Manager
NHL (2000-2003, Edmonton)

Paul Coffey

At the ripe old age of 24, Paul Coffey couldn't help but laugh at his days as a National Hockey League neophyte.

"I remember the cocktail party they were having for Peter Gzowski (author of the 1981 Oiler chronicle *The Game of Our Lives*)," said Coffey. "Invitations were from 5 to 7. I got there at exactly five minutes to seven. Heck, I was so worried about being on time, I sat in my car for 10 minutes before going in. Boy, was I stupid."

Then there was the time he drove into radio play-by-play broadcaster Rod Phillips' truck in the parking lot. "It was snowing and the lot was slippery," said Coffey. "I started spinning and all I could see was the long Lincoln Gretz (Wayne Gretzky) was driving in those days and Rod's truck. I thought quick and decided it was better to hit Rod than Wayne."

If Coffey did some growing up off the ice during his seven seasons with the Edmonton Oilers, he did just as much on it. The Oilers' first-round pick in the 1980 entry draft, the defenceman stepped straight into the team lineup, but his forays into the offensive zone often left him down and out of the play. "The worst smell at the Coliseum was burnt Coffey," said a radio colour-commentator.

But what soon emerged was a tremendously gifted offensive player, a marvellous skating ability that could lift a crowd off its feet from the time he hit his own blue-line until he blasted his feared slapshot into the opposition net.

"He's outstanding, a great player. His skating ability and shot are something else," said Bobby Orr, who would surrender more than one of his NHL records to Coffey.

"He's like a fourth forward on our team and, if we get caught, he can be four strides behind somebody and catch up," said Gretzky. "He's amazing."

"(Mark) Messier chews up the ice, skates through it," said Minnesota North Stars general manager Lou Nanne. "Coffey seems to float on top of it."

The reason may have been the way his skates were sharpened. "I don't have that much of a hollow in the blade," Coffey explained. "It seems like I can glide. It's really hard to get used to the feel they give you ... it feels like you've got no edge, but it makes me feel really light-footed."

> "I don't have much of a hollow in the blade. It seems like I can glide. It's really hard to get used to the feel they give you ... it feels like you've got no edge, but it makes me feel really light-footed."
>
> *Paul Coffey*

PROFILE

PAUL COFFEY

Born
June 1, 1961, Weston, Ont.

Regular Season
NHL (1980-2001; Edmonton, Pittsburgh, Los Angeles, Detroit, Hartford, Philadelphia, Chicago, Carolina, Boston):
1,409 games, 396 goals,
1,135 assists, 1,531 points

Playoffs
NHL: 194 games, 59 goals,
137 assists, 196 points

NHL Trophies
3 James Norris

NHL All-Stars
4 First Team, 4 Second Team.

Stanley Cups
4

In 1984-85, Coffey set NHL records for most goals, assists and points in a playoff season for defencemen. Then during 1985-86, he set defenceman records with 48 goals in the season, plus six assists and eight points in a game. Three times he won the Norris Trophy as the league's top defenceman.

If there was any one play that turned his image and confidence around, it came in the 1984 Canada Cup. During the semifinals against the Soviet Union, he broke up a two-on-one rush, raced up ice and ripped a shot that Mike Bossy deflected in for the winning goal.

But coach Glen Sather's constant prodding of Coffey to be more motivated finally wore him down, and by 1987 he was asking to be traded. Sather finally obliged in late November, sending him to the Pittsburgh Penguins.

"Going into this thing, I was hoping either to be going back to the Oilers or, if traded, that both teams made out," said Coffey. "I just hope it works out for both clubs."

In early 2003, after retiring following more than 20 NHL seasons, Coffey was brought in by Gretzky, the managing partner of the Phoenix Coyotes, to improve the team's power play. Seems like Coffey made the right choice when he decided to miss the big Gretzky Lincoln all those years back.

Glenn Anderson

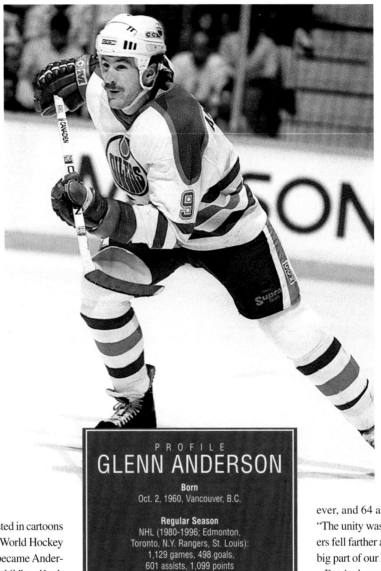

"Sure I'm different. Why would you want to be the same as everybody else? It's just that I'm willing to take the risk and put myself on the edge."

There is a defining picture of Glenn Anderson after the Edmonton Oilers won the 1982-83 Clarence Campbell Conference title.

Wearing the lid of the Campbell Bowl on his head and a huge grin under a walrus moustache, Anderson resembled a Roman centurian who had just conquered the world.

His image was that of the free spirit, never bothered by anything, never worried about what the next day would bring.

"There is a serious side to me but life is too short to be really serious," he said in a 1990 interview. "Timing is everything but I don't stay within the dots; I go outside the dots.

"Sure I'm different. Why would you want to be the same as everybody else? It's just that I'm willing to take the risk and put myself on the edge. My style of hockey shows it too. I'm willing to take a chance to see what will happen."

His style was described as kamikaze. And with it came a tremendous ability to skate. It was a scary combination — taking huge risks at top speed, pressing the envelope, as the fighter pilots say.

Anderson grew up in Vancouver, interested in cartoons on TV. Then Don Berry, who had won a World Hockey championship with the Penticton Vees, became Anderson's coach and made hockey fun. Glenn's childhood buddies included Berry's son Doug, later a centre with the World Hockey Association Oilers, and Mike Fox, who now calls himself Michael J. Fox.

After being sick for four straight days the first time he went on the fishing boat his father Magnus owned, Glenn decided hockey suited him better. He advanced from the University of Denver to Canada's Olympic team in 1980.

"From the time I was growing up, I always had a dream that I won a medal playing for Canada at the Olympics," said Anderson. "When that dream didn't come true at the 1980 Winter Olympics in Lake Placid, I cried big time."

As the speedy sidekick to the thundering Mark Messier, Anderson scored 54 goals twice for the Oilers, in 1982-83 and 1985-86. He made four straight All-Star Game appearances.

Then disaster struck. Twice.

Anderson's best friend George Varvis died after collapsing in Anderson's swimming pool.

PROFILE
GLENN ANDERSON

Born
Oct. 2, 1960, Vancouver, B.C.

Regular Season
NHL (1980-1996; Edmonton,
Toronto, N.Y. Rangers, St. Louis):
1,129 games, 498 goals,
601 assists, 1,099 points

Playoffs
NHL: 225 games, 93 goals,
121 assists, 214 points.

Stanley Cups
6

Then Wayne Gretzky was traded from the Oilers.

"It was a year of devastation," said Anderson. "I went through a lot of turmoil. George's death hit me in my heart and in my soul. Then Wayne got traded. I couldn't understand how anyone could trade someone we were so close to. It was like another death."

Anderson's production in the 1988-89 season fell to 16 goals, his fewest ever, and 64 assists, the fewest since his rookie year. "The unity wasn't there. Some guys came together; others fell farther apart. We had lost the heart and soul and a big part of our hockey team."

But Anderson picked himself up by the bootstraps at the 1989 world championship, with his parents and brother in attendance. He won a fifth Stanley Cup with the Oilers in 1990, then was traded with Grant Fuhr to the Toronto Maple Leafs in 1991, and won a sixth Cup with the New York Rangers in 1994.

Later that year, he tried to fulfil his original dream by joining the Canadian national team. And in 1996, he wanted to play for the Vancouver Canucks in front of his parents, but general manager Glen Sather brought him back to the Oilers instead. "This team doesn't have much experience and winning is a learned thing," said an exasperated Anderson. He was soon off to the St. Louis Blues and retired that season.

When Sather left the Oilers in 2000, he reflected on the stars of Edmonton's glory years. "There was a real caring, sincere attitude about all those guys," said Sather. "Even a guy like Glenn Anderson, who had this reputation as lackadaisical ... as a space cadet, he wasn't like that all the time. He was a solid guy. I liked him."

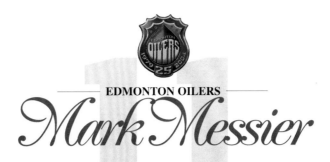

Mark Messier

His fantasy was to be Mick Jagger, belting out *Jumpin' Jack Flash*, jolted by the electricity from tens of thousands of fans. But Mark Messier would have to become a "gas, gas, gas" through hockey.

The bloodlines were there. His father Doug had been a rock solid defenceman with the minor-pro Edmonton Flyers and Portland Buckeroos of the Western Hockey League.

"He survived on a lot of guts and determination," said Mark. "He knew better than anybody what it took to win."

And Mark's older brother Paul led the Spruce Grove Mets, coached by father Doug, to the 1975 Centennial Cup as Canada's Tier II junior hockey champs.

Two years later, Mark made the same junior team, still coached by his father, at age 15.

"Yeah, I wanted to take after Paul," said Mark. "He's a heck of a hockey player — but I wanted to make it for myself, too."

As a 17-year-old, he started the 1978-79 season with his dad's team, making $7 for a win, $4 for a tie and $2 for a loss. But he soon jumped to the NHL rival World Hockey Association, playing five games with the Indianapolis Racers and 47 for the Cincinnati Stingers.

The Edmonton Oilers chose him second, 48th overall, in the 1979 NHL entry draft, but Messier balked at coming to camp, wanting a four-year contract at $50,000 a season, plus a bonus. It was a gutsy move for a fellow who had scored one goal in 52 games the previous year.

But he eventually signed and played with the Oilers that year. But not all went smoothly. During the season, he went to the wrong airport and missed a team flight, prompting coach Glen Sather to send him a new ticket — to the minor league Houston Apollos for four games.

The Oilers squeaked into the playoffs in the team's first year in the NHL, but when they lost the first playoff round to Philadelphia, the Flyers' Bill Barber said: "That Messier. Well, he convinced me he's going to turn out to be just super."

Two years later, in 1981-82, Messier hit the 50-goal plateau.

Off the ice, there were fines for refusing a breathalyser and failing to leave identification at the scene of an accident.

On the ice, he was accused of being undisciplined. Most memorable was an

"There's only a certain amount of room on the ice and everybody has to have a little respect in order to get the room they want."

elbow that nearly took off the head of Soviet Vladimir Kovin during the 1984 Canada Cup.

Naturally, TV analyst Don Cherry was impressed, saying: "The Russians were never the same."

Messier won the Conn Smythe Trophy as best playoff performer in 1984 when the Oilers won their first of five Stanley Cups.

"I can't ever see Mark getting out of hockey, whether he is coaching or playing until he is 40," said his girlfriend Cathy Day in 1986. "It's his love."

During the summer of 1990, Messier celebrated a fifth Stanley Cup with the Oilers and the Hart Trophy as the league's most valuable player.

"There's only a certain amount of room on the ice and everybody has to have a little respect in order to get the room they want," said Messier. "I just like to get the job done when it counts."

As team captain he would speak at length about teammates, but it was almost impossible to get him to talk about himself. "It's important to make sure there is no animosity or disharmony or cliques among the players. When you're winning, none of that comes out into the forefront, but when you're losing, it all comes out."

In 1991, Messier went to the New York Rangers, saying: "I had a fantastic 12 years in Edmonton but I'm looking forward to the new challenge ahead of me."

When he hit 1,000 career points that year, he said: "Two thousand, why not?" adding that he wanted to play until he was 40.

Another Hart Trophy came his way in 1992, and another Stanley Cup in 1994. Messier, 42, entered the 2003-04 season with 1,804 points.

PROFILE
MARK MESSIER

Born
Jan. 18, 1961, Edmonton, Alta.

Regular Season
1. WHA (1978-79; Indianapolis, Cincinnati): 52 games, 1 goal, 10 assists, 11 points
2. NHL (1979-2003; Edmonton, N.Y. Rangers, Vancouver): 1,680 games, 676 goals, 1,168 assists, 1,844 points

Playoffs
NHL: 236 games, 109 goals, 186 assists, 295 points

NHL Trophies
2 Hart, 1 Conn Smythe

NHL All-Stars
4 First Team, 1 Second Team

Stanley Cups
6

Jari Kurri

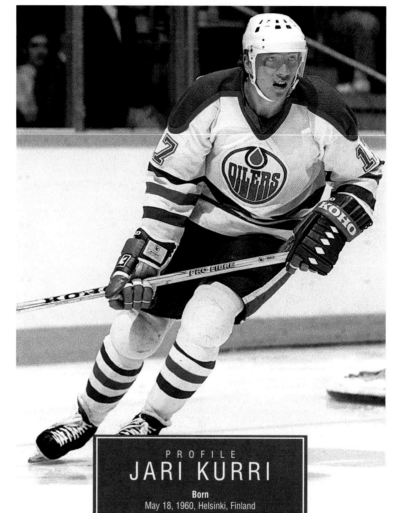

He learned to speak English as a 20-year-old by watching endless episodes of *Happy Days* on TV in an apartment with teammate Paul Coffey.

But before too long, Jari Kurri had introduced a term of his own to the hockey vernacular.

The one-timer. Blasting the puck on the fly without stopping to control the pass.

Kurri and Coffey and Wayne Gretzky on the power play became the stuff of legends.

"I'd hate to tell (Paul Coffey), but I was never looking for him," said Gretzky. "I was always looking for Jari for the one-timer."

"On those two-on-ones with Wayne, you knew the pass was going to Jari, but you couldn't defend against it," said former Winnipeg Jets coach Barry Long. "It was always a completed play. When he got it away, it almost never went off the glass. He never wasted any shots, they were always on the net."

"We used to practise those religiously for 20 minutes every single day," said Gretzky.

> *"On those two-on-ones with Wayne, you knew the pass was going to Jari, but you couldn't defend against it.*
>
> *Barry Long*

When Glen Sather went about building the Edmonton Oilers, he modelled the team after the Winnipeg Jets, who had surrounded scoring star Bobby Hull with speedy playmakers from Europe, namely Ulf Nilsson, Kent Nilsson and Anders Hedberg.

With that in mind during the 1980 NHL entry draft, Sather got Kurri, who had been playing hockey since age seven in Helsinki, Finland, to play along Wayne Gretzky's right side.

There were adjustments, coming to the NHL.

PROFILE
JARI KURRI

Born
May 18, 1960, Helsinki, Finland

Regular Season
NHL (1980-1998; Edmonton, Los Angeles, N.Y. Rangers, Anaheim, Colorado):
1,251 games, 601 goals, 797 assists, 1,398 points

Playoffs
NHL: 200 games, 106 gaols, 127 assists, 233 points

NHL Trophies
1 Lady Byng

NHL All-Stars
2 First Team, 3 Second Team

Stanley Cups
5

"The boards," said Kurri. "I had to learn to use the boards. The rinks are smaller. And you have to keep your mind on shooting all the time."

But Kurri didn't think it was enough to just be Gretzky's setup man. Before the 1982-83 season, Gretzky asked if he was going for a 50-goal season, and Kurri said no, because he was a two-way player.

"He was maybe the most unselfish player I've every played with," said Gretzky.

However, they clicked together too well for Kurri to be harnessed. He scored 52 goals in 1983-84 and hit 71 in 1984-85. Yet he was as soft-spoken and low key as they come.

Kurri spent 10 years with the Oilers and 15 in the NHL.

"He was a pioneer who became a leader," said Sather. "He had a certain grace that only the great players possess."

In the fall of 2001, Kurri entered the Hockey Hall of Fame and his No. 17 was retired at Skyreach Centre.

> *"I'd hate to tell (Paul Coffey), but I was never looking for him. I was always looking for Jari for the one-timer."*
>
> *Wayne Gretzky*

"This is a very emotional night for me," said Kurri, who returned with his 16-year-old twin sons, Ville and Joonas, the godsons of Gretzky. "This rink, this city, having my number up beside Wayne Gretzky and Al Hamilton ... it's amazing.

"I want to thank all my old teammates out here with me, and (Oiler coaches) Craig MacTavish and Charlie Huddy, who I played with on the Stanley Cup teams. And the fans ... they gave me so much support. I always felt appreciated."

His banner rose at Skyreach to flutter to the right of Gretzky's banner.

Just like he had been on the ice, Gretzky's right-hand man.

EDMONTON OILERS

Grant Fuhr

The morning after Grant Fuhr had flummoxed the New York Islanders 1-0 in the opening game of the 1984 Stanley Cup finals, a New York writer sought out Fuhr's meaning of life.

"When there were seven seconds left, you looked at the clock. What was on your mind?" asked the scribe.

"I wanted to know how much time was left," said the Edmonton Oilers goalie.

Fuhr later laughed at any suggestion that he was a complex man who kept his feelings behind his mask. "I don't worry about anything," he said. "As you get old you start to worry. I'll be young for a long time yet. When you do worry a lot, it's time to get out."

Fuhr was a direct contrast to Glenn Hall, who was famed for getting so worked up before games that be vomited. Ironically, as Fuhr grew up in Spruce Grove, it was Hall from nearby Stony Plain who was his inspiration. "He gave me the push to become a goalie," said Fuhr.

Fuhr's simplistic approach to the game was exemplified one year when he and a friend drove 30 hours from Los Angeles, arriving in Edmonton the night before Oilers training camp started. He hadn't been on a sheet of ice for four months, since the Oilers' last playoff game. Then he put on new skates, took his factory-new pads and gloves out of their plastic bags, and started stopping shots.

"Unbelievable," said Ron Low, an assistant coach at the time. "Couldn't get anything by him."

Fuhr, who's black, was adopted by white parents when he was 17 days old. Once cut by the Sherwood Park Crusaders Tier II junior team, he was the Oilers' first-round selection in the 1981 entry draft.

"Are you sure we need another goalie with our first pick?" coach Glen Sather asked his chief scout, Barry Fraser. "We've got Andy Moog — he just beat the (Montreal) Canadiens in the playoffs."

But Fraser was adamant about the 18-year-old Fuhr: "He's the best pro prospect since Bernie Parent."

Fuhr piled up a 23-game unbeaten streak in his rookie season and made the second NHL all-star team.

"The NHL isn't much different from junior, except we travel first class," he

said, at age 19, after meeting U.S. President Ronald Reagan at the White House.

But he arrived at his second Oilers training camp 20 pounds overweight, and during a January night in 1983 he called the Edmonton fans "a bunch of jerks." Days later he was sent to the Oilers' farm team in Moncton to collect himself.

He won the Vezina Trophy as the league's top netminder in 1988.

One summer he announced his retirement on a golf cart, then came out of retirement, then fired his agent Rich Winters — all because the league nixed a $500,000 offer he got from Pepsi to wear the name on his goal pads.

In September of 1991, he was suspended by NHL president John Ziegler for substance abuse, namely cocaine, and missed the first 59 games of the season.

He went to the Toronto Maple Leafs the next year, shared the Jennings Trophy for best goals-against average with Buffalo in 1994, and retired in 2000.

> *"I don't worry about anything. As you get older, you start to worry. I'll be young for a long time yet. When you do worry a lot, it's time to get out."*
>
> *Grant Fuhr*

"The thing that made Grant so great was you never knew what style he was playing," said Low, himself a former Oiler goalie.

"One night he'd be out 15 feet in front of the net challenging the shooter, the next he'd be standing on his goal line."

In 2003, Fuhr was selected to the Hockey Hall of Fame, and his No. 31 would be retired at Skyreach Centre.

"I couldn't ask for a better job than playing hockey," he said.

PROFILE
GRANT FUHR

Born
Sept. 29, 1962, Spruce Grove, Alberta

Regular Season
NHL (1981-2000; Edmonton, Toronto, Buffalo, Los Angeles, St. Louis, Calgary): 868 games, 403 wins, 295 losses, 114 ties, 25 shutouts, 3.38 goals-against average

Playoffs
NHL: 150 games, 92 wins, 50 losses, 6 shutouts, 2.92 goals against

NHL Trophies
1 Vezina, 1 Jennings

NHL All-Stars
1 First Team, 1 Second Team

Stanley Cups
5

Glen Sather

He has been described as obnoxious and arrogant. A cut on his lip from his early playing days has ironed what looks like a permanent smirk on his face.

But it was all part of a persona Glen Sather would use with great aplomb in dealing with players, executives and the media. He managed by control, usually through fear and intimidation. And the result — after 25 years as a player, coach and general manager of the Edmonton Oilers dating back to 1976 — was membership in the Hockey Hall of Fame.

A graduate of the junior Edmonton Oil Kings, Sather managed a mere 80 goals in 10 NHL seasons with six different teams, and in 1976 left the Minnesota North Stars to become captain of the World Hockey Association Edmonton Oilers. On Jan. 27, 1977, he became the head coach.

"It didn't look like we were going to make the playoffs, so Bep (coach Guidolin) bailed out. He gave me a choice. He said I could either sit in the stands or coach."

"I'd spent 10 years running hockey schools so I had some experience in coaching, but I wouldn't say I have the personality that makes me appealing," he said in 1984. "I'm described as being caustic, that I irritate people. I've always been that kind of person who will take abuse and fight back, just a lot of times I don't win friends. But all through my (playing) career if a big guy was bothering me I wasn't going to let him get away with it. I'd fight him. That's just the way I am."

Sather always surmised that had he would wind up a businessman. Early on he owned two restaurants and a number of rental units in Banff.

But coaching did offer one lure. "It was a challenge, and how many things are there in the world that are? Today, it's triathlons and climbing mountains. Coaching beats 9 to 5 everyday. It's interesting, different."

As general manager, he prevented the Oiler teams of the 1980s — filled with gifted individuals — from self-destructing by stepping on landmines that were their egos. He negotiated contracts with players offering bonus clauses for team achievements, like conference titles, rather

than individual milestones.

As the Oilers had continually finished near the top in the standings, he realized he would no longer be able to build through late-round picks in the entry draft — where the top choices can be a crapshoot and the bottom ones certainly are.

His new philosophy was to build through trades, acquiring an undervalued commodity, but one that was somewhat of a known quantity.

He also stayed behind the Oilers bench through the 1988-89 season, then handed the coaching chores to John Muckler, so he could concentrate on the general manager duties.

"It's not an easy job," said Sather, of coaching. "A lot of nights you go home and go to bed at 2 in the morning. At 2:30 you're up, then again at 3, and 3:30, then 4."

Sather proved in 1990 that you could still win the Stanley Cup without a huge payroll. But that came to a crashing halt later that year, when the St. Louis Blues signed Scott Stevens as a free agent for $5.1 million over four years, a 325-per-cent raise over his previous annual salary of $300,000.

Sather's long-standing campaign to keep player salaries affordable to small market teams had fallen on deaf ears.

Inducted into the Hockey Hall of Fame in 1997, Sather hung on as Oilers general manager through the 1999-2000 season. But with his friend Peter Pocklington no longer owning the team, other challenges beckoned, and Sather went to the New York Rangers.

"It wasn't work coaching those guys, it was fun," he said, of players like Wayne Gretzky and Mark Messier and Kevin Lowe. "To be around Wayne and Mark and Kevin and the rest of those players, to see them grow up, was special."

He said beating the Montreal Canadiens in the 1981 playoffs had been the stepping stone for the team.

"The players were so eager to try new things. We started the motion and free-flow game, but I'm not going to take credit. The ideas I got came from going to Finland in the WHA and watching a bunch of peewees practise in Turku."

His Oiler legacy: five Stanley Cups.

PROFILE
GLEN SATHER

Born
Sept. 2, 1943, High River, Alta.

Player

Regular Season

1. NHL (1966-1976; Boston, Pittsburgh, N.Y. Rangers, St. Louis, Montreal, Minnesota) : 658 games, 80 goals, 113 asists, 193 points

2. WHA (1976-77; Edmonton): 81 games, 19 goals, 34 assists, 53 points

Playoffs

1. NHL: 72 games, 1 goal, 5 assists, 6 points

2. WHA: 5 games, 1 goal, 1 assist, 2 points

Coach

Regular Season

1. WHA (1977-1979, Edmonton): 178 games, 95 wins, 76 losses, 7 ties

2. NHL (1979-1989, 1993-94, Edmonton; 2003, N.Y. Rangers): 870 games, 475 wins, 281 losses, 113 ties, 4 Stanley Cups

General Manager

NHL (1980-2000, Edmonton; 2000-2003, N.Y. Rangers)

EDMONTON OILERS

Peter Pocklington

As a child, Peter Pocklington sold his Christmas gifts to raise cash.

As an adult, he sold his wife's 12-carat diamond ring, a Renoir painting, took over a $1.4-million bank loan and tossed in another million dollars for operational expenses to purchase the Edmonton Oilers hockey club, with a partner, from Nelson Skalbania in 1976.

"A pretty good deal. Yeah, I'd say so," said Pocklington in 1997, who had long since bought the franchise outright for $6.5 million.

He arrived in Edmonton from Ontario in 1971 and purchased a Ford dealership. "It was the West," Pocklington said. "You didn't have to have a school tie. I didn't think there was much establishment here to stop a young guy from getting on in life."

He soon owned the Drillers soccer club, the Oilers and the Trappers baseball club.

But it was his 1978 acquisition of Wayne Gretzky from Skalbania's Indianapolis Racers that got the Oilers into the National Hockey League in 1979 and propelled Pocklington into the international spotlight.

While Gretzky was leading the Oilers to four of their five Stanley Cups, Pocklington was golfing with "my pal Gerry Ford," the former president of the United States.

Of course fame came with a price tag — in 1982 he was held hostage for 11 hours after a botched kidnapping attempt on his wife Eva.

But in 1983, he was back in the spotlight, running unsuccessfully for the leadership of the federal Progressive Conservatives.

The Oilers won their first Stanley Cup in 1984, in their fifth season of NHL operation, just as Pocklington had predicted to broadcaster Dick Beddoes on national TV. "I'm just totally excited," said Pocklington after the win. "I've got to say this is the biggest high I've had in my 42 years — that, and meeting my second wife."

As he and Eva were bathed in dressing room champagne, he denied reports he was having financial problems and would sell the Oilers to the highest bidder.

"Of course there's a general depression in Alberta, but this helps the people here feel better and it sure helps me feel better."

Two years later, in 1986, came a six-month strike at his Gainers meatpacking plant. And two years after that, in 1988, came a much larger public outcry over his shocking sale of Gretzky to the Los Angeles Kings.

In a 1994 deal with the City of Edmonton and Northlands by which Pocklington agreed to keep the team in Edmonton until at least 2004, his Coliseum Management Inc. took control of the Coliseum. He filled it promoting a Luciano Pavarotti concert.

But Coliseum income wasn't enough to solve his financial woes. In late 1997, Alberta Treasury Branches took control of the Oilers as payment towards Pocklington's debt, and the next spring the team was sold to the Edmonton Oilers Investors Group.

In 2000, Pocklington left Edmonton to spend his time in Toronto and Indian Wells, Calif.

"A lot of people don't like what I do or say, but I have to look at the results," said Pocklington.

"You've got five Stanley Cups, the PCL (Pacific Coast League) championships, a Driller championship years ago. We've had more speakers in this city in 20 years — some of the things other people don't do."

In 2002, he acquired controlling interest in Golfgear International Inc, a small company that makes golfing equipment.

> "A lot of people don't like what I do or say, but I have to look at the results. You've got five Stanley Cups, the PCL championships, a Driller championship years ago."

PROFILE
PETER POCKLINGTON

Born
1941, Regina, Sask.
1971
Arrives in Edmonton and buys a Ford dealership
1976
With a partner, buys the Edmonton Oilers of the World Hockey Association
1978
As sole owner of the Oilers, acquires Wayne Gretzky
1979
Oilers join NHL
1982
Held at gunpoint for 11 hours after a botched attempt to kidnap his wife Eva
1983
Runs unsuccessfully for leadership of the federal Progressive Conservatives
1986
Violent, six-month strike at Pocklington-owned Gainers
1988
Sells Gretzky to Los Angeles for $18 million
1998
Oilers are sold to local ownership group for $70 million US
2000
Leaves Edmonton, takes up residence in Toronto and California

EDMONTON OILERS
1979-2003
ALL-TIME OILERS

As part of the celebration of 25 years in the National Hockey League, the Edmonton Oilers joined with the *Edmonton Journal* to let fans select the All-Time Oiler teams over the Internet.

Lists were generated by *Journal* writer Jim Matheson, a member of the Hockey Hall of Fame, and fans also had the opportunity of writing in additional selections.

Nearly 11,000 votes were received.

Not surprisingly, the overall top vote-getter was Wayne Gretzky, with 9,183 votes, roughly 84 per cent of all votes for centres. The rest of the first team was also definitive: Grant Fuhr in goal, 7,797 votes; Paul Coffey, 8,591, and current general manager Kevin Lowe, 7,109, on defence; plus Jari Kurri, 8,997, and Glenn Anderson, 4,185, as the wingers.

Glen Sather was selected the coach, with 7,544 votes.

Named to the second team were goalie Bill Ranford, 1,081 votes, defencemen Eric Brewer, 985, and Charlie Huddy, 908; centreman Mark Messier, 1,023; plus wingers Ryan Smyth, 3,226, and Esa Tikkanen, 1,387. The team is coached by current Oiler head coach Craig MacTavish, with 1,529 votes.

Of interest were the top two vote-getters among write-in candidates. Al Hamilton, the first Oiler to have his number retired after playing most of his time with the team in the World Hockey Association, attracted 56 votes.

And, presumably in the vacuuming category, longtime dressing room attendant Joey Moss garnered 47 votes.

KEVIN LOWE
FIRST TEAM: DEFENCE
NUMBER OF VOTES:
7,109

GRANT FUHR
FIRST TEAM: GOALIE
NUMBER OF VOTES:
7,797

PAUL COFFEY
FIRST TEAM: DEFENCE
NUMBER OF VOTES:
8,591

JARI KURRI
FIRST TEAM: WINGER
NUMBER OF VOTES:
8,997

WAYNE GRETZKY
FIRST TEAM: CENTRE
NUMBER OF VOTES:
9,183

GLENN ANDERSON
FIRST TEAM: WINGER
NUMBER OF VOTES:
4,185

ESA TIKKANEN
SECOND TEAM: WINGER
NUMBER OF VOTES:
1,387

MARK MESSIER
SECOND TEAM: CENTRE
NUMBER OF VOTES:
1,023

RYAN SMYTH
SECOND TEAM: WINGER
NUMBER OF VOTES:
3,226

CHARLIE HUDDY
SECOND TEAM: DEFENCE
NUMBER OF VOTES:
908

BILL RANFORD
SECOND TEAM: GOAL
NUMBER OF VOTES:
1,081

ERIC BREWER
SECOND TEAM: DEFENCE
NUMBER OF VOTES:
985

Appendices

1972-1996
Primary Logo

1978-1979
Primary Logo

1996-2003
Primary Logo

EVOLUTION OF THE OILERS JERSEY

When the Edmonton Oilers wanted to tinker with their sweater design in 1996, there was good reason why the National Hockey League insisted on some loyalty to the original version of the jersey.

The franchise, unlike many newer NHL teams, actually has some tradition, with five Stanley Cup championships.

The name itself has been around Alberta sporting circles for some time.

The Leduc Oilers baseball and hockey teams — the latter with an oil derrick crest — were born shortly after Leduc No. 1 oil well blew in 1947. The Edmonton Oil Kings first played for the Memorial Cup, emblematic of Canadian junior hockey supremacy, in 1954. The Edmonton Oilers baseball team, a semi-pro squad of American and Canadian college players, existed in the early 1960s.

And on Nov. 1, 1971, Bill Hunter registered the Edmonton Oil Kings as a fran-

chise in the upstart World Hockey Association, a league he helped create. But when the Calgary Broncs failed to put up a $100,000 bond to be part of the league, Hunter changed his team's name to Alberta Oilers — with thoughts of playing some games in Calgary during the inaugural 1972-73 WHA season. The next season, with the franchise firmly ensconced in Edmonton, the team was renamed the Edmonton Oilers.

"I chose Oilers because of the area," wrote Hunter, in his 2000 autobiography *Wild Bill*. "Many Edmontonians earned their living directly or indirectly from the oil patch: on the rigs, in refinery row or out in one of the industrial parks. A local artist drew the familiar oil-drop logo, and I designed the uniforms and chose the colours. The colours were part of a larger idea."

Hunter met with Charlie Hay, head of Gulf Western oil company, and showed

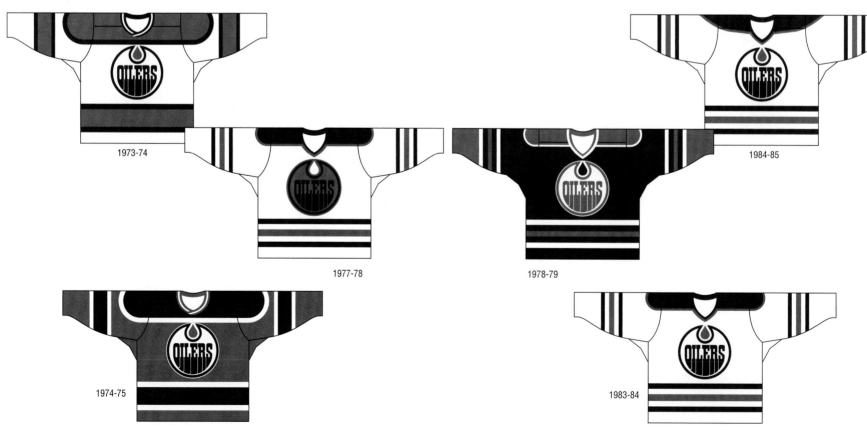

1973-74

1977-78

1974-75

1984-85

1978-79

1983-84

1996-2003
Secondary Logo

2001-2003
Third Jersey Crest

2001-2003
Third Jersey Shoulder Patch

how the Oilers' logo complimented the Gulf Western logo. By using Gulf's orange and blue colours, Hunter suggested the logo would be subliminal advertising for the company. Hunter and Gulf shook hands on a $10-million sponsorship agreement. But the Gulf board of directors said Imperial Oil was already identified with hockey through its sponsorship of *Hockey Night in Canada* and squashed the deal. Hunter was stuck with the name, the colours and the crest.

During the outrageous 1970s, the Oilers' WHA colour combinations switched often. Sometimes the sweaters were predominantly orange, sometimes mostly blue. The crest sometimes had orange lettering with a blue oil drop, other times a blue crest on an orange background.

In 1996, after 17 years, came the first major makeover. Copper and red trim replaced the old orange. And the blue, predominant especially on the road uniform, was much darker.

That came despite a study by Buffalo psychologist Alan Reifman and colleague Neil McGillicuddy, which showed that teams with black or near-black uniforms get penalized more. One theory was that dark uniforms are more visible to referees — a reverse stealth effect — while another was that players played more aggressively wearing black. The Oilers also came out with a secondary logo, a roughneck yanking on a hockey stick.

By 2001, after other NHL teams found that creating a third jersey was a marketing bonanza, the Oilers decided to follow suit. Calgary-born Todd McFarlane, creator of SPAWN comics and a member of the Edmonton Oilers Investors Group, joined with Brent Ashe to design Edmonton's third jersey.

The sweater features a new silver alternate logo resembling a blazing missile. Rivets mark the 10 captains in the team's NHL history and skate blades represent the five Stanley Cups, centred around the traditional oil drop, now turned over and coloured blue.

Wrote *The Journal*'s fashion critic Jean Fraser: "The lace-up retro detail, silver-navy colour mix and hip-hop sensibility mark it a winner from a fashion point of view."

The Oilers' sweater became the fastest-selling third jersey in NHL history.

In 2003-2004, NHL teams will go back to the future, wearing their dark jerseys at home and whites on the road, breaking a 23-year tradition.

1987-88

1996-97

1999-2000

2001-2002
Alternate Jersey

1989-90

2000-2001

EDMONTON OILERS STATS AND FACTS

Edmonton Oilers Award Winners 1979-80 to 2002-03

ZANE FELDMAN TROPHY (MVP)
1979-80	Blair MacDonald	1992-93	Bill Ranford
1980-81	Wayne Gretzky	1993-94	Bill Ranford
1981-82	Wayne Gretzky	1994-95	Jason Arnott
1982-83	Wayne Gretzky	1995-96	Doug Weight
1983-84	Wayne Gretzky	1996-97	Curtis Joseph
1984-85	Wayne Gretzky	1997-98	Doug Weight
1985-86	Wayne Gretzky	1998-99	Bill Guerin
1986-87	Wayne Gretzky	1999-00	Tommy Salo
1987-88	Wayne Gretzky	2000-01	Tommy Salo
1988-89	Jari Kurri	2001-02	Tommy Salo
1989-90	Mark Messier	2002-03	Tommy Salo &
1990-91	Bill Ranford		Todd Marchant
1991-92	Bill Ranford		

TOP FIRST YEAR OILER
1979-80	Dave Lumley	1992-93	Shayne Corson
1980-81	Glenn Anderson	1993-94	Jason Arnott
1981-82	Grant Fuhr	1994-95	Todd Marchant
1982-83	Randy Gregg	1995-96	Curtis Joseph
1983-84	Mark Messier*	1996-97	Mike Grier
1984-85	Mike Krushelnyski	1997-98	Roman Hamrlik
1985-86	Craig MacTavish	1998-99	Tom Poti
1986-87	Craig Muni	1999-00	Jim Dowd
1987-88	Craig Simpson	2000-01	No winner announced
1988-89	Jimmy Carson	2001-02	No winner announced
1989-90	Geoff Smith	2002-03	Ales Hemsky
1990-91	Anatoli Semenov	*Presented to the top playoff	
1991-92	Vincent Damphousse	performer 1983-84 only.	

UNSUNG HERO
1987-88	Charlie Huddy	1995-96	Zdeno Ciger
1988-89	Charlie Huddy	1996-97	Doug Weight
1989-90	Bill Ranford	1997-98	Dean McAmmond
1990-91	Petr Klima	1998-99	Mike Grier
1991-92	Joe Murphy	1999-00	Ethan Moreau
1992-93	Craig MacTavish	2000-01	No winner announced
1993-94	Shayne Corson	2001-02	Steve Staios
1994-95	David Oliver	2002-03	Ethan Moreau

COMMUNITY SERVICE AWARD
1987-88	Mike Krushelnyski	1995-96	Luke Richardson
1988-89	Kevin Lowe	1996-97	Jason Arnott
1989-90	Craig Simpson	1997-98	Todd Marchant
1990-91	Craig Simpson	1998-99	Pat Falloon
1991-92	Kevin Lowe	1999-00	Todd Marchant
1992-93	Craig Simpson	2000-01	No winner announced
1993-94	Kelly Buchberger	2001-02	Georges Laraque
1994-95	Bill Ranford	2002-03	Georges Laraque

DEFENCEMAN OF THE YEAR
1979-80	Doug Hicks	1991-92	Norm Maciver
1980-81	Lee Fogolin	1992-93	Luke Richardson
1981-82	Kevin Lowe	1993-94	Igor Kravchuk
1982-83	Charlie Huddy	1994-95	Luke Richardson
1983-84	Paul Coffey	1995-96	Bryan Marchment
1984-85	Paul Coffey	1996-97	Bryan Marchment
1985-86	Paul Coffey	1997-98	Boris Mironov
1986-87	Kevin Lowe	1998-99	Roman Hamrlik
1987-88	Kevin Lowe	1999-00	Jason Smith
1988-89	Charlie Huddy	2000-01	Jason Smith
1989-90	Craig Muni	2001-02	Janne Niinimaa
1990-91	Steve Smith	2002-03	Steve Staios

TOP DEFENSIVE FORWARD
1987-88	Craig MacTavish	1995-96	Kelly Buchberger
1988-89	Esa Tikkanen	1996-97	Kelly Buchberger
1989-90	Craig MacTavish	1997-98	Mats Lindgren
1990-91	Craig MacTavish	1998-99	Todd Marchant
1991-92	Craig MacTavish	1999-00	Mike Grier
1992-93	Kelly Buchberger	2000-01	Todd Marchant
1993-94	Kelly Buchberger	2001-02	Todd Marchant
1994-95	Kelly Buchberger	2002-03	Todd Marchant

MOST POPULAR PLAYER
1987-88	Wayne Gretzky	1995-96	Doug Weight
1988-89	Mark Messier	1996-97	Curtis Joseph
1989-90	Mark Messier	1997-98	Curtis Joseph
1990-91	Mark Messier	1998-99	Doug Weight
1991-92	Kelly Buchberger	1999-00	Georges Laraque
1992-93	Kelly Buchberger	2000-01	Doug Weight
1993-94	Shayne Corson	2001-02	Mike Comrie
1994-95	Kirk Maltby	2002-03	Ryan Smyth

Edmonton Oilers All-Star Selections

1980
SECOND TEAM
Wayne Gretzky, Centre

1981
FIRST TEAM
Wayne Gretzky, Centre

1982
FIRST TEAM
Wayne Gretzky, Centre
Mark Messier, Left Wing
SECOND TEAM
Grant Fuhr, Goal
Paul Coffey, Defence

1983
FIRST TEAM
Wayne Gretzky, Centre
Mark Messier, Left Wing
SECOND TEAM
Paul Coffey, Defence

1984
FIRST TEAM
Wayne Gretzky, Centre
SECOND TEAM
Mark Messier, Left Wing
Jari Kurri, Right Wing
Paul Coffey, Defence

1987
FIRST TEAM
Wayne Gretzky, Centre
Jari Kurri, Right Wing

1985
FIRST TEAM
Wayne Gretzky, Centre
Jari Kurri, Right Wing
Paul Coffey, Defence

1986
FIRST TEAM
Wayne Gretzky, Centre
Paul Coffey, Defence
SECOND TEAM
Jari Kurri, Right Wing

1988
FIRST TEAM
Grant Fuhr, Goal
SECOND TEAM
Wayne Gretzky, Centre

1989
SECOND TEAM
Jari Kurri, Right Wing

1990
FIRST TEAM
Mark Messier, Centre

Edmonton Oilers in the NHL All-Star Game

1979-80 (Detroit): Wayne Gretzky (F), Blair MacDonald (F); Total – 2

1980-81 (Los Angeles): Wayne Gretzky (F); Total – 1

1981-82 (Washington): Paul Coffey (D), Grant Fuhr (G), Wayne Gretzky (F), Mark Messier (F); Total – 4

1982-83 (NY Islanders): Paul Coffey (D), Wayne Gretzky (F), Jari Kurri (F), Mark Messier (F); Total – 4

1983-84 (New Jersey): Glenn Anderson (F), Paul Coffey (D), Grant Fuhr (G), Wayne Gretzky (F), Jari Kurri (F)*, Kevin Lowe (D), Mark Messier (F), Glen Sather (Coach); Total – 8

1984-85 (Calgary): Glenn Anderson (F), Paul Coffey (D), Grant Fuhr (G), Wayne Gretzky (F), Mike Krushelnyski (F), Jari Kurri (F), Kevin Lowe (D), Andy Moog (G), Glen Sather (Coach); Total – 9

1985-86 (Hartford): Glenn Anderson (F), Paul Coffey (D), Lee Fogolin (D), Grant Fuhr (G), Wayne Gretzky (F), Jari Kurri (F), Kevin Lowe (D), Mark Messier (F), Andy Moog (G), Glen Sather (Coach); Total – 10

1986-87 (Rendez-Vous '87): Glenn Anderson (F), Paul Coffey (D)*, Grant Fuhr (G), Wayne Gretzky (F), Jari Kurri (F), Mark Messier (F), Esa Tikkanen (F); Total – 7

1987-88 (St. Louis): Glenn Anderson (F), Grant Fuhr (G), Wayne Gretzky (F), Jari Kurri (F), Kevin Lowe (D), Mark Messier (F), Glen Sather (Coach); Total – 7

1988-89 (Edmonton): Jimmy Carson (C), Grant Fuhr (G), Jari Kurri (RW), Kevin Lowe (D), Mark Messier (C), Glen Sather (Coach); Total – 6

1989-90 (Pittsburgh): Jari Kurri (RW), Kevin Lowe (D), Mark Messier (C); Total – 3

1990-91 (Chicago): Mark Messier (C), Bill Ranford (G), Steve Smith (D), John Muckler (Coach); Total – 4

1991-92 (Philadelphia): Vincent Damphousse (LW); Total – 1

1992-93 (Montreal): Dave Manson (D); Total – 1

1993-94 (NY Rangers): Shayne Corson (LW); Total – 1

1995-96 (Boston): Doug Weight (C); Total – 1

1996-97 (San Jose): Jason Arnott (C); Total – 1

1997-98 (Vancouver): Doug Weight (C); Total – 1

1998-99 (Tampa Bay): Roman Hamrlik (D); Total – 1

1999-00 (Toronto): Tommy Salo (G); Total – 1

2000-01 (Colorado): Janne Niinimaa (D), Doug Weight (C); Total – 2

2001-02 (Los Angeles): Tommy Salo (G); Total – 1
Note: Mike Comrie (C) selected to NHL YoungStars Game

2002-03 (Florida): Eric Brewer (D); Total – 1
Note: Ales Hemsky (RW) selected to NHL YoungStars Game, but was replaced by Shawn Horcoff (C) due to injury.

* Selected to team but did not play.

Edmonton Oilers Yearly Molson Cup Winners
1979-80 to 2002-03

1979-80	Wayne Gretzky	1991-92	Joe Murphy
1980-81	Wayne Gretzky	1992-93	Bill Ranford
1981-82	Wayne Gretzky	1993-94	Bill Ranford
1982-83	Wayne Gretzky	1994-95	Bill Ranford
1983-84	Wayne Gretzky	1995-96	Doug Weight
1984-85	Wayne Gretzky	1996-97	Curtis Joseph
1985-86	Wayne Gretzky	1997-98	Curtis Joseph
1986-87	Wayne Gretzky	1998-99	Bill Guerin
1987-88	Wayne Gretzky	1999-00	Tommy Salo
1988-89	Grant Fuhr	2000-01	Tommy Salo
1989-90	Mark Messier	2001-02	Tommy Salo
1990-91	Bill Ranford	2002-03	Tommy Salo

Edmonton Oilers NHL Award Winners

HART MEMORIAL TROPHY
(Most Valuable Player)
Wayne Gretzky
1980-87
Mark Messier
1989-90

JAMES NORRIS MEMORIAL TROPHY
(Outstanding Defenceman)
Paul Coffey
1984-85
1985-86

EMERY EDGE AWARD
(Plus-Minus Leader)
Charlie Huddy
1982-83
Wayne Gretzky
1983-84
1984-85
1986-87

ART ROSS TROPHY
(Leading Scorer)
Wayne Gretzky
1981-87

LADY BYNG MEMORIAL TROPHY
(Most Gentlemanly Player)
Wayne Gretzky
1979-80
Jari Kurri
1984-85

JACK ADAMS AWARD
(Coach of the Year)
Glen Sather
1985-86

LESTER B. PEARSON AWARD
(Outstanding Player as selected by the NHL Player's Association)
Wayne Gretzky
1982-85
1987
Mark Messier
1989-90

CONN SMYTHE TROPHY
(Stanley Cup MVP)
Mark Messier
1983-84
Wayne Gretzky
1984-85
1987-88
Bill Ranford
1989-90

VEZINA TROPHY
(Outstanding Goaltender)
Grant Fuhr
1987-88

KING CLANCY MEMORIAL TROPHY
Kevin Lowe
1989-90

BUDWEISER/NHL MAN OF THE YEAR
Kevin Lowe
1989-90

EDMONTON OILERS STATS AND FACTS

Edmonton Oilers All-Time Sweater Numbers (1979-80 to 2002-03)

Players listed have played in at least one regular season or playoff game as an Oiler.
The most recent player to wear the number is listed first.

1 - Ty Conklin, Mike Minard, Joaquin Gage, Wayne Cowley, Ron Tugnutt, Peter Ing, Kari Takko, Grant Fuhr, Peter LoPresti, Don Cutts.

2 - Eric Brewer, Igor Ulanov, Brett Hauer, Boris Mironov, Bob Beers, Chris Joseph, Jim Ennis, Lee Fogolin.

3 - Al Hamilton. Number was retired following the 1979-80 season.

4 - Kevin Lowe.

5 - Alexei Semenov, Tom Poti, Greg de Vries, Brett Hauer, Brad Werenka, Steve Smith, Jim Playfair, Doug Hicks.

6 - Bobby Dollas, Bryan Muir, Jeff Norton, Ken Sutton, Gord Mark, Ian Herbers, Brian Glynn, Jeff Beukeboom, Rick Chartraw, Dean Clark, Garry Lariviere, John Hughes, Colin Campbell.

7 - Daniel Cleary, Fredrik Lindquist, Jason Arnott, Martin Gelinas, Mark Lamb, Paul Coffey, Ron Chipperfield.

8 - Ales Pisa, Frank Musil, Doug Friedman, Ray Whitney, Sean Brown, Michel Petit, Zdeno Ciger, Joe Murphy, John LeBlanc, Doug Smith, John Miner, Wayne Van Dorp, Stu Kulak, Dave Lumley, Gord Sherven, Reg Kerr, Steve Graves, Kari Jalonen, Risto Siltanen.

9 - Bill Guerin, Mike Watt, Ralph Intranuovo, Glenn Anderson, Shayne Corson, Bernie Nicholls, Glenn Anderson, Kari Makkonen, Jim Harrison.

10 - Shawn Horcoff, Kevin Brown, Pat Falloon, Steve Kelly, Mariusz Czerkawski, Ryan Smyth, Ilya Byakin, Esa Tikkanen, Jaroslav Pouzar, Matti Hagman, Ron Areshenkoff.

11 - Mark Messier.

12 - Bobby Allen, Josh Green, Michel Picard, Joe Hulbig, Jesse Belanger, Tyler Wright, Micah Aivazoff, Steve Rice, David Maley, Troy Mallette, Adam Graves, Jimmy Carson, Dave Hannan, Dave Hunter.

13 - German Titov, Ken Linseman, Risto Jalo, Ken Linseman.

14 - Jani Rita, Domenic Pittis, Bert Robertsson, Mats Lindgren, Kent Nilsson, Craig MacTavish, Esa Tikkanen, Ray Cote, Laurie Boschman, Walt Poddubny, Blair MacDonald.

15 - Brad Isbister, Marty Reasoner, Chad Kilger, Dan LaCouture, Drake Berehowsky, Joe Hulbig, David Roberts, Fredrik Olausson, Kevin Todd, Scott Thornton, Steve Rice, Greg Hawgood, Steve Rice, Dan Currie, David Haas, Tomas Srsen, Trevor Sim, Miroslav Frycer, Geoff Courtnall, Steve Graves, Kent Nilsson, Steve Graves, Jeff Brubaker, Mike Moller, Pat Conacher, Curt Brackenbury, Alex Tidey, Wayne Bianchin.

16 - Mike York, Rem Murray, Kelly Buchberger, Selmar Odelein, Pat Hughes, Bobby Schmautz, Dan Newman.

17 - Rem Murray, Scott Thornton, Jari Kurri, Cam Connor. Number was retired on October 6, 2001.

18 - Ethan Moreau, Scott Fraser, Barrie Moore, Miroslav Satan, Dan McGillis, Kirk Maltby, Craig Simpson, Mark Lamb, Danny Gare, Mark Napier, Terry Martin, Ken Berry, Brett Callighen.

19 - Marty Reasoner, Sven Butenschon, Chris Hajt, Boyd Devereaux, Kent Manderville, Tyler Wright, Brian Benning, Tyler Wright, Anatoli Semenov, Normand Lacombe, Danny Gare, Mike Rogers, Willy Lindstrom, Ken Berry, Don Ashby, Bill Flett.

20 - Radek Dvorak, Marc-Andre Bergeron, Jochen Hecht, Jason Chimera, Josef Beranek, Tony Hrkac, Barrie Moore, David Oliver, Boris Mironov, Brad Zavisha, Jozef Cierny, Jeff Chychrun, Marc Laforge, Mike Hudson, Shaun Van Allen, Martin Gelinas, Steve Dykstra, Keith Acton, Moe Mantha, Scott Metcalfe, Jaroslav Pouzar, Dave Lumley, Billy Carroll, Dave Lumley.

21 - Jason Smith, Daniel Lacroix, Ladislav Benysek, Valeri Zelepukin, Mariusz Czerkawski, Igor Kravchuk, Shayne Corson, Vincent Damphousse, Randy Gregg, Stan Weir.

22 - Anson Carter, Roman Hamrlik, Luke Richardson, Charlie Huddy, Ron Carter, Poul Popiel.

23 - Cory Cross, Sean Brown, Dan McGillis, Nick Stajduhar, Jason Bonsignore, Vladimir Vujtek, Dan Currie, Martin Rucinsky, Dave Manson, Greg Hawgood, Tommy Lehmann, Tomas Jonsson, Keith Acton, Moe Lemay, Jim Wiemer, Marc Habscheid, Tom Roulston, Tom Bladon, Mike Forbes.

24 - Steve Staios, Christian Laflamme, Janne Niinimaa, Bryan Marchment, Dave Manson, Dan Currie, Brad Aitken, Kevin McClelland, Tom Roulston, Peter Driscoll.

25 - Mike Grier, Greg de Vries, Mike Stapleton, Geoff Smith, Greg C. Adams, Mike Moller, Raimo Summanen, Reg Kerr, Todd Strueby, Don Jackson, Mike Toal.

26 - Todd Marchant, Shjon Podein, Dan Currie, David Shaw, David Haas, Shaun Van Allen, Max Middendorf, Reijo Ruotsalainen, Peter Eriksson, Craig Redmond, Ken Hammond, Mike Krushelnyski, Tom Gorence, Todd Strueby, Don Nachbaur, Mike Forbes, Pat Price.

27 - Georges Laraque, Ralph Intranuovo, Peter White, Todd Elik, Scott Mellanby, Dave Hunter, Kim Issel, Reed Larson, Ron Shudra, Dave Semenko.

28 - Jason Chimera, Alex Selivanov, Bill Huard, Jiri Slegr, Roman Oksiuta, Mike Stapleton, Roman Oksiuta, Craig Muni, Ken Solheim, Gord Sherven, Larry Melnyk, John Blum, Lance Nethery, Todd Strueby, Roy Sommer, Dave Dryden.

29 - Kari Haakana, Patrick Cote, Alex Selivanov, Steve Passmore, Jason Bowen, Louie DeBrusk, Josef Beranek, Igor Vyazmikin, Vladimir Ruzicka, Daryl Reaugh, Reijo Ruotsalainen, Jim Playfair, Don Jackson.

30 - Jussi Markkanen, Dominic Roussel, Bill Ranford, Bob Essensa, Bill Ranford, Warren Skorodenski, Mike Zanier, Ron Low.

31 - Joaquin Gage, Curtis Joseph, Fred Brathwaite, Grant Fuhr, Eddie Mio. Number was retired on October 9, 2003.

32 - Scott Ferguson, Craig Millar, Miroslav Satan, Dean Kennedy, Gord Mark, Ron Tugnutt, Dave Brown, Alan May, Nick Fotiu, Jim Wiemer, Daryl Reaugh.

33 - Jiri Dopita, Dan LaCouture, Marty McSorley, Dan McGillis, Marko Tuomainen, Scott Pearson, Norm Foster, Eldon Reddick, Kim Issel, Marty McSorley, Marco Baron, Lindsay Middlebrook, Gary Edwards, Bob Dupuis, Bryon Baltimore, John Bednarski.

34 - Fernando Pisani, Sergei Zholtok, Michel Riesen, Jim Dowd, Vladimir Vorobiev, Jim Dowd, Donald Dufresne, Ryan McGill, Len Esau, Brent Grieve, Gord Mark, Darcy Martini, Alexander Kerch, Todd Elik, Greg Hawgood, Mike Ware, Glen Cochrane, Scott Metcalfe, Dave Donnelly, Dean Hopkins.

35 - Tommy Salo, Mikhail Shtalenkov, Bryan Muir, Craig Millar, Bryan Muir, Adam Bennett, Francois Leroux, Mike Greenlay, Randy Exelby, Francois Leroux, Andy Moog, Jim Corsi.

36 - Jarret Stoll, Shawn Horcoff, Dennis Bonvie, Ralph Intranuovo, Todd Marchant, Brad Werenka, Norm Maciver, Bruce Bell, Norm Maciver, Selmar Odelein.

37 - Brian Swanson, Daniel Cleary, Dean McAmmond, Doug Halward, Dave Hunter, Tom McMurchy.

38 - Chris Ferraro, Terran Sandwith, Iain Fraser.

39 - Doug Weight.

40 - Scott Ferguson, Fred Brathwaite, Ken Sutton.

41 - Bill McDougall, Brent Gilchrist.

42 - Kevin Brown, Doug Weight, Josef Beranek.

43 - Dennis Bonvie.

44 - Janne Niinimaa.

45 - Ales Pisa.

46 - Jani Rita, Todd Reirden.

47 - Marc-Andre Bergeron, Paul Comrie, Don Murdoch.

51 - Andrei Kovalenko.

55 - Alex Henry, Igor Ulanov, Drew Bannister.

64 - Jason Bonsignore.

65 - Mark Napier.

77 - Garry Unger.

83 - Ales Hemsky.

85 - Petr Klima.

89 - Mike Comrie.

94 - Ryan Smyth.

99 - Wayne Gretzky. Number was retired on October 1, 1999.

EDMONTON OILERS

1979-2003

EDMONTON OILERS STATS AND FACTS

Edmonton Oilers All-Time NHL Roster (1979-80 to 2002-03)

A total of 343 players have played at least one regular season and/or playoff game with the Edmonton Oilers during the team's 24 seasons in the National Hockey League between 1979-80 and 2002-03.

		REGULAR SEASON					PLAYOFFS				
PLAYER (NUMBERS)	**SEASONS**	**GP**	**G**	**A**	**PTS**	**PIM**	**GP**	**G**	**A**	**PTS**	**PIM**
ACTON, Keith (20,23)	1988-89	72	14	21	35	68	7	2	0	2	16
ADAMS, Greg C. (25)	1989	49	4	5	9	82	–	–	–	–	–
AITKEN, Brad (24)	1991	3	0	1	1	0	–	–	–	–	–
AIVAZOFF, Micah (12)	1995	21	0	1	1	2	–	–	–	–	–
ALLEN, Bobby (12)	2003	1	0	0	0	0	–	–	–	–	–
ANDERSON, Glenn (9)	1981-91, 96	845	417	489	906	798	164	81	102	183	314
ARESHENKOFF, Ron (10)	1980	4	0	0	0	0	–	–	–	–	–
ARNOTT, Jason (7)	1994-98	286	100	139	239	489	12	3	6	9	18
ASHBY, Don (19)	1980-81	24	12	12	24	2	3	0	0	0	0
BALTIMORE, Bryon (33)	1980	2	0	0	0	4	–	–	–	–	–
BANNISTER, Drew (55)	1997-98	35	0	3	3	42	12	0	0	0	30
BARON, Marco (G) (33)	1985	1	0	0	0	0	–	–	–	–	–
BEDNARSKI, John (33)	1980	1	0	0	0	0	–	–	–	–	–
BEERS, Bob (2)	1994	66	10	27	37	74	–	–	–	–	–
BELL, Bruce (36)	1990	1	0	0	0	0	–	–	–	–	–
BELANGER, Jesse (12)	1997	6	0	0	0	0	–	–	–	–	–
BENNETT, Adam (35)	1994	48	3	6	9	49	–	–	–	–	–
BENNING, Brian (19)	1993	18	1	7	8	59	–	–	–	–	–
BENYSEK, Ladislav (21)	1998	2	0	0	0	0	–	–	–	–	–
BERANEK, Josef (29, 42, 20)	1992-93,1999-2000	208	42	60	102	108	14	2	1	3	4
BEREHOWSKY, Drake (15)	1998	67	1	6	7	169	12	1	2	3	14
BERGERON, Marc-Andre (20, 47)	2003	5	1	1	2	9	1	0	1	1	0
BERRY, Ken (19, 18)	1982, 84	28	4	6	10	19	–	–	–	–	–
BEUKEBOOM, Jeff (6)	1986-92	284	12	57	69	733	29	1	3	4	50
BIANCHIN, Wayne (15)	1980	11	0	0	0	7	–	–	–	–	–
BLADON, Tom (23)	1981	1	0	0	0	0	–	–	–	–	–
BLUM, John (28)	1983-84	9	0	4	4	26	–	–	–	–	–
BONSIGNORE, Jason (23, 64)	1995-96	21	1	2	3	4	–	–	–	–	–
BONVIE, Dennis (43, 36)	1995-96, 98	14	0	0	0	74	–	–	–	–	–
BOSCHMAN, Laurie (14)	1982-83	73	10	15	25	220	3	0	1	1	4
BOWEN, Jason (29)	1998	4	0	0	0	10	–	–	–	–	–
BRACKENBURY, Curt (15)	1981-82	72	2	9	11	165	2	0	0	0	0
BRATHWAITE, Fred (G) (31, 40)	1994-96	40	0	0	0	2	–	–	–	–	–
BREWER, Eric (2)	2001-03	238	22	53	75	143	12	2	8	10	18
BROWN, Dave (42)	1989-91	140	3	12	15	361	26	0	1	1	36
BROWN, Kevin (42, 10)	1999-2000	19	4	2	6	0	1	0	0	0	0
BROWN, Sean (8, 23)	1997-2002	269	12	23	35	664	4	0	0	0	33
BRUBAKER, Jeff (15)	1986	4	1	0	1	12	–	–	–	–	–
BUCHBERGER, Kelly (16)	1987-99	795	82	158	240	1747	78	9	15	24	116
BUTENSCHON, Sven (19)	2001-02	21	1	1	2	6	–	–	–	–	–
BYAKIN, Ilja (10)	1994	44	8	20	28	30	–	–	–	–	–
CALLIGHEN, Brett (18)	1980-82	160	56	89	145	132	14	4	6	10	8
CAMPBELL, Colin (6)	1980	72	2	11	13	196	3	0	0	0	11
CARROLL, Billy (20)	1985-86	70	8	11	19	22	9	0	0	0	4
CARSON, Jimmy (12)	1989-90	84	50	53	103	36	7	2	1	3	6
CARTER, Anson (22)	2001-03	211	69	88	157	68	6	3	1	4	4
CARTER, Ron (22)	1980	2	0	0	0	0	–	–	–	–	–
CHARTRAW, Rick (6)	1984	24	2	6	8	21	1	0	0	0	2
CHIMERA, Jason (20, 28)	2001-03	70	15	9	24	36	2	0	2	2	0
CHIPPERFIELD, Ron (7)	1980	67	18	19	37	24	–	–	–	–	–
CHYCHRUN, Jeff (20)	1994	2	0	0	0	0	–	–	–	–	–
CIERNY, Jozef (20)	1994	1	0	0	0	0	–	–	–	–	–
CIGER, Zdeno (8)	1993-96	204	64	91	155	55	–	–	–	–	–
CLARK, Dean (6)	1984	1	0	0	0	0	–	–	–	–	–
CLEARY, Daniel (37, 7)	2000-03	220	31	55	86	127	10	1	2	3	10
COCHRANE, Glen (34)	1989	12	0	0	0	52	–	–	–	–	–
COFFEY, Paul (7)	1981-87	532	209	460	669	693	94	36	67	103	167
COMRIE, Mike (89)	2001-03	192	61	72	133	149	12	2	2	4	10
COMRIE, Paul (47)	2000	15	1	2	3	4	–	–	–	–	–
CONACHER, Pat (15)	1984	45	2	8	10	31	3	1	0	1	2
CONKLIN, Ty (G) (1)	2002	4	0	0	0	0	–	–	–	–	–
CONNOR, Cam (17)	1980	38	7	13	20	136	–	–	–	–	–
CORSI, Jim (G) (35)	1980	26	0	3	3	6	–	–	–	–	–
CORSON, Shayne (21, 9)	1993-95	192	53	84	137	413	–	–	–	–	–
COTE, Patrick (29)	2001	6	0	0	0	18	–	–	–	–	–
COTE, Ray (14)	1983-85	15	0	0	0	4	14	3	2	5	4
COURTNALL, Geoff (15)	1988	12	4	4	8	15	19	0	3	3	23
COWLEY, Wayne (G) (1)	1994	1	0	0	0	0	–	–	–	–	–
CROSS, Cory (23)	2003	11	2	3	5	8	6	0	1	1	2
CURRIE, Dan (15, 24, 23, 26)	1991-93	17	1	0	1	6	–	–	–	–	–
CUTTS, Don (1)	1980	6	0	0	0	6	–	–	–	–	–
CZERKAWSKI, Mariusz (10, 21)	1996-97	113	38	38	76	24	12	2	1	3	10
DAMPHOUSSE, Vincent (21)	1992	80	38	51	89	53	16	6	8	14	8
DeBRUSK, Louie (29)	1992-97	228	19	12	31	797	6	0	0	0	4
DEVEREAUX, Boyd (19)	1998-2000	175	15	31	46	49	1	0	0	0	0
de VRIES, Greg (25, 5)	1996-98	115	8	9	17	144	19	0	1	1	29
DOLLAS, Bobby (6)	1998	52	2	6	8	49	11	0	0	0	16
DONNELLY, Dave (34)	1988	4	0	0	0	4	–	–	–	–	–
DOPITA, Jiri (33)	2003	21	1	5	6	11	–	–	–	–	–
DOWD, Jim (36)	1999-2000	70	5	18	23	45	5	2	1	3	4
DRISCOLL, Peter (24)	1980-81	60	3	8	11	97	3	0	0	0	0
DRYDEN, Dave (G) (28)	1980	14	0	0	0	0	–	–	–	–	–
DUFRESNE, Donald (34)	1996-97	64	1	7	8	31	3	0	0	0	0
DUPUIS, Bob (G) (33)	1980	1	0	0	0	0	–	–	–	–	–
DVORAK, Radek (20)	2003	12	4	4	8	14	4	1	0	1	0
DYKSTRA, Steve (20)	1988	15	2	3	5	39	–	–	–	–	–
EDWARDS, Gary (G), (33)	1981	15	0	2	2	0	1	0	0	0	0
ELIK, Todd (24, 27)	1993-94	18	1	9	10	14	–	–	–	–	–
ENNIS, Jim (2)	1988	5	1	0	1	10	–	–	–	–	–
ERIKSSON, Peter (26)	1990	20	3	3	6	24	–	–	–	–	–
ESAU, Len (34)	1995	14	0	6	6	15	–	–	–	–	–
ESSENSA, Bob (G) (30)	1997-99	74	0	1	1	4	1	0	0	0	0
EXELBY, Randy (G) (35)	1990	1	0	0	0	0	–	–	–	–	–
FALLOON, Pat (10)	1999-2000	115	22	36	58	24	4	0	1	1	4
FERGUSON, Scott (40, 32)	1998, 2001-03	149	6	8	14	208	11	0	0	0	8
FERRARO, Chris (38)	1999	2	1	0	1	0	–	–	–	–	–
FLETT, Bill (19)	1980	20	5	2	7	2	–	–	–	–	–
FOGOLIN, Lee (2)	1980-87	586	36	124	160	886	78	5	13	18	115
FORBES, Mike (23, 26)	1980, 82	18	1	7	8	26	–	–	–	–	–
FOSTER, Norm (G) (33)	1992	10	0	0	0	2	–	–	–	–	–
FOTIU, Nick (32)	1989	1	0	0	0	0	–	–	–	–	–
FRASER, Iain (38)	1995	13	3	0	3	0	–	–	–	–	–
FRASER, Scott (18)	1998	29	12	11	23	6	11	1	1	2	0
FRIEDMAN, Doug (8)	1998	16	0	0	0	20	–	–	–	–	–
FRYCER, Miroslav (15)	1989	14	5	5	10	18	–	–	–	–	–
FUHR, Grant (G) (1, 31)	1982-1991	423	0	36	36	48	111	0	12	12	14
GAGE, Joaquin (G) (1, 31)	1995-96, 2001	23	0	1	1	4	–	–	–	–	–
GARE, Danny (19, 18)	1987	18	1	3	4	6	–	–	–	–	–
GELINAS, Martin (20, 7)	1989-1993	258	60	60	120	156	53	6	12	18	41
GILCHRIST, Brent (41)	1993	60	10	10	20	47	–	–	–	–	–
GLYNN, Brian (6)	1992-93	89	6	18	24	66	16	4	1	5	8
GORENCE, Tom (26)	1984	12	1	1	2	0	–	–	–	–	–
GRAVES, Adam (12)	1990-91	139	16	30	46	250	40	7	10	17	39
GRAVES, Steve (8, 15)	1984, 87-88	35	5	4	9	10	–	–	–	–	–
GREEN, Josh (12)	2001-03	81	10	7	17	64	3	0	0	0	0
GREGG, Randy (21)	1982-90	453	40	148	188	309	130	13	37	50	121
GREENLAY, Mike (G) (35)	1990	2	0	1	1	0	–	–	–	–	–
GRETZKY, Wayne (99)	1980-88	696	583	1086	1669	323	120	81	171	252	56
GRIER, Mike (25)	1997-2002	448	81	102	183	292	34	6	4	10	31
GRIEVE, Brent (34)	1994	24	13	5	18	14	–	–	–	–	–
GUERIN, Bill (9)	1998-2001	211	79	82	161	354	20	10	5	15	28
HAAKANA, Kari (29)	2003	13	0	0	0	4	–	–	–	–	–
HAAS, David (15, 26)	1991	5	1	0	1	0	–	–	–	–	–
HABSCHEID, Marc (23)	1982-85	74	10	16	26	26	–	–	–	–	–
HAGMAN, Matti (10)	1981-82	147	41	71	112	34	12	5	1	6	6
HAJT, Chris (19)	2001	1	0	0	0	0	–	–	–	–	–
HALWARD, Doug (37)	1989	24	0	7	7	25	2	0	0	0	0
HAMILTON, Al (3)	1980	31	4	15	19	20	1	0	0	0	0
HAMMOND, Ken (26)	1989	5	0	1	1	8	–	–	–	–	–
HAMRLIK, Roman (22)	1998-00	196	22	81	103	186	20	0	7	7	18
HANNAN, Dave (12)	1988	51	9	11	20	43	12	1	1	2	8
HARRISON, Jim (9)	1980	3	0	0	0	0	–	–	–	–	–
HAUER, Brett (5,2)	1996, 2000	34	4	4	8	32	–	–	–	–	–
HAWGOOD, Greg (23, 15, 34)	1991-93	55	7	25	32	63	13	0	3	3	23
HECHT, Jochen (20)	2002	82	16	24	40	60	–	–	–	–	–
HEMSKY, Ales (83)	2003	59	6	24	30	14	6	0	0	0	0
HENRY, Alex (55)	2003	3	0	0	0	0	–	–	–	–	–
HERBERS, Ian (6)	1994	22	0	2	2	32	–	–	–	–	–
HICKS, Doug (5)	1980-82	186	17	67	84	183	12	1	1	2	6
HOPKINS, Dean (34)	1986	1	0	0	0	0	–	–	–	–	–
HORCOFF, Shawn (36, 10)	2001-03	188	29	42	71	83	11	3	1	4	6
HRKAC, Tony (20)	1998	36	8	11	19	20	12	0	3	3	2
HUARD, Bill (28)	1998-99	33	0	1	1	72	4	0	0	0	2
HUDDY, Charlie (22)	1981-91	694	81	287	368	500	138	16	61	77	104
HUDSON, Mike (20)	1993	5	0	1	1	2	–	–	–	–	–
HUGHES, John (6)	1981	18	0	3	3	30	–	–	–	–	–
HUGHES, Pat (16)	1981-85	300	88	83	171	330	55	7	23	30	52
HULBIG, Joe (15, 12)	1997-99	24	2	2	4	4	6	0	1	1	2
HUNTER, Dave (12, 37, 27)	1980-89	653	119	171	290	776	105	16	24	40	211
ING, Peter (G) (1)	1992	12	0	3	3	0	–	–	–	–	–
INTRANUOVO, Ralph (36, 27, 9)	1995-97	22	2	4	6	4	–	–	–	–	–
ISBISTER, Brad (15)	2003	13	3	2	5	9	6	0	1	1	12
ISSEL, Kim (27, 33)	1989	4	0	0	0	0	–	–	–	–	–
JACKSON, Don (25, 29)	1982-86	262	15	45	60	508	53	4	5	9	147
JALO, Risto (13)	1986	3	0	3	3	0	–	–	–	–	–
JALONEN, Kari (8)	1984	3	0	0	0	0	–	–	–	–	–
JONSSON, Tomas (23)	1989	20	1	10	11	22	4	2	0	2	6
JOSEPH, Chris (2)	1988-94	154	12	39	51	205	5	1	3	4	2
JOSEPH, Curtis (G) (31)	1996-98	177	0	5	5	28	24	0	0	0	4
KELLY, Steve (10)	1997-98	27	1	2	3	14	6	0	0	0	2
KENNEDY, Dean (32)	1995	40	2	8	10	25	–	–	–	–	–
KERCH, Alexander (34)	1994	5	0	0	0	2	–	–	–	–	–
KERR, Reg (25, 8)	1984	3	0	0	0	0	–	–	–	–	–
KILGER, Chad (15)	1999-2001	87	9	5	14	39	7	0	0	0	4
KLIMA, Petr (85)	1990-93, 97	291	120	97	217	343	60	13	10	23	36
KOVALENKO, Andrei (51)	1997-99	176	51	58	109	139	13	4	3	7	8
KRAVCHUK, Igor (21)	1993-96	160	27	61	88	57	–	–	–	–	–
KRUSHELNYSKI, Mike (26)	1985-88	290	95	131	226	213	68	16	23	39	68
KULAK, Stu (8)	1987	23	3	1	4	41	–	–	–	–	–
KURRI, Jari (17)	1981-90	754	474	569	1043	348	146	92	110	202	101
LACOMBE, Normand (19)	1987-90	133	30	22	52	116	26	5	1	6	49
LaCOUTURE, Dan (15, 33)	1999-2001	45	2	4	6	39	1	0	0	0	0
LACROIX, Daniel (21)	1999	4	0	0	0	13	–	–	–	–	–

EDMONTON OILERS STATS AND FACTS

		REGULAR SEASON					PLAYOFFS				
PLAYER (NUMBERS)	SEASONS	GP	G	A	PTS	PIM	GP	G	A	PTS	PIM
LAFLAMME, Christian (24)	1999-2000	61	0	6	6	32	4	0	1	1	2
LAFORGE, Marc (20)	1994	5	0	0	0	21	–	–	–	–	–
LAMB, Mark (18, 7)	1988-92	176	24	54	78	127	59	7	19	26	40
LARAQUE, Georges (27)	1998-2003	352	35	47	82	654	21	2	5	7	20
LARIVIERE, Garry (6)	1981-83	92	1	25	26	61	14	0	5	5	6
LARSON, Reed (27)	1989	10	2	7	9	15	–	–	–	–	–
LeBLANC, John (8)	1989	2	1	0	1	0	1	0	0	0	0
LEHMANN, Tommy (23)	1990	1	0	0	0	0	–	–	–	–	–
LEMAY, Moe (23)	1987-88	14	1	2	3	38	9	2	1	3	11
LEROUX, Francois (35)	1989-93	11	0	3	3	11	–	–	–	–	–
LINDGREN, Mats (14)	1997-99	199	29	39	68	76	24	1	5	6	10
LINDQUIST, Fredrik (7)	1999	8	0	0	0	2	–	–	–	–	–
LINDSTROM, Willy (19)	1983-85	163	40	41	81	58	53	12	17	29	22
LINSEMAN, Ken (13)	1983-84, 91	202	58	120	178	394	37	16	13	29	87
LoPRESTI, Peter (G) (1)	1981	2	0	0	0	0	–	–	–	–	–
LOW, Ron (G) (30)	1980-83	67	0	4	4	2	3	0	0	0	0
LOWE, Kevin (4)	1980-92, 97-98	1037	74	309	383	1236	172	9	43	52	156
LUMLEY, Dave (20, 8)	1980-87	386	90	140	230	582	61	6	8	14	131
MacDONALD, Blair (14)	1980-81	131	65	72	137	33	3	0	3	3	0
MACIVER, Norm (36)	1990-92	79	8	39	47	65	31	1	6	7	18
MacTAVISH, Craig (14)	1986-94	801	155	176	331	680	113	13	24	37	143
MAKKONEN, Kari (9)	1980	9	2	2	4	0	–	–	–	–	–
MALEY, David (12)	1992-93	36	4	7	11	75	10	1	1	2	4
MALLETTE, Troy (12)	1992	15	1	3	4	36	–	–	–	–	–
MALTBY, Kirk (18)	1994-96	164	21	17	38	184	–	–	–	–	–
MANDERVILLE, Kent (19)	1996	37	3	5	8	38	–	–	–	–	–
MANSON, Dave (23, 24)	1992-94	219	33	75	108	570	16	3	9	12	44
MANTHA, Moe (20)	1988	25	0	6	6	26	–	–	–	–	–
MARCHANT, Todd (36, 26)	1994-2003	678	136	207	343	490	43	7	6	13	42
MARCHMENT, Bryan (24)	1995-98	216	7	37	44	576	3	0	0	0	4
MARK, Gord (34, 32, 6)	1994-95	30	0	3	3	78	–	–	–	–	–
MARKKANEN, Jussi (G) (30)	2002-03	36	0	1	1	2	1	0	0	0	0
MARTIN, Terry (18)	1985	4	0	2	2	0	–	–	–	–	–
MARTINI, Darcy (34)	1994	2	0	0	0	0	–	–	–	–	–
MAY, Alan (32)	1989	3	1	0	1	7	–	–	–	–	–
McAMMOND, Dean (37)	1994-99	303	61	100	161	149	12	1	4	5	12
McCLELLAND, Kevin (24)	1984-90	428	56	94	150	1298	95	10	17	27	276
McDOUGALL, Bill (41)	1994	4	2	1	3	4	–	–	–	–	–
McGILL, Ryan (34)	1995	8	0	0	0	8	–	–	–	–	–
McGILLIS, Dan (18, 23)	1997-98	140	16	31	47	126	12	0	5	5	24
McMURCHY, Tom (37)	1988	9	4	1	5	8	–	–	–	–	–
McSORLEY, Marty (33)	1986-88, 99	206	24	36	60	768	48	4	8	12	184
MELLANBY, Scott (27)	1992-93	149	38	44	82	344	16	2	1	3	29
MELNYK, Larry (28)	1984-86	34	2	14	16	36	18	1	4	5	26
METCALFE, Scott (20, 34)	1988	2	0	0	0	0	–	–	–	–	–
MESSIER, Mark (11)	1980-91	851	392	642	1034	1122	166	80	135	215	175
MIDDENDORF, Max (26)	1991	3	1	0	1	2	–	–	–	–	–
MIDDLEBROOK, Lindsay (g) (33)	1983	1	0	0	0	0	–	–	–	–	–
MILLAR, Craig (35, 32)	1997-99	36	4	2	6	29	–	–	–	–	–
MINARD, Mike (G) (1)	2000	1	0	0	0	0	–	–	–	–	–
MINER, John (8)	1988	14	2	3	5	16	–	–	–	–	–
MIO, Eddie (G) (31)	1980-81	77	0	6	6	10	–	–	–	–	–
MIRONOV, Boris (20, 2)	1994-99	320	42	118	160	444	24	5	11	16	43
MOLLER, Mike (15, 25)	1986-87	7	2	1	3	0	–	–	–	–	–
MOOG, Andy (G) (35)	1981-87	235	0	11	11	46	37	0	1	1	4
MOORE, Barrie (18)	1997	4	0	0	0	0	–	–	–	–	–
MOREAU, Ethan (18)	1999-2003	313	52	47	99	353	19	0	5	5	24
MUIR, Bryan (35, 6)	1996-98	12	0	0	0	23	5	0	0	0	4
MUNI, Craig (28)	1987-93	493	24	87	111	492	83	0	15	15	94
MURDOCH, Don (47)	1980-81	50	15	11	26	22	3	2	0	2	0
MURPHY, Joe (8)	1990-92	222	69	100	169	91	53	16	29	45	42
MURRAY, Rem (17, 16)	1997-2002	416	72	90	162	121	38	5	8	13	16
MUSIL, Frank (8)	1998-2001	69	1	7	8	46	8	0	0	0	8
NACHBAUR, Don (26)	1983	4	0	0	0	17	2	0	0	0	7
NAPIER, Mark (18, 65)	1985-87	175	41	71	112	35	28	6	9	15	7
NETHERY, Lance (28)	1982	3	0	2	2	2	–	–	–	–	–
NEWMAN, Dan (16)	1980	10	3	1	4	0	–	–	–	–	–
NICHOLLS, Bernie (9)	1992-93	95	28	61	89	80	16	8	11	19	25
NIINIMAA, Janne (24, 44)	1998-2003	399	34	154	188	419	26	1	5	6	22
NILSSON, Kent (15, 14)	1987, 95	23	6	12	18	4	21	6	13	19	11
NORTON, Jeff (6)	1996-97	92	6	27	33	58	–	–	–	–	–
ODELEIN, Selmar (16, 36)	1986-89	18	0	2	2	35	–	–	–	–	–
OKSUITA, Roman (28)	1994-95	36	12	4	16	12	–	–	–	–	–
OLAUSSON, Fredrik (15)	1994-96	108	9	35	44	54	–	–	–	–	–
OLIVER, David (20)	1995-97	141	37	35	72	58	–	–	–	–	–
PASSMORE, Steve (G) (29)	1999	6	0	1	1	2	–	–	–	–	–
PEARSON, Scott (33)	1994-95	100	20	22	42	219	–	–	–	–	–
PETIT, Michel (8)	1997	18	2	4	6	20	–	–	–	–	–
PICARD, Michel (12)	2000	2	0	0	0	2	–	–	–	–	–
PISA, Ales (45,8)	2002-03	50	1	3	4	26	–	–	–	–	–
PISANI, Fernando (34)	2003	35	8	5	13	10	6	1	0	1	2
PITTIS, Domenic (14)	2001-02	69	4	11	15	57	3	0	0	0	2
PLAYFAIR, Jim (5, 29)	1984	2	1	1	2	2	–	–	–	–	–
PODDUBNY, Walt (14)	1982	4	0	0	0	0	–	–	–	–	–
PODEIN, Shjon (26)	1993-94	68	16	11	27	33	–	–	–	–	–
POPIEL, Paul (22)	1980	10	0	0	0	0	–	–	–	–	–
POTI, Tom (5)	1999-2002	285	27	78	105	209	15	0	4	4	4
POUZAR, Jaroslav (10, 20)	1983-85, 87	186	34	48	82	135	29	6	4	10	16
PRICE, Pat (26)	1980-81	134	19	45	64	327	3	0	0	0	11
RANFORD, Bill (G) (30)	1988-96, 2000	449	0	19	19	46	41	0	2	2	4
REAUGH, Daryl (G) (32, 29)	1985, 88	7	0	0	0	0	–	–	–	–	–
REASONER, Marty (15)	2002-03	122	17	25	42	69	6	1	0	1	2
REDDICK, Eldon (G) (33)	1990-91	13	0	0	0	0	1	0	0	0	0
REDMOND, Craig (26)	1989	21	3	10	13	12	–	–	–	–	–
REIRDEN, Todd (46)	1999	17	2	3	5	20	–	–	–	–	–
RICE, Steve (15, 12)	1992-94	94	19	20	39	66	–	–	–	–	–
RICHARDSON, Luke (22)	1992-97	436	13	65	78	630	28	0	7	7	59
RIESEN, Michel (34)	2001	12	0	1	1	4	–	–	–	–	–
RITA, Jani (46, 14)	2002-03	13	3	1	4	0	–	–	–	–	–
ROBERTS, David (15)	1996	6	2	4	6	6	–	–	–	–	–
ROBERTSSON, Bert (14)	2000	52	0	4	4	34	5	0	0	0	0
ROGERS, Mike (19)	1986	8	1	0	1	0	–	–	–	–	–
ROULSTON, Tom (23, 24)	1981-84	137	36	32	68	64	18	2	2	4	2
ROUSSEL, Dominic (G) (30)	2001	8	0	0	0	2	–	–	–	–	–
RUCINSKY, Martin (23)	1992	2	0	0	0	0	–	–	–	–	–
RUOTSALAINEN, Reijo (29, 26)	1987, 90	26	6	15	21	12	43	4	16	20	22
RUZICKA, Vladimir (29)	1990	25	11	6	17	10	–	–	–	–	–
SALO, Tommy (G) (35)	1999-2003	290	0	3	3	18	21	0	1	1	2
SANDWITH, Terran (38)	1998	8	0	0	0	6	–	–	–	–	–
SATAN, Miroslav (32, 18)	1996-97	126	35	28	63	44	–	–	–	–	–
SCHMAUTZ, Bobby (16)	1980	29	8	8	16	20	–	–	–	–	–
SELIVANOV, Alexander (28, 29)	1999-2000	96	35	26	61	70	7	0	1	1	10
SEMENKO, Dave (27)	1980-87	454	59	77	136	976	69	6	6	12	193
SEMENOV, Anatoli (19)	1990-92	116	35	38	73	42	22	6	6	12	12
SEMENOV, Alexei (5)	2003	46	1	6	7	58	6	0	0	0	0
SHAW, David (26)	1992	12	1	1	2	8	–	–	–	–	–
SHERVEN, Gord (8, 28)	1984-86	44	11	8	19	14	–	–	–	–	–
SHTALENKOV, Mikhail (G) (35)	1999	34	0	0	0	2	–	–	–	–	–
SHUDRA, Ron (27)	1988	10	0	5	5	6	–	–	–	–	–
SILTANEN, Risto (8)	1980-82	206	38	113	151	104	16	5	2	7	20
SIM, Trevor (15)	1990	3	0	1	1	2	–	–	–	–	–
SIMPSON, Craig (18)	1988-93	419	185	180	365	475	67	36	32	68	56
SKORODENSKI, Warren (G) (30)	1988	3	0	0	0	0	–	–	–	–	–
SLEGR, Jiri (28)	1995-96	60	5	18	23	88	–	–	–	–	–
SMITH, Doug (8)	1989	19	1	1	2	9	–	–	–	–	–
SMITH, Geoff (25)	1990-94	306	11	56	67	192	12	0	1	1	6
SMITH, Jason (21)	1999-2003	316	18	48	66	358	21	0	4	4	33
SMITH, Steve (5)	1985-91	385	46	172	218	1080	87	10	29	39	216
SMYTH, Ryan (10, 94)	1995-2003	560	175	196	371	441	44	15	12	27	54
SOLHEIM, Ken (28)	1986	6	1	0	1	5	–	–	–	–	–
SOMMER, Roy (28)	1981	3	1	0	1	7	–	–	–	–	–
SRSEN, Tomas (15)	1991	2	0	0	0	0	–	–	–	–	–
STAIOS, Steve (24)	2002-03	149	10	26	36	204	6	0	0	0	4
STAJDUHAR, Nick (23)	1996	2	0	0	0	4	–	–	–	–	–
STAPLETON, Mike (28, 25)	1994-95	69	11	20	31	49	–	–	–	–	–
STOLL, Jarret (36)	2003	4	0	1	1	0	–	–	–	–	–
STRUEBY, Todd (28, 25, 26)	1982-84	5	0	1	1	2	–	–	–	–	–
SUMMANEN, Raimo (25)	1984-87	132	30	33	63	33	10	2	5	7	0
SUTTON, Ken (40, 6)	1995-96	44	3	9	12	51	–	–	–	–	–
SWANSON, Brian (37)	2001-03	68	4	12	16	16	–	–	–	–	–
TAKKO, Kari (G) (1)	1991	11	0	1	1	0	–	–	–	–	–
THORNTON, Scott (17, 15)	1992-96	209	23	30	53	385	1	0	0	0	0
TIDEY, Alex (15)	1980	5	0	0	0	8	–	–	–	–	–
TIKKANEN, Esa (14, 10)	1985-93	522	178	258	436	759	114	51	46	97	171
TITOV, German (13)	2000	7	0	4	4	4	5	1	1	2	0
TOAL, Mike (25)	1980	3	0	0	0	0	–	–	–	–	–
TODD, Kevin (15)	1993	25	4	9	13	10	–	–	–	–	–
TUGNUTT, Ron (G) (1, 32)	1992-93	29	0	0	0	4	2	0	0	0	0
TUOMAINEN, Marko (33)	1995	4	0	0	0	0	–	–	–	–	–
ULANOV, Igor (2, 55)	2000-01	81	3	23	26	100	11	0	0	0	10
UNGER, Garry (77)	1981-83	75	9	13	22	83	13	1	0	1	25
Van ALLEN, Shaun (26, 20)	1991, 93	23	1	4	5	6	–	–	–	–	–
VAN DORP, Wayne (8)	1987	3	0	0	0	25	3	0	0	0	2
VOROBIEV, Vladimir (34)	1999	2	2	0	2	2	1	0	0	0	0
VUJTEK, Vladimir (23)	1993-94	70	5	25	30	22	–	–	–	–	–
VYAZMIKIN, Igor (29)	1991	4	1	0	1	0	–	–	–	–	–
WARE, Mike (34)	1989-90	5	0	1	1	15	–	–	–	–	–
WATT, Mike (9)	1998	14	1	2	3	4	–	–	–	–	–
WEIGHT, Doug (42, 39)	1993-2001	588	157	420	577	445	39	10	23	33	58
WEIR, Stan (21)	1980-82	200	48	66	114	93	10	0	0	0	4
WERENKA, Brad (36, 5)	1993-94	42	5	7	12	38	–	–	–	–	–
WHITE, Peter (27)	1994-96	61	10	12	22	2	–	–	–	–	–
WHITNEY, Ray (8)	1998	9	1	3	4	0	–	–	–	–	–
WIEMER, Jim (23, 32)	1988	12	1	2	3	15	2	0	0	0	2
WRIGHT, Tyler (19, 12)	1993-96	41	3	1	4	70	–	–	–	–	–
YORK, Mike (16)	2002-03	83	24	31	55	10	6	0	2	2	2
ZANIER, Mike (G) (30)	1985	3	0	0	0	0	–	–	–	–	–
ZAVISHA, Brad (20)	1994	2	0	0	0	0	–	–	–	–	–
ZELEPUKIN, Valeri (21)	1998	33	2	10	12	57	8	1	2	3	2
ZHOLTOK, Sergei (34)	2001	37	4	16	20	22	3	0	0	0	0

EDMONTON OILERS STATS AND FACTS
Current NHL Individual Records Established or Tied By Edmonton Oilers

REGULAR SEASON RECORDS (24)

MOST GOALS, ONE SEASON:
92 – Wayne Gretzky, 1981-82

MOST GOALS, ONE SEASON, BY A DEFENCEMAN:
48 – Paul Coffey, 1985-86

MOST ASSISTS, ONE SEASON:
163 – Wayne Gretzky, 1985-86

MOST POINTS, ONE SEASON:
215 – Wayne Gretzky, 1985-86

MOST GAMES SCORING THREE-OR-MORE GOALS,
ONE SEASON:
10 – Wayne Gretzky, 1981-82 and 1983-84

HIGHEST ASSIST-PER-GAME AVERAGE,
ONE SEASON (35 or more):
2.04 – Wayne Gretzky, 1985-86

HIGHEST POINTS PER-GAME AVERAGE, ONE SEASON
(among players with 50 or more):
2.77 – Wayne Gretzky, 1983-84

MOST GOALS, ONE SEASON, INCLUDING PLAYOFFS:
100 – Wayne Gretzky, 1983-84

MOST ASSISTS, ONE SEASON, INCLUDING PLAYOFFS:
174 – Wayne Gretzky, 1985-86

MOST POINTS, ONE SEASON, INCLUDING PLAYOFFS:
255 – Wayne Gretzky, 1984-85

MOST GOALS ONE SEASON, BY A CENTRE:
92 – Wayne Gretzky, 1981-82

MOST ASSISTS ONE SEASON, BY A CENTRE:
163 – Wayne Gretzky, 1985-86

MOST POINTS ONE SEASON, BY A CENTRE:
215 – Wayne Gretzky, 1985-86

FASTEST TWO SHORTHANDED GOALS:
12 Seconds – Esa Tikkanen, at Toronto,
November 12/88, 1st period.
Goals scored at 10:44 and 10:56.

MOST GOALS, MINIMUM 50 GAMES, FROM THE START
OF THE SEASON:
61 – Wayne Gretzky, 1981-82 and 1983-84

LONGEST CONSECUTIVE POINT-SCORING STREAK:
51 Games – Wayne Gretzky, 1983-84;
October 5, 1983 through January 27, 1984

LONGEST CONSECUTIVE POINT-SCORING STREAK FROM
THE START OF A SEASON:
51 Games – Wayne Gretzky, 1983-84;
October 5, 1983 through January 27, 1984

MOST ASSISTS, ONE GAME:
7 – Wayne Gretzky, February 15, 1980 vs
Washington; December 11, 1985 at Chicago;
February 14, 1986 vs Quebec (Ties NHL record)

MOST ASSISTS, ONE GAME, BY A DEFENCEMAN:
6 – Paul Coffey, March 14, 1986 vs Detroit
(Ties NHL record)

MOST ASSISTS, ONE ROAD GAME:
7 – Wayne Gretzky December 11, 1985 at
Chicago (Ties NHL record)

MOST ASSISTS, ONE GAME, BY A PLAYER IN HIS FIRST
NHL SEASON:
7 – Wayne Gretzky, February 15, 1980 vs
Washington

MOST POINTS, ONE GAME, BY A DEFENCEMAN:
8 – Paul Coffey, March 14, 1986 vs Detroit;
2 goals, 6 assists (Ties NHL record)

MOST GOALS, ONE PERIOD:
4 – Wayne Gretzky, February 18, 1981,
3rd period vs St. Louis (Ties NHL record)

MOST ASSISTS, ONE SEASON, BY A GOALTENDER:
14 – Grant Fuhr, 1983-84

STANLEY CUP PLAYOFF RECORDS (27)

MOST CAREER PLAYOFF POINTS:
382 – Wayne Gretzky, 1979-80 through
1998-99

MOST CAREER PLAYOFF GOALS:
122 – Wayne Gretzky, 1979-80 through
1998-99

MOST CAREER PLAYOFF ASSISTS:
260 – Wayne Gretzky, 1979-80 through
1998-99

MOST CAREER THREE-OR-MORE GOAL GAMES:
10 – Wayne Gretzky, 1979-80 through
1998-99

MOST CAREER SHORTHANDED GOALS:
14 – Mark Messier, 1979-80 through 1997-98

MOST POINTS, ONE PLAYOFF YEAR:
47 – Wayne Gretzky, 1984-85; 17 goals,
30 assists

MOST GOALS, ONE PLAYOFF YEAR:
19 – Jari Kurri, 1984-85
(Ties NHL record)

MOST ASSISTS, ONE PLAYOFF YEAR:
31 – Wayne Gretzky, 1987-88

MOST POINTS BY A DEFENCEMAN ONE PLAYOFF YEAR:
37 – Paul Coffey, 1984-85; 12 goals, 25 assists

MOST GOALS BY A DEFENCEMAN, ONE PLAYOFF YEAR:
12 – Paul Coffey 1984-85

MOST ASSISTS BY A DEFENCEMAN ONE PLAYOFF YEAR:
25 – Paul Coffey, 1984-85

MOST SHORTHANDED GOALS, ONE PLAYOFF YEAR:
3 – Wayne Gretzky, 1982-83 (Ties NHL record)
– Todd Marchant, 1996-97 (Ties NHL record)

MOST THREE-OR-MORE GOAL GAMES ONE PLAYOFF
YEAR:
4 – Jari Kurri, 1984-85

MOST WINS BY A GOALTENDER ONE PLAYOFF YEAR:
16 – Grant Fuhr, 1987-88
– Bill Ranford, 1989-90 (Ties NHL record)

MOST POINTS, IN FINAL SERIES:
13 – Wayne Gretzky, 1987-88, scored 3 goals
10 assists during 4 game Stanley Cup Final
against Boston.

MOST ASSISTS, IN FINAL SERIES:
10 – Wayne Gretzky, 1987-88, during 4 game
Stanley Cup Final against Boston.

MOST GOALS IN ONE SERIES
OTHER THAN FINAL):
12 – Jari Kurri, 1984-85, during 6 game
Conference Final against Chicago

MOST ASSISTS IN ONE SERIES
(OTHER THAN FINAL):
14 – Wayne Gretzky, 1984-85, during 6 game
Conference Final against Chicago
(Ties NHL record)

MOST THREE-OR-MORE GOAL GAMES, ONE PLAYOFF
SERIES:
3 – Jari Kurri, 1984-85, during 6 game
Conference Final against Chicago.

MOST POINTS, ONE GAME, BY A DEFENCEMAN:
6 – Paul Coffey, May 14, 1985 vs Chicago;
1 goal, 5 assists

MOST ASSISTS, ONE GAME:
6 – Wayne Gretzky, April 9, 1987 vs Los Angeles
(Ties NHL record)

MOST POWERPLAY GOALS, ONE GAME:
3 – Jari Kurri, April 9, 1987 vs Los Angeles
(Ties NHL record)

MOST SHORTHANDED GOALS, ONE GAME:
2 – Wayne Gretzky, April 6, 1983 vs Winnipeg
(Ties NHL record)
– Jari Kurri, April 24, 1983 vs Chicago
(Ties NHL record)

MOST POINTS, ONE PERIOD:
4 – Wayne Gretzky, April 12, 1987 at
Los Angeles, 3rd period; 1 goal, 3 assists
– Glenn Anderson, April 6, 1988 vs Winnipeg,
3rd period; 3 goals, 1 assist
(Ties NHL record)

MOST ASSISTS, ONE PERIOD:
3 – Wayne Gretzky, 5 times; April 8/81,
April 24/83, April 25/85, April 9/87,
April 12/87 (Tied NHL record)

MOST SHORTHANDED GOALS, ONE PERIOD:
2 – Jari Kurri, April 24, 1983 vs Chicago,
3rd period (Ties NHL record)

MOST PENALTY SHOTS FACED AND STOPPED,
ONE PLAYOFF YEAR AND SERIES:
2 – Grant Fuhr, 1984-85, Stanley Cup Final
against Philadelphia, May 28 and
May 30, 1985

ALL STAR GAME RECORDS (3)

MOST GOALS, ONE GAME:
4 – Wayne Gretzky, 1983 at Uniondale

MOST GOALS, ONE PERIOD:
4 – Wayne Gretzky, 3rd period, 1983 at
Uniondale

EDMONTON OILERS STATS AND FACTS

NHL Team Records Held or Co-Held By The Edmonton Oilers (Regular Season)

MOST GOALS, ONE SEASON:
446 – 1983-84 (NHL record)

HIGHEST GOALS PER-GAME AVERAGE, ONE SEASON:
5.58 – 1983-84, 446 goals in 80 games (NHL record)

MOST SHORTHANDED GOALS, ONE SEASON:
36 – 1983-84 (NHL record)

MOST SCORING POINTS, ONE SEASON:
1,182 – 1983-84 (NHL record)

MOST 50-OR-MORE GOAL SCORERS, ONE SEASON:
3 – 1983-84, Wayne Gretzky 87; Glenn Anderson 54; Jari Kurri 52 (NHL record)
3 – 1985-86, Jari Kurri 68; Glenn Anderson 54; Wayne Gretzky 52 (NHL record)

MOST 40-OR MORE GOAL SCORERS, ONE SEASON:
4 – 1982-83, Wayne Gretzky 71; Glenn Anderson, Mark Messier 48; Jari Kurri 45 (Ties NHL record)
– 1983-84, Wayne Gretzky 87; Glenn Anderson 54; Jari Kurri 52; Paul Coffey 40 (Ties NHL record)
– 1984-85, Wayne Gretzky 73; Jari Kurri 71; Mike Krushelnyski 43; Glenn Anderson 42 (Ties NHL record)
– 1985-86, Jari Kurri 68; Glenn Anderson 54; Wayne Gretzky 52; Paul Coffey 48 (Ties NHL record)

MOST 100-OR-MORE POINT SCORERS, ONE SEASON:
4 – 1982-83, Wayne Gretzky 196; Mark Messier 106; Glenn Anderson, Jari Kurri 104 (Ties NHL record)
– 1983-84, Wayne Gretzky 205; Paul Coffey 126; Jari Kurri 113; Mark Messier 101 (Ties NHL record)
– 1985-86, Wayne Gretzky 215; Paul Coffey 138; Jari Kurri 131; Glenn Anderson 102 (Ties NHL record)

MOST ASSISTS ONE SEASON:
737 – 1985-86 (NHL record)

FASTEST TWO GOALS FROM THE START OF A GAME, ONE TEAM:
24 Seconds
– Oilers at Los Angeles, March 28/82. Scorers: Mark Messier, 0:14; Dave Lumley, 0:24, Edmonton won 6-2 (NHL record)

LONGEST UNDEFEATED STREAK FROM START OF SEASON:
15 Games
– October 11/84 through November 9/84 (12 wins, 3 ties) (NHL record)

FEWEST SHUTOUTS ONE SEASON:
0 – 1980-81 (Ties NHL record)
– 1981-82 (Ties NHL record)
– 1986-87 (Ties NHL record)

FEWEST SHOTS, ONE PERIOD:
0 – Edmonton at Minnesota, February 20/91, 2nd period. (Ties NHL record)

MOST POINTS, BOTH TEAMS, ONE GAME:
62 – Edmonton at Chicago, December 11, 1985. Edmonton won 12-9 and had 24 assists, Chicago 17. (NHL record)

MOST GOALS, BOTH TEAMS, ONE PERIOD:
12 – Edmonton at Chicago, December 11, 1985. second period. Edmonton scored 6 goals and Chicago 6 in a 12-9 Oilers win (Ties NHL record)

MOST POINTS, BOTH TEAMS, ONE PERIOD:
35 – Edmonton at Chicago, December 11, 1985. second period. Edmonton scored 18 points (6 goals, 12 assists) and Chicago scored 17 points (6 goals, 11 assists) in a 12-9 Oilers win. (NHL record)

MOST PENALTIES, BOTH TEAMS, ONE GAME:
85 Penalties
– Edmonton at Los Angeles, February 28/90. Edmonton received 26 minors, 7 majors, 6 misconducts, 4 game misconducts, 1 match penalty for 44 penalties. Los Angeles received 26 minors, 9 majors, 3 misconducts and 3 game misconducts for 41 penalties. (NHL record)

MOST PENALTIES, ONE TEAM, ONE GAME:
44 Penalties
– Edmonton at Los Angeles, February 28/90. Edmonton received 26 minors, 7 majors, 6 misconducts, 4 game misconducts and 1 match penalty.

Edmonton Oilers Career Scoring – 1979-80 to 2002-03

	PLAYER	GP	G	A	PTS	PIM	PPG	SHG	WG	TG	HT	ENG
1.	Wayne Gretzky	696	583	1086	1669	323	125	55	61	14	43	25
2.	Jari Kurri	754	474	569	1043	348	107	31	60	16	20	8
3.	Mark Messier	851	392	642	1034	1122	89	36	43	14	13	12
4.	Glenn Anderson	845	417	489	906	798	126	13	73	9	20	8
5.	Paul Coffey	532	209	460	669	693	69	15	19	3	4	1
6.	Doug Weight	588	157	420	577	527	39	2	17	4	1	9
7.	Esa Tikkanen	522	178	258	436	759	36	21	30	1	5	4
8.	Kevin Lowe	1037	74	309	383	1236	16	5	10	0	0	3
9.	Ryan Smyth	560	175	196	371	441	76	1	26	7	4	3
10.	Charlie Huddy	694	81	287	368	500	25	2	6	3	0	0
11.	Craig Simpson	419	185	180	365	475	75	0	21	1	2	3
12.	Todd Marchant	678	136	207	343	490	17	20	18	5	0	4
13.	Craig MacTavish	701	155	176	331	680	10	29	25	2	2	4
14.	Dave Hunter	653	119	171	290	776	3	6	15	4	0	1
15.	Kelly Buchberger	795	82	158	240	1747	5	12	24	2	1	0
16.	Jason Arnott	286	100	139	239	489	36	1	12	3	2	3
17.	Dave Lumley	386	90	140	230	582	8	1	15	4	2	2
18.	Mike Krushelnyski	290	95	131	226	213	24	1	7	3	1	0
19.	Steve Smith	385	46	172	218	1080	15	0	6	0	0	1
20.	Petr Klima	274	119	90	209	337	32	1	10	0	3	1
21.	Randy Gregg	453	40	148	188	309	3	3	7	0	0	1
	Janne Niinimaa	399	34	154	188	419	16	2	4	0	0	2
23.	Mike Grier	448	81	102	183	292	10	10	11	1	1	6
24.	Ken Linseman	202	58	120	178	394	17	6	7	0	1	1
25.	Pat Hughes	300	88	83	171	330	9	11	20	2	1	0
26.	Joe Murphy	222	69	100	169	143	16	3	6	3	1	1
27.	Rem Murray	416	72	90	162	121	10	8	13	3	1	3
28.	Bill Guerin	211	79	82	161	354	36	0	7	1	0	3
	Dean McAmmond	303	61	100	161	149	19	0	9	0	0	1
30.	Boris Mironov	320	42	118	160	444	24	1	7	2	0	1
	Lee Fogolin	586	36	124	160	886	0	6	2	1	0	0
32.	Anson Carter	211	69	88	157	68	29	1	11	1	0	3
33.	Zdeno Ciger	204	64	91	155	55	21	0	6	2	0	2
34.	Risto Siltanen	206	38	113	151	104	14	1	4	2	1	1
35.	Kevin McClelland	428	56	94	150	1298	0	2	7	0	0	0
36.	Brett Callighen	160	56	89	145	132	17	0	2	3	0	0
37.	Blair MacDonald	131	65	72	137	33	18	2	7	1	4	2
	Shayne Corson	192	53	84	137	413	22	2	5	1	1	3
39.	Dave Semenko	454	59	77	136	976	9	0	8	0	1	1
40.	Mike Comrie	192	61	72	133	149	19	0	12	3	0	3
41.	Martin Gelinas	258	60	60	120	156	10	0	5	3	1	1
42.	Stan Weir	200	48	66	114	93	5	2	5	3	0	0
43.	Matti Hagman	147	41	71	112	34	7	0	2	0	0	0
	Mark Napier	175	41	71	112	35	6	2	4	2	0	0
45.	Craig Muni	493	24	87	111	492	0	3	3	0	0	0
46.	Andrei Kovalenko	176	51	58	109	139	17	0	7	2	0	0
47.	Dave Manson	219	33	75	108	570	16	1	3	1	0	1
48.	Tom Poti	285	27	78	105	209	11	1	7	0	0	0
49.	Jimmy Carson	84	50	53	103	36	20	0	5	1	1	0
	Roman Hamrlik	196	22	81	103	186	12	1	3	1	0	1
51.	Josef Beranek	208	42	60	102	108	10	0	4	0	0	0
52.	Ethan Moreau	313	52	47	99	353	3	6	10	2	0	4
53.	Vincent Damphousse	80	38	51	89	53	12	1	8	1	1	0
	Bernie Nicholls	95	28	61	89	80	11	0	3	0	0	0
55.	Igor Kravchuk	160	27	61	88	57	12	1	2	0	0	0
56.	Daniel Cleary	220	31	55	86	127	0	0	1	1	0	2
57.	Doug Hicks	186	17	67	84	183	7	3	1	0	0	0
58.	Scott Mellanby	149	38	44	82	344	13	0	8	1	0	0
	Georges Laraque	352	35	47	82	654	2	0	4	1	1	0
	Jaroslav Pouzar	186	34	48	82	135	4	0	4	0	0	1
61.	Willy Lindstrom	163	40	41	81	58	3	0	4	1	1	0

MOLSON

Congratulations on the first 25 years! There are very few organizations
that can look back at as many accomplishments as those of the Oilers.
Five Stanley Cups, some of the greatest players ever to lace
them up and thousands of fans. What a history!
What a team! What an organization! What a partnership we have!
Molson is proud to have been part of it.

Best personal regards,

Daniel J. O'Neill
President & Chief Executive Officer
Molson Inc.

NAME / NOM   Edmonton Oilers

No.